Third Edition

READING IN FOCUS
Learning to Get the Message

Esta de Fossard

M. Ed. in Reading

EG40CB1
PUBLISHED BY
SOUTH-WESTERN PUBLISHING CO.
CINCINNATI, OH   WEST CHICAGO, IL   DALLAS, TX   LIVERMORE, CA

De Fossard, Esta.
    Reading in focus : learning to get the message / Esta de Fossard.
— 3rd ed.
        p. cm.
    ISBN 0-538-70048-3 (module A) — ISBN 0-538-70049-1 (module B)
— ISBN 0-538-70050-5 (module C)
    1. Readers (Adult) I. Title
PE1126.A4D36   1990
428.6—dc20   89-6167
                                                                  CIP

1 2 3 4 5 6 7 W 5 4 3 2 1 0 9

Printed in the United States of America

PREFACE

The Purpose of This Course

This course will assist you to:

- understand and remember what you read.
- recognize different types of writing.
- know how to read each of these different types of writing.
- understand and use reading as a *means to an end*: to gain knowledge, opinions, ideas, and/or enjoyment.

Using This Book

This book can be used in three different ways. You and your instructor will decide how you will use it. It can be used with a class that meets every day. In that case, you will do *all* the exercises in the book. Or it can be used with a class that meets only two or three times a week. Then you will *not* do the exercises marked with a star (★). Or you can use it for studying alone. In that case, you should do *all* the exercises.

Plan of the Book

The book has ten sections. Each section has three articles in it. Each set of three articles is about the same subject, but with different points of view. Each article trains you in some of the skills that will help you be a better reader. One article and the exercises that go with it make up one lesson. There are seven steps to go through when you do each lesson:

■ Introduction

The Introduction will explain the type of writing you will be reading in the article and give you guidelines on how to read and make use of this type of writing.

■ Word Study

The Word Study section includes a practice exercise (indicated by ★), Dictionary Definitions, and an exercise using the selected words. The answers to these exercises will be in the back of this book in the Answer Key. Do not do the exercise marked ★ if you are doing the short course.

You will record your Word Study score along with all other scores for each article on the Development Chart that is explained later in this preface.

■ Article

Begin by reading the title of the article and the Paragraph Key instructions. Then fill in your starting time like this:

Time Key

Finishing Time _____

Starting Time _**11:05**_

Total Reading Time _____ minutes

When you finish reading the article, fill in your Finishing Time and your Total Reading Time like this:

Finishing Time _**11:25**_

Starting Time _**11:05**_

Total Reading Time _**:20**_ minutes

To find your Total Reading Time, subtract your Starting Time from your Finishing Time. Record your Total Reading Time on the Development Chart.

◼ Paragraph Key

As you read the article, stop at the end of each paragraph, and write a brief Paragraph Key note in the space provided. This Paragraph Key note will be a very short statement of what the paragraph is about.

Example:

The American flag is a symbol of all that America stands for: liberty, truth, justice, and freedom for all. During the War of Independence the flag was given the name "Old Glory" and that name is still used for it today.

flag – symbol of America
called Old Glory

Check your Paragraph Key answers with the Answer Key in the back of this book. Record your score on the Development Chart.

◼ Summary

On the summary page you will make a short outline of the main points of the article. You make a summary to help you remember what you have read.

Example:

1 Flag stands for *liberty, truth, justice, and freedom.*
2 Flag often called *"Old Glory"*

The answers to the summary are not in this book. They will be checked by your instructor. If you are working alone, you will check your answers in the manual. Record your score on the Development Chart.

■ Recalling the Details

This page gives you a final check to see if you understand and recall what you have read. It is a page of statements about the article. You must choose the correct ending for each statement. Circle the letter of the correct ending. Example:

1 *Old Glory* is the name given to

    a George Washington
    b the United States flag
    c the Capitol building

The answers to this section are not in this book. They will be checked by your instructor. If you are working alone, you will check your answers in the manual. Record your score on the Development Chart.

★ Personal Opinion

The Personal Opinion page will give you a chance to use the study words again. It also allows you to give some of your own ideas on the topic of the sentence that you will complete. At the top of the page under the instructions, you will find a list of words like this:

| accident | future | sport |
| admire | raise | vacation |

Under the words will be a group of sentences. Each sentence has two blanks. One short, solid blank like this _____, and one longer blank like this . . . . You must choose the best word from the list to fill in the short, solid blank (_____) in each sentence. You will fill in the other longer blank (. . . . .) with ideas of your own that complete the sentence intelligently. Here is an example, using the words from the list:

1 The ____*sport*____ I like best is
. . . . *football* . . . .

2 When I have a ____*vacation*____ from work, I like to
. . . . *go to the beach* . . . .

3 The person I ____*admire*____ most is
my father who is a great teacher. . .

4 The worst ____*accident*____ I ever had was
a car crash which put me in the hospital

For practice, finish these two sentences using the remaining words from the list:

5 We should always _____ the flag

. . . .

6 I believe in the _____ of America

. . . .

The answers for the Personal Opinion section are not in this book. They will be checked by your instructor. If you are working alone, you will check your answers in the manual. Then record your score on the Development Chart. You will score two points for each correct word you put in the short blanks. You will not be graded on the personal ideas you put in the long blanks. If you are doing the short course, you will not do the Personal Opinion page.

Try to discuss your personal ideas with friends or with other people in your class. Reading should not stop when you finish the page. It is important to use the ideas you get from reading. You can start using them by discussing them with others.

★ **Speed Exercise**

The Speed Exercise will help you read faster. You will have one minute to read the Speed Exercise. Your instructor will time this and tell you when to start and stop. If you are working alone, you will have to time yourself. When you are told to stop (or at the end of one minute), put an X after the last word you read. Then count the number of words you read. This will tell you how fast you are reading. Record your reading speed on the Development Chart. You will learn to read faster as you practice.

After each Speed Exercise, there are some questions about it. Answer these questions each time. This will tell you how well you are understanding what you read. If you cannot answer the questions, you may be trying to read too fast or you may not be concentrating on what you are reading.

The answers to the Speed Exercise questions are not in the back of the book. You can check the answers yourself by looking back at the contents of the exercise. Record your score on the Development Chart. (If you are doing the short course, you will not do the Speed Exercise in class. It is a good idea, however, to find time to do it alone so that you can improve your reading speed.)

Here is a Speed Exercise to practice. You can see that the words are put into groups. This will teach you to read more than one word at a time. It will help you learn to read faster. You will have one minute to read this Speed Exercise. Your instructor will tell you when to start and stop. If you are working alone, give yourself one minute to see how much of this you can read.

Everyone should learn to read. We need to read many things every day. We read labels on food boxes and cans. We read newspapers and magazines. We read street signs and directions. We read instructions at work. We read textbooks in school and college. Reading also helps us think better. When we read a lot of ideas, it helps us find new ideas of our own. Reading is a useful skill for everyone.

(73 words)

How many words did you read? _____ Answer these questions about what you read:

1 Three things we read are _____ ,

_____ and _____

2 Reading helps us _____

3 Reading is a useful skill for _____

(Check all your answers by looking back at the Speed Exercise.)

Other Parts of This Book

This book also has a glossary, an alphabet, a pronunciation key, a grammatical key, and a Development Chart.

■ Glossary

The glossary gives the meanings of special words used in this book. All the words are about reading. Use the glossary to check the meanings of words about reading that are new to you. The glossary also gives the number of the article in which the word is first used. It begins on page xii.

■ Alphabet

The alphabet is listed on the left edge of the inside front cover. It shows you the order in which letters appear in the alphabet. Many things in this book are given in alphabetical order. The glossary is in alphabetical order. The Dictionary Definitions are in alphabetical order. Use the alphabet to help you follow things that are listed in alphabetical order.

■ Pronunciation Key

The pronunciation key will help you learn how to say new words. There are special marks in a dictionary that tell you how to say a word. The pronunciation key will help you understand these marks. These marks are used in the Dictionary Definitions. Get used to using them. The pronunciation key is on the inside front cover.

Practice using the pronunciation key by doing this exercise. Each word in the list is followed by the correct dictionary pronunciation in parentheses ( ). Following the pronunciation are the definition and two possible pronunciations. Use the pronunciation key to find out which of the two pronunciations is correct. Put a circle around the right answer.

1 acquiesce (ak' w es') give consent by keeping silent.

   a ak you es
   b ak wee es

2 calipers (kal' prz) instrument used to measure the diameter or thickness of something.

   a kal e purz
   b kal ee fers

3 phraseology (fr ' z ol' j) selection and arrangement of words.

   a fray zee ol o jee
   b prayz ol o jee

4 syllogism (sil' jiz' m) a form of argument consisting of two propositions containing a common term and a third proposition (the conclusion) following logically from them.

   a sigh low jiz em
   b sill e jiz em

5 xenophobia (zen' f b) hatred or fear of foreigners or strangers.

   a zen h foe bee ah
   b zeen ah fobe ah

■ Grammatical Key

The grammatical key is a list of the parts of speech. It also shows the short forms (abbreviations) that the dictionary uses for these parts of speech. The grammatical key is on the inside front cover. You will learn more about parts of speech as you study the Word Study pages.

■ Development Chart

The Development Chart is on page xv. This is where you write your scores when you have finished each exercise. You must also record here the scores you make on the exercises that are corrected by your instructor. The Development Chart will show you how your reading is improving and in which areas you need to study harder.

There are two charts, Chart A and Chart B. Use Chart A if you are doing the full course or if you are working alone. Use Chart B if you are doing the short course. You will see that some squares have an X in them. In these sections, there will be no score for that particular exercise.

You will see that there is a place for your test scores at the bottom of the page too. You will have a test in the middle of the course and at the end of the course. Fill in your test scores in the places provided.

CONTENTS

GLOSSARY

This is the list of words related to reading. You will use many of them in this course. A number in brackets after a word indicates the article in this book where the word is used.

abbreviation: a short form of something written. There are standard abbreviations for the parts of speech. These are listed in the grammatical key in the inside front cover of this book. [P]

acknowledgment: the names of people who have helped with a book or names of sources from which articles or information have been taken. [4]

adjective: a word that gives more information about a noun (abbreviated: adj) [5]

adverb: a word that gives more information about a verb, adjective, or another adverb (abbreviated: adv) [10]

alphabet: the 26 letters that are used to spell the words in our language [P]

alphabetical order: the order in which words are given in a dictionary from a to z [1]

anecdote: a very short story used within an article, book, etc., to demonstrate a point or give an example [11]

antonym: A single word that has the opposite or almost opposite meaning to another word [26]

application letter: a letter written when applying for a job. There are certain pieces of information that should be included in an application letter. [20]

ARCHAIC: a restrictive label that indicates a word or meaning which is very rare except in old books or in books written in the style of an earlier period [17]

article: a short piece of writing, based on either facts or opinions, that gives information about something [3]

authority: the names, dates, and other information that help you know if the person writing the article and the content in the article can be relied upon to be correct [5]

autobiography: the story of a person's life, written directly by that person [8]

bibliography: a list of books or articles that are all about the same subject [2]

biography: a book or article telling about a person's life but written by someone else [8]

business letter: a very common form of written communication between companies or individuals in business [20]

by-line: a line giving the name of the writer of a news story [22]

characters: the people in a story [18]

contents: a list of the names of the chapters in a book, and the page where each new chapter starts [2]

context: the way a word is used in a sentence, which can help you understand the meaning of the word [1]

date line: a statement of the place from which a news story comes and the time it occurred [22]

DIALECT: a restrictive label that indicates a word or meaning which is used only in the folk speech of a certain geographical area [17]

dictionary: a book that gives information about each word in our language—its meanings, spelling, pronunciation, parts of speech, history, etc. [1]

editorial: an article that gives opinions about the news, often written by an editor of the newspaper [24]

emotional appeal: the use of words and phrases that appeal to the reader's emotions in order to encourage the reader to read the facts [27]

entry: a dictionary listing of a word, with its meaning and other information [12]

etymology: the history of a word [24]

fact: a thing that is known to be true or to have really happened [5]

fiction: literature that tells of imaginary people, places, things [28]

5W + H Question Frame: questions that can be used to help you understand and remember almost anything you read: who, what, when, where, why, and how [4]

footnote: a note, usually situated at the bottom of the page, telling where certain information came from [5]

foreword: another name for an introduction (see "introduction" in this list) [2]

generalization: the forming of a general statement or rule from a limited number of examples. Generalizations must always be thought about before being assumed to be correct.

glossary: a list of special words and meanings that are often used in the subject area that the textbook is about [2] [14]

grammatical label: an italicized abbreviation in a dictionary entry that gives the part of speech of the word being defined (also called "part of speech label") [4]

graph: an illustration that summarizes information which would be more difficult to explain in words [21]

hard news: news that reports the facts of current events [24]

homonyms: words that sound exactly the same but have different spellings [6]

hypothesis: (in an editorial) the main idea or point of view [24]

illustrative sentence or phrase: a sentence or phrase, usually italicized, which is included in some dictionary entries to show how a word can be used

index: a long alphabetical list of all the things that are in a book [2]

inference: knowledge arrived at on the evidence of other information provided. We gain a lot of information from inference rather than direct statement when we read. [13]

inflected forms: any changes made in the spelling of a word when it is used in different ways [17]

INFORMAL: a restrictive label that indicates a word or meaning which is used in everyday speech or writing, but not in formal speech or writing [17]

interpretive journalism: editorial opinions, giving the writer's view of the news [24]

intransitive verb: a verb that does not need an object to complete its meaning (abbreviated v.i.)

introduction: 1. a short chapter at the beginning of a book, which tells about the book and how to use it 2. one or more paragraphs at the beginning of an article, which present either an outline of the information to be given, a "teaser" to get the reader interested, or information about the author [2]

irony: ordinary meaning of words is the opposite of what is in the writer's mind; event or outcome opposite of what is expected [29]

journalism: the writing of material for presentation in newspapers or radio or television news programs [22]

language label: a label used to indicate a word borrowed directly from another language

letter of application: a letter containing information that would help a possible employer assess the applicant's qualifications for a job [20]

memorandum: an informal note sent from one department to another within a business or office [19]

news service: organization that supplies news to various newspapers [22]

news story: an article that reports the news [22]

noun: a naming word that tells you the person, place, thing, or idea you are reading about (abbreviated: n) [5]

opinion: a personal belief, idea, or point of view that is not necessarily based on fact [6]

paragraph: a group of sentences in an essay, article, or story that all relate to the same topic [3] [17]

paragraph key: a set of brief notes giving the main points or facts of each paragraph [1]

paragraph summary: a summary that gives the main points of an article or chapter in the form of a paragraph, rather than in outline form [1]

parenthesis: part of a sentence set off from the rest with punctuation marks like these ( ) [P]

part of speech: the work that a word does in a sentence: noun, verb, adjective, adverb, etc. [4]

persuasive article: one that tries to attract you to the point of view of the writer

plot: the sequence of events that happen in a story [18]

preface: another word for an introduction (see "introduction" in this list) [2]

prefix: a short group of letters added to the front of a root word to change its meaning [21]

pro and con: for and against. A pro and con article is one that shows both sides of a question.

prologue (or prolog): another word for an introduction (see "introduction" in this list) [2]

pronunciation key: a special system that the dictionary uses to show you how to say a word [P]

report: detailed information of a particular subject, arranged in a formal, organized pattern [16]

restrictive label: a label in a dictionary, printed in capital letters or enclosed in parentheses, that introduces a special meaning of a word and tells you the special circumstances in which it applies [17]

root: the main part of a word not including the suffix or the prefix [30]

satire: use of sarcasm, irony, or wit to attack a

custom, idea, or habit [30]

scholarly article: article written by someone knowledgeable in the field [26]

setting: the time and place in which a story happens [18]

skim: build a mental outline of a chapter by briefly looking at the title, subtitle, headings, and subheadings

SLANG: a restrictive label that indicates a word usage which is acceptable in very informal speaking but not in formal writing

slant: a particular viewpoint in reporting the news, or certain stress put on one part of a news story [23]

speed reading: reading a large amount of material in a small amount of time [1]

Standard Business English: the preferred way of using the English language for business letters and transactions: a form of the language that has been standardized so everyone can use and understand it [20]

stress: the accent that is put on a syllable in a word when it is said. It is indicated in the dictionary by a mark like this ' [1]

subtitle: a short heading listed after the main title of a book or used in the chapters of a book to help you understand the main points of each chapter [2]

suffix: a group of letters added to the end of a word

to change its part of speech

summary: a brief restatement of the main ideas of a chapter, article, or story [1]

supposition: thing supposed; belief, opinion [25]

syllable: the smallest unit of a word. A word is broken into syllables as we pronounce it. [2]

synonym: one word with the same or nearly the same meaning as another word [4]

tense: the time when the action of a verb occurs, often indicated by different inflected forms [17]

textbook: a book of factual information on a particular topic, particularly used in schools and colleges [2]

theme: the particular aspect of life or a character that a story makes you think about [18]

title: the name given to something, such as a book, play, poem, etc. [2]

topic: subject that people think, write, or talk about [2]

topic sentence: the sentence that states the main point of a paragraph [3]

transitive verb: a verb that has a direct object (abbreviated: v.t.) [4]

verb: a word that tells you what action a noun is doing or what the noun is feeling, being, or seeming (abbreviated: v) [4]

yellow press: sensational or lurid writing or presentation of the news [22]

DEVELOPMENT CHART

Use Chart A if your course is 5 hours a week or if you are working alone. Use Chart B if you are doing the shorter course.
Fill in the chart when you complete the work for each article. The chart will show your progress, and it will also show where your weaknesses are.
This will help you to know where you must work harder.

CHART A – FOR FULL COURSE AND INDIVIDUAL STUDY COURSE

Article Number	Points	1	2	3	4	5	6	7	8	9	10	11	12	13	14	15	16	17	18	19	20	21	22	23	24	25	26	27	28	29	30
* Word Study	10																														
Using the Words	10																														
Paragraph Key	20																														
Summary	10																														
Recalling the Details	10																				X		X								
* Personal Opinion	20																														
* Speed Exercise	20																														
Total	100																														

Possible Score, 100

CHART B – FOR SHORT COURSE

Article Number	Points	1	2	3	4	5	6	7	8	9	10	11	12	13	14	15	16	17	18	19	20	21	22	23	24	25	26	27	28	29	30
Using the Words	10																														
'Paragraph Key	20																														
Summary	10																														
Recalling the Details	10																				X		X								
Total	50																														

Possible Score, 50

| Total Reading Time | | | | | | | | | | | | | | | | | | | | X | | X | | | | | | | | |

Minutes

TEST SCORES: TEST 1 _____   TEST 2 _____

SECTION A.
Reading Is a Means to an End

ARTICLE 1.
Reading Made Easy
Introduction

Reasons for Reading

■ Reading means making sense of the printed word. You read for a number of different reasons. You can read to find facts and learn from them. You can read to get instructions to make something, such as a cake. You can read to learn about the daily news. You can also read just for fun.

■ Reading is easier if you have a purpose for reading. You can understand what you read more easily if you know why you are reading. You will remember more of what you read, if you read with a purpose.

■ Anyone can learn to be a good reader. A good reader is curious and wants to discover new ideas. A good reader likes to think about facts and opinions. A good reader likes words and enjoys finding and using new words correctly.

■ As you begin this course, ask yourself, "Why do I want to improve my reading?" Your answer will give you the motive to study hard. This course can help you improve your reading. Use it well.

Reading Made Easy
Word Study, Using the Words

Word Study—Dictionary Contents

■ Words are the tools of reading. The best way to get to know words is to use them. Do not be afraid of new words. If you don't know a word, find out about it.

■ A *dictionary* tells you all about words. A dictionary tells you:

1 What a word means.
2 How to pronounce (say) the word. The dictionary uses a special system to show you how to say a word.
3 Where to put stress on the word.
4 How to spell the word. Some words can be spelled correctly in more than one way. The dictionary will show you this.
5 Any special meanings the word has.
6 The etymology (et′ ə mol′ ə jē) or history of the word; where the word comes from.

■ Words in the dictionary are put in *alphabetical order*. Words on the first page of the dictionary begin with *aa*. The first three words in the Scott, Foresman Advanced Dictionary are: *aardvark, aardwolf,* and *Aaron*. After the *aa* words, you will find words that begin with *ab: abaca, aback,* and *abacterial*.

★ ■ Put these words in alphabetical order. Write them in a list on the lines at the right. Then check your answers in the Answer Key in the back of this book. The first one is done for you.

reading	freeze
judge	_____
freeze	_____
picnic	_____
panic	_____
read	_____
impact	_____
judging	_____
reader	_____
improve	_____

■ Check your answers in the Answer Key.
■ Record your score on the Development Chart in the front of this book.
■ Look for the correct answers to any you had wrong.

NUMBER CORRECT _____ (Possible 10)
(1 point for each answer; the first one is a free point)

Using the Words

■ Some words have more than one meaning. When more than one meaning is given in the dictionary, each meaning has a number in front of it. Example: **concentrate 1** bring together in one place. **2** pay close attention.

■ For this exercise, use the Dictionary Definitions that follow. Find the right meaning for each boldfaced word in the following sentences. Be sure the meaning you choose makes sense in the sentence.

■ Write the number of the meaning you choose in the parentheses ( ) at the beginning of the sentence.

1 (   ) The basketball <u>coach</u> made the team train for an hour a day.
2 (   ) If you want to understand what you read, you must <u>concentrate</u>.
3 (   ) You can often tell what a word means from its <u>context</u> in the sentence.
4 (   ) You can work out your own test grade if you look at the answer <u>key</u>.
5 (   ) Make a <u>summary</u> of important points when you finish reading.

■ Check your answers in the Answer Key.
■ Record your score on the Development Chart.

NUMBER CORRECT _____ (Possible 10)
(2 points for each answer)

Dictionary Definitions

coach (kōch), *n.* **1** a large, four-wheeled, usually closed carriage with seats inside and often on top, formerly used in carrying passengers and mail. **2** a railroad car with seats for passengers at lower fares than sleeping accommodations. **3** bus. **4** a class of passenger accommodations on a commercial aircraft at lower rates than first class. **5** person who teaches or trains athletic teams, etc.: *a swimming coach.* **6** (in baseball) a person who directs base runners and the batter. **7** instructor who supervises the training of actors, singers, etc.: *a drama coach, a music coach.* **8** a private teacher who helps a student prepare for a special test.
concentrate (kon' sən trāt), *v.,* **-trated, -trating,** *v.i.* **1** bring together in one place. **2** pay close attention; focus the mind (*on* or *upon*): *She concentrated upon the problem.*
context (kon' tekst), *n.* **1** parts directly before and after a word, sentence, etc., that influence its meaning: *You can often tell the meaning of a word from its context.*
key (kē), *n., pl.* **keys. 1** a small metal instrument for locking and unlocking the lock of a door, a padlock, etc. **2** anything shaped or used like it: *a key to open a tin can.* **3** the answer to a puzzle or problem. **4** sheet or book of answers: *a key to a test.* **5** a systematic explanation of abbreviations and symbols used in a dictionary, map, etc. The pronunciation key in this dictionary lists all the symbols of the sounds in English that are used in the pronunciations, and also gives examples of words that contain these sounds. **6** place that commands or gives control of a sea, a district, etc., because of its position: *Gibraltar is the key to the Mediterranean.* **7** an important or essential person, thing, etc. **8** pin, bolt, wedge, or other piece put in a hole or space to hold parts together. **9** one of a set of levers pressed down by the fingers in playing some musical instruments, such as a piano, and in operating a typewriter or other instrument. **10** a mechanical device for opening and closing an electric circuit, as in a telegraph. **11** scale or system of related tones in music which are based on a keynote: *a song written in the key of C.* **12** device to turn a bolt or nut. Watches used to be wound with keys. **13** tone of voice; style of thought or expression: *The poet wrote in a melancholy key.* **14** key fruit, samara. **15** a guide to the identification of a group of plants or animals, having the outstanding determining characteristics arranged in a systematic way.
summary (sum' ər ē), *n., pl.* **-maries,** *adj.—n.* **1** a brief statement giving the main points. **2** an outline at the beginning or end of a book chapter: *The history book had a summary at the end of each chapter.*

Reading Made Easy
Article

Paragraph Key

■ Complete each Paragraph Key note when you have finished reading the paragraph. (The first one has been done for you.)

---

¹Many people find reading difficult. Perhaps this is because reading is not a natural ability like breathing or walking. Reading is a skill, and like all skills it needs practice before it becomes easy.

a Reading is a skill that needs practice.

²In that way, reading is something like playing football. The more you practice, the more skilled you become. The beginner in football has the help of a **coach** who gives advice on how to improve the needed skills.

b Reading is like _____

³This book can be used as a reading coach. It will give you advice on how to improve your reading skills. It will help you, however, only if you decide to work with it. Coaching is no use unless the coaching advice is followed.

c This book is like a _____

⁴You must begin your reading study with the understanding that reading is work. Like football training, it requires hard and consistent work if you want to succeed at it. No serious player would go to football training and do something else at the same time. Similarly, when you read, you cannot do other things at the same time. When you read seriously, therefore, you should neither watch TV nor have the radio or stereo playing.

d Reading is_____ _____

⁵When you read, you must have a good light. You should also have a pencil, paper, and a dictionary, and be prepared to **concentrate**. When you are a more experienced reader, you will be able to manage without these things, but at first you should follow all the rules.

e Be prepared to _____ when you read

The following rules can help you learn to be a more effective reader:

Reading Rules:

⁶Become acquainted with words and their meanings. Learn how to make use of a wide variety of words and how to use a dictionary to help you understand words. Make it a practice to write down words you do not know. Try to work out their meaning from their **context** in the sentence. If this does not help your understanding, check the meaning later in the dictionary.

f Get to know_____ and _____

⁷It is better not to look up a new word as you read, unless you cannot make sense of the sentence without it. You should, however, look up the word when you finish reading and then try to use it in your own writing and conversation.

g New words: _____ _____

[8]Do not read too slowly. It is tempting to think that slower reading will lead to greater comprehension. This is not true. Reading slowly allows the mind time to think about other things. Keep the pace up within each paragraph.

[9]Keep your concentration fixed on the words you are reading and the author's meaning. Do not explore your own interpretation of the subject as you read. Keep that for later and explore your own ideas when you have finished the reading.

[10]Read to remember. You waste time if you have to read the same thing two or three times to get the message. You can increase your ability to remember what you read if you learn to use the Paragraph **Key** like this:
■ Stop reading at the end of each paragraph.
■ In the margin, write a brief note on the main point of the paragraph.

[11]If you cannot capture the point of the paragraph in your own words, it means you have not understood what you read. You should study the paragraph again before you move on. When you have completed the article, reread the Paragraph Key notes, and you will see that you have a quick **summary** of the main points of the article.

[12]Because much of your reading in school is done for tests, summary writing can be very helpful. The summary lists the main points, and when you wish to restudy that material, you can work from the summary. It will not always be necessary to reread the whole chapter or article.

[13]Learn to think about what you read and to discuss it with other people. Discussion is a good way to develop your own ideas and viewpoints. Reading can expose you to ideas, but reading is just the start. The important thing is what you do with what you read.

[14]You should be able to discuss what you read. It is important to recall enough of the details to talk about the subject accurately and intelligently. Your ability to recall what you read will be helped by making a Paragraph Key and a summary. Make it a practice to check what you recall of the important things you read.

[15]Read with questions in mind. Reading to find the answers to questions will provide you with a motive to read. It is not enough to simply read the words. The important thing is to use what you read to stimulate your own ideas and enquiries.

[16]There are different ways to read different things. This book will guide you in reading such things as a story, an article, a report, and a newspaper. Each of these is easier to read if you know the best method.

[17]How fast should you read? Is speed reading a valuable skill? These are good questions. Most people read about as fast as they talk, which is about 150 words per minute. Their reading speed is determined by their speaking speed because they pronounce each word mentally as they read.

h Do not read

_____

_____

i Explore your own ideas

_____

j Read to _____

_____

k A Paragraph Key is like

a _____

l A summary _____

_____

m Use what you read by

_____

n Learn to _____

_____

o Read with _____

_____

p There are _____

_____

q Most people read ____

_____

Reading Made Easy
Article

[18]Silent pronunciation is not necessary, however. You can learn to look at words and read them without saying them. This will increase the speed of your reading. The speed exercises in this book are designed to help you learn to read without saying each word mentally.

r Learn to_____

_____

[19]Speed reading is a skill that needs daily practice. It is a valuable skill, however, only if you comprehend and remember what you read. A good workable speed is about 300 words per minute. A reading speed of 500 words per minute is about as good as the average reader really needs to have.

s Speed reading needs

_____

[20]You can be a better reader. You can make reading work for you if you learn how.

t You can_____

_____

- Write in your Finishing Time and subtract to find your Total Reading Time.
- Record your Total Reading Time on the Development Chart.
- Check your answers in the Answer Key.
- Record your score.
- Look for the correct answers to any you had wrong.

NUMBER CORRECT _____ (Possible 20)
(1 point for each answer)

Reading Made Easy
Summary

Summary

■ The ideas in this article are important if you want to learn to read better. You should be able to make a summary of the main points in your own words. This will ensure that you understand the points.

■ Read your Paragraph Key again up to the end of paragraph 18. The comments about speed reading are not really part of what you need to know to read better. Do not put them in the summary.

■ Now see if you can fill in the blanks in the summary points without looking back at the article. If you get stuck, look at the paragraph number that is given in the parentheses ( ).

■ There are ten main points to remember for this article.

1 Reading is a _____ that we have to learn. (par. 1)

2 You have to _____ to get better at it. (par. 2)

3 You must _____ when you read (par. 5)

4 To improve your reading, get to know _____ . (par. 6)

5 It does not help to read too _____ . (par. 8)

6 Read to _____ . (par. 10)

7 Learn to make _____ in your own words. (par. 11)

8 Learn to _____ about what you read. (par. 13)

9 Always read with _____ in mind. (par. 15)

10 Read different things in _____ ways. (par. 16)

■ Check with your teacher or with the manual for the correct answers.

■ Record your score.

■ Look for the correct answers to any you had wrong.

NUMBER CORRECT _____ (Possible 10)
(1 point for each answer)

Article 1 ● Reading Made Easy   7

Reading Made Easy
Recalling the Details

Recalling the Details

■ Your summary was a brief restatement of the main points of the article.

■ If you want to make any article really useful to you, you must learn to recall more than just the main points. You can practice recalling details with this article.

■ Reread your Paragraph Key notes to refresh your memory. Then read these sentences and choose the ending that would finish the sentence with the same idea that the article had. Circle the letter of the correct ending.

1 The article said that reading is not natural like

   a eating and drinking
   b breathing and walking
   c sleeping and waking

2 When you start to read, you should have

   a good light, pencil, and paper
   b the radio or stereo playing
   c a coach standing beside you

3 When you come to a word that you don't know, you should

   a underline it and look it up later
   b always look it up right away
   c forget about it and go on reading

4 When you are trying to understand something, you should

   a read very slowly so you take it all in
   b not read slowly or your mind will wander
   c read as fast as you can, even if you don't understand

5 You should think about your own ideas on the subject

   a before you begin to read
   b as you read
   c when you have finished reading

6 A Paragraph Key is

   a a book that tells you what words mean
   b a few words jotted down beside each paragraph
   c a summary

7 If you cannot fill in a Paragraph Key, it means

   a you did not understand the paragraph very well
   b the paragraph was badly written
   c it really doesn't matter

8 A good way to remember what you read for a test is to

   a learn it by heart
   b make a summary of it in your own words
   c read the chapter over and over again

9 The main trouble with speed reading is

   a it costs a lot to learn
   b it only works if you're very smart
   c it does not last unless you practice every day

10 A good comfortable reading speed is

   a 150 words per minute
   b 300 words per minute
   c 500 words per minute

■ Check with your teacher or with the manual for the correct answers.
■ Record your score.
■ Look for the correct answers to any you had wrong.

NUMBER CORRECT _____ (Possible 10)
(1 point for each answer)

★ Personal Opinion

■ On this page you will have a chance to use the vocabulary words from the article again. This will help you to be sure you understand the words and their meanings.

■ At the same time, you will have a chance to give some of your own ideas.

■ In the sentences that follow, you should choose the right word from the list to fill in the short blanks. Then finish the sentence **in your own words** so that it gives your ideas on the subject. This will help you remember that the most important part of reading is using what you have read and thinking when you finish reading.

■ Here again are the five words:

coach   context   summary
concentrate   key

■ Now work on the sentences:

1 It seems to me that an important _____ to good reading is

. . . .

2 If I could have a _____ for reading, I would like special help with

. . . .

3 A _____ is a brief statement of. . . . .

4 If I cannot get the meaning of a word from its _____ in the article, I find it helpful

to. . . . .

5 I think one way to be sure you _____ when you read, is to

. . . .

■ Check with your teacher or with the manual for the correct answers.

■ Record your score.

■ Look for the correct answers to any you had wrong.

■ Discuss your ideas with friends or with other students who have finished this work.

NUMBER CORRECT _____ (Possible 20)
(4 points for each word)

Reading Made Easy

★ Speed Exercise

■ The Speed Exercise will be timed by your teacher. You will be given exactly one minute to read the article or as much of it as you can. You are not asked to answer the questions within that minute, just read the article. Start reading when your teacher says "Start." Stop reading when your teacher says "Stop." Put an X after the last word you read so you can see how far you got. (If you are working alone, you must time one minute for yourself.)

At the end of each section of work you will find a short article like this. This is to help you to learn to read faster. You will have one minute to read the whole of this short article. Then answer the questions which follow it. The words are spread out to help you to learn to read words in groups rather than one at a time. As you read these short pieces you will learn how to read faster and at the same time you will find your own reading speed getting better. (94 words)

1 Why are the words written in groups? _____

2 Where will the Speed Exercises be? _____

3 What will follow each Speed Exercise? _____

■ There is no Answer Key for the Speed Exercises. You can check your answers by looking back at the Speed Exercise article.

NUMBER CORRECT _____ (Possible 20)
You will score 14 points if you read the whole article, and 2 points for each correct answer. Check your answers by looking back at the article. Deduct 1 point for every line you did not read.

Reading a Textbook

■ What is the purpose of a textbook? It is to provide facts (and sometimes opinions) on a particular topic. When you are using a textbook, therefore, your aim is to find and understand the facts, and find and consider the opinions.

■ The opinions in the textbook will be the writer's ideas. As you study the textbook, you may also develop opinions of your own.

■ A textbook can be very dull reading if you use it only to learn the facts it presents. On the other hand, a textbook can be very interesting reading if you use it to start your own ideas.

■ As you read the articles in this book, think about the differences between facts and opinions. Learn to distinguish facts from opinions or ideas.

■ *Think* when you read. The end result of reading a textbook should be the gaining of knowledge and the stimulation of your ideas.

What's in a Textbook?
Word Study, Dictionary Definitions

Word Study—Syllabication

■ The units that make up words are called syllables (sil′ ə bəlz). A syllable consists of a vowel alone or a vowel with one or more consonants. The vowels are *a, e, i, o,* and u; *y* can also be used as a vowel. The word *chapter* has two syllables: chap ter. The first syllable (chap) has the vowel "a" in it. The second syllable (ter) has the vowel "e" in it. The dictionary shows you the syllables in a word. In the *Scott, Foresman Advanced Dictionary*, there is a small space after each syllable: chap ter. A word is simpler to read if you break it into syllables.

★ ■ Make a Word List. Write the following words in their syllables. You will find the words in the Dictionary Definitions.

	NUMBER OF SYLLABLES	MEANING	WORD LIST
1	3	a list of special words in the subject area of the book	_____
2	2	a list of the names of chapters	_____
3	5	a list of books or articles on the same subject	_____
4	3	a short piece of writing on a topic	_____
5	2	a list of all the things in a book	_____
6	2	a name of a book, film, or person	_____
7	2	a subject people talk or write on	_____
8	3	part of a word pronounced as a unit	_____
9	2	an introduction to a book	_____
10	2	a list of information	_____

■ Check your answers in the Answer Key.
■ Record your score.
■ Look for the correct answers to any you had wrong.

NUMBER CORRECT _____ (Possible 10)
(1 point for each answer)

Dictionary Definitions

article (ar′ tə kəl), *n.* a short piece of writing on a certain topic. When used in law, it can mean a clause in a contract.
bibliography (bib′ lē og′ rə fē), *n.* a list of other books or articles you can read that are about the same subject as the textbook. You will find the bibliography at the end of each chapter, or it may be at the end of the whole book.
contents (kon′ tents), *n.* a list that tells you the names of the chap-

ters and the page where each new chapter starts. It may also have a short outline of what each chapter has in it. It is sometimes called the table of contents. It is in the front of the book.
glossary (glos′ ər ē), *n.* a list of special words that are often used in the subject area that the text-book is about. It may be at the beginning or end of the book.
index (in′ deks), *n.* a long list of all the things that are in a book. This

list is put in alphabetical order (beginning with words that start with a) and it will help you find the information you are looking for in the book. It is always at the end of a book.
preface (pref′ is), *n.* another word for introduction.
syllable (sil′ əb əl), *n.* this is the part of the word that is pronounced as a unit. A syllable usually has a vowel in it. In the word *camel, ca* is one syllable, and *mel*

is the other syllable.

table (tā' bəl), *n*. a piece of furniture having a smooth flat top and legs. It can also mean a list of information.

title (tī' tl), *n*. the name given to something, like a book or a film or a person.

topic (top' ik), *n*. a subject that people think about or write about or talk about. A topic sentence is the sentence that tells you what a paragraph is all about.

Using the Words

■ Choose the right word from the Dictionary Definitions to fill in the blank in each of these sentences. The definitions should help you in your choice. Use each word only once.

1 The table of _____ is found in the front of a textbook.

2 Another word for _____ is "introduction."

3 A chapter deals with one _____ of a subject.

4 A _____ is the smallest unit of a word.

5 A _____ is a list of special words about a subject.

6 The _____ is found at the back of a textbook.

7 You should understand the _____ of a textbook before you read it.

8 Each _____ in this book is on a new topic.

9 A _____ is a list of books about a subject.

10 The _____ of contents is a list of the topics in a textbook.

■ Check your answers in the Answer Key.
■ Record your score.

NUMBER CORRECT _____ (Possible 10)
(1 point for each answer)

What's in a Textbook?
Article

Paragraph Key

■ Make a brief note about the most important points of the indicated paragraphs.

---

¹One of the most important tools of learning you use in college is the textbook. Another is your teacher. The best aid to good learning, however, is your own will to learn.

²A textbook is a tool that helps you acquire knowledge about a particular subject. Like any other tool, a textbook is useful only if you know how to use it. You will have to make use of textbooks in almost every college subject you study, so it is wise to know how to make the best use of them.

³There are certain things you can do that will help you make better use of textbooks. You can begin by carefully examining each of your books to see what it contains and how it should be used. If possible, you should become familiar with the textbook before you have to use it in class.

⁴You should be aware of these parts of a textbook:

⁵The **title**: Be sure you understand the title. If it contains words that are new to you, check their meanings. The title of this book is *Reading in Focus*. Do you understand the meaning of that title? Try to express it in words of your own to be sure you understand it.

⁶The subtitle: A subtitle is like an extension that adds a bit more to the title. Not all textbooks have subtitles. This one does. It is *Learning to Get the Message*. So, the title of this book advises you that the subject is reading. The subtitle expands this and tells you that the book will deal particularly with understanding and using what you read.

⁷Every textbook contains some or all of these things:

1 Table of contents
2 Index
3 Glossary
4 Bibliography

⁸The **table** of **contents** is placed in the front of the book. It is on pages ix–xi. Its function is to identify what the book contains. Look at the table of contents now. You will see an overview of the subjects covered in the book.

⁹The **index** is usually found in the back of the book. The index is presented in alphabetical order, with each index entry being on a separate **topic**.The

a Best aid to learning is

————————————

b A textbook is a ————

————————————

c Get to know a textbook before ————————

————————————

d ————————————

e ————————————

————————————

f ————————————

————————————

g ————————————

————————————

h ————————————

————————————

entry word is followed by the numbers of the pages that contain information about or references to this topic. There is no index to this book.

¹⁰The **glossary** is a list of words that relate to the particular topic of the book—in this case reading. The glossary in this book comes on page xii.

¹¹The glossary is alphabetized and can be used to check the way certain words are used when they relate to reading. Look at the glossary now and see how it works.

¹²A **bibliography** is a list of books on a particular topic. It will enable you to read more about any subject that is of special interest to you. This book does not have a bibliography.

¹³Not all textbooks contain all these features. Some do not provide a bibliography. Others have no glossary or index.

¹⁴If a book has no glossary, you can make your own. For each subject you are studying, you can make a glossary of the words that belong to that subject. Keep your glossary on a blank page at the back of the textbook.

¹⁵You might have noticed that some textbooks have a **preface**. A preface is the same as an introduction, and it tells you three things: why the book was written, what the book is about, and the best way to use the book.

¹⁶If you have not so far read the preface to this book, you should do so when you finish this article. It will help you to use this book correctly. You will find it on page iii.

¹⁷Almost all textbooks are made up of chapters. Each chapter deals with a separate topic of the main subject of the textbook. For example, the main subject of a book about using a computer is computers. Each chapter, therefore, would deal with a separate topic of this subject. There might be chapters on Start Up, DOS, and Programs—all topics on the main subject of computers.

¹⁸This book is made up of ten groups of **articles**. Like a book, each group has a central subject. For example, the second group is on the subject of dreams, and each article in that group deals with a different idea about dreams. Each group in the book contains three articles. They are like chapters, since each article presents a separate topic on the main subject of the group.

¹⁹When you read a chapter, look for these things:

1 Heading
2 Subheadings
3 Boldfaced or colored words
4 Summary
5 Questions

i _____
   _____

j _____
   _____

k _____
   _____

l _____
   _____

m _____
   _____

n _____
   _____

o _____
   _____

What's in a Textbook?
Article

6 Pictures
7 Review exercises

[20]The heading tells you the topic of the chapter while the subheadings indicate the aspects of the topic that the chapter will cover. Boldfaced or colored words are key words or new words. If they are not familiar to you, you might be able to read them more easily if you break them into **syllables**.

p _____

_____

[21]The summary can appear at the beginning or at the end of a chapter. It gives a short outline of the main points of the chapter. The summary might take the form of questions that will tell you what to look for as you read. Pictures can also give you a quick indication of the chapter subject matter, while review questions can help you to be sure you understand the chapter.

q _____

_____

[22]Carefully examine each of your textbooks. Find out how the chapters are organized. You will find it much easier to make effective use of your textbook if you know how it works.

r _____

_____

[23]Where a chapter has no summary provided, you should write your own, because it is much easier to study and review work from a summary.

s _____

_____

[24]A textbook is a tool. If you learn how to use the textbook effectively, you can make it work for you.

t _____

_____

- Write in your Finishing Time and subtract to find your Total Reading Time.
- Record your Total Reading Time on the Development Chart.
- Check your answers in the Answer Key.
- Record your score.
- Look for the correct answers to any you had wrong.

NUMBER CORRECT _____ (Possible 20)
(1 point for each answer)

Summary

■ A summary of this article should give you a list of the major parts of a textbook and the work each part does. Reread your Paragraph Key notes and then complete the summary. (The points of the summary are taken from paragraphs 1–17 of the article.)

1 A textbook is a _____

2 A textbook can help you if _____

When you get a new textbook, look for these parts:

3 _____

4 _____

5 _____

6 _____

7 _____

8 _____

9 _____

10 A textbook is divided into _____

■ Check with your teacher or with the manual for the correct answers.
■ Record your score.

NUMBER CORRECT _____ (Possible 10)
(1 point for each answer)

What's in a Textbook?
Recalling the Details

Recalling the Details

■ Using a textbook may be a big part of the work you do in college, so it is a good idea to know how to use a textbook well. As you choose the right ending for each of these statements, you can check your own understanding of how a textbook is put together. Circle the letter of the group of words that is given for each statement in the article.

1 A textbook is a tool that

    a builds your career
    b helps you learn
    c is used only by teachers

2 You can learn to use a textbook by

    a reading it aloud
    b going to class
    c knowing how it works

3 The title of a textbook
    a tells what the book is about
    b is at the back of the book
    c is a list of other books

4 The subtitle of a textbook

    a comes before the title
    b gives the author's name
    c tells more about the title

5 The table of contents

    a comes after each chapter
    b shows what the book contains
    c is not of much use

6 The index is

    a another word for introduction
    b at the end of each chapter
    c in alphabetical order

7 The glossary

    a is a list of special words
    b is at the end of the book
    c must be written by the student

8 The bibliography

    a tells about the author's life
    b is a list of other books on the subject
    c tells why the book was written

9 The preface

    a is another word for introduction
    b is a list of special words
    c tells about one topic of a subject

10 A chapter

    a is found only at the back of the book
    b must have its own glossary
    c deals with a particular topic

■ Check with your teacher or with the manual for the correct answers.
■ Record your score.

NUMBER CORRECT _____ (Possible 10)
(1 point for each answer)

★ Personal Opinion

■ Here again are the ten words used for special study with this article. Select the correct word to fill in the blank in each of the following sentences, then complete each sentence **in your own words** so it expresses your ideas on the topic.

article	contents	index	syllables	title
bibliography	glossary	preface	table	topic

1 A textbook should have a _____ to tell you the meanings of special words. If it does not have one, you...................................... /

2 A _____ is like an introduction. It tells...

3 If you break a word into _____ , you might find it

....

4 A textbook may have a _____ and a subtitle, which together will tell you

....

5 You can use the _____ if you want to find the names of other books

....

6 In the _____ of contents, you will find

....

7 The _____ is at the back of a book. It is always listed in

....

8 You can find out what a textbook is about if you read the table of _____ . It is found..

9 A chapter contains information on a new _____ of a

....

10 In this book, each _____ in a group is on a new topic of a subject. All the subjects deal with..

■ Check with your teacher or with the manual for the correct answers.
■ Record your score.

NUMBER CORRECT _____ (Possible 20)
(2 points for each word)

What's in a Textbook?

★ Speed Exercise

■ The Speed Exercise will be timed by your teacher. You will be given exactly one minute to read the article or as much of it as you can. You are not asked to answer the questions within that minute, just read the article. Start reading when your teacher says "Start." Stop reading when your teacher says "Stop." Put an X after the last word you read so you can see how far you got. (If you are working alone, you must time one minute for yourself.)

Reading uses two things: your eyes and your brain. Both of them need training. Train your eyes to move quickly. Train them to see more than one word at a time. Your eyes may get tired. Stop now and then and blink. That will give your eyes a rest. You can do eye exercises too. Do this every day: Look straight ahead. Now move your eyes from left to right without moving your head. Do it five or six times. Do that every day until you can do it twenty times. Your eyes will get stronger. (96 words)

1 Reading uses the _____ and the _____ .

2 Both of them need _____ .

3 Rest your eyes by _____ .

4 To begin with, do the exercises _____ times.

5 Work up to _____ times.

NUMBER CORRECT _____ (Possible 20)
Score 10 points if you read the whole article, and 2 points for each correct answer. Check your answers by looking back at the article. Deduct 1 point for each line you did not read.

GETTING THE POINT

Finding the Topic

- Whenever you read, you should have a purpose in mind. You should understand everything you read.

- Your reading in this book consists of articles. An article is a piece of writing on a particular topic. An article is made up of a number of paragraphs, each of which deals with one idea relating to the topic.

- Your purpose in reading an article is to gain information and ideas from it. You will understand the article if you find and understand the main point of each paragraph. The main point is frequently found in the first sentence or, alternatively, in the last sentence. Occasionally, the main point will be found in one of the other sentences in the paragraph.

- Read carefully to find the main point, and then make a note of it in the Paragraph Key. Stop at the end of each paragraph and ask yourself, "What was that paragraph about?" If you cannot make a brief note on its contents, you should read it again.

Why Read?
Word Study, Dictionary Definitions

Word Study—Finding Meanings in the Dictionary

■ A dictionary tells you what words mean. If a word has more than one meaning, the dictionary will give all the meanings. The meanings have numbers in front of them. The most common meaning is listed first. Some words have only one meaning. Some words have several meanings. You must look through the dictionary meanings to find the one that suits the word you are reading.

★ ■ Here is a list of words to study with this article. Look in the Dictionary Definitions to find the first meaning for each of these words. Write that meaning on the line beside the word. The first one is done for you.

1 acquire   get by one's own efforts or actions _____

2 acquisition _____

3 dogma _____

4 dogmatically _____

5 familiar _____

6 familiarize _____

7 media _____

8 medium _____

9 opinion _____

10 opinionated _____

■ Check your answers in the Answer Key.
■ Record your score.
■ Look for the correct answers to any you had wrong.

NUMBER CORRECT _____ (Possible 10)
(1 point for each answer; the first one is a free point)

Dictionary Definitions

acquire (ə kwīr'), v. **1** get by one's own efforts or actions. **2** come into the possession of.

acquisition (ak' wə zish' ən), n. **1** act of acquiring or getting. **2** something acquired or gained.

dogma (dôg' mə, dog' mə), n. **1** belief taught or held as true, especially by authority of a church. **2** any system of established principles and tenets.

dogmatically (dôg mat' ik lē, dog mat' ik lē), adv. done with dogmatism; emphatically.

familiar (fə mil' yər), adj. **1** known from constant association; well known. **2** of everyday use; common; ordinary. **3** well acquainted; versed.

familiarize (fə mil' yə rīz'), v. make (a person) well acquainted with something.

media (mē' dē ə), n. **1** a plural of medium. **2** mass media.

medium (mē' dē əm), n. **1** something that is in the middle in nature or degree; neither one extreme nor the other. **2** sub-

stance or agent through which anything acts; a means. **3** substance in which something can live; environment.

opinion (ə pin' yən), n. **1** what one thinks; belief not so strong as knowledge; judgment. **2** an impression or estimation of quality, character, or value. **3** a formal judgment by an expert; professional advice.

opinionated (ə pin' yə nā' tid), adj. obstinate or conceited with regard to one's opinions.

Using the Words

■ Choose the right word from the Word List to fill in the blank in each of these sentences. Use each word only once.

   1 A personal point of view that is not a fact is called an _____ .

   2 It is helpful to _____ yourself with a textbook before you have to use it in class.

   3 Our opinions are often formed by what we learn from the _____ .

   4 It is hard to have a worthwhile conversation with an _____ person.

   5 If you want to state your ideas _____ , you'd better be sure of your facts.

   6 It is helpful to _____ the habit of making a summary of what you read.

   7 Television is a _____ that stimulates the visual senses.

   8 New ideas often come from things with which we are already _____ .

   9 The _____ of wealth is a strong motivator in the lives of many people.

   10 Members of a religious group should agree to obey the _____ it teaches.

■ Check your answers in the Answer Key.
■ Record your score.

NUMBER CORRECT _____ (Possible 10)
(1 point for each answer)

Why Read?
Article

[1]When we consider that we have radio to listen to and television to watch, we may ask why we need to read at all.

a _____

_____

[2]There are four very good reasons for reading. We read to **acquire** facts, such as the price of goods in shops, the content of packaged goods, or how to use them. Food containers offer a lot of information that must be read before it can be helpful to us.

First Reason:

b We read to _____

_____

[3]We also acquire facts from reading the newspaper—facts such as the daily news, entertainment, and sports information. Newspapers also contain advertisements that give us information about job possibilities or goods that we must buy. We can, of course, find out about daily news from television. But the newspaper contains more information than we usually get from television.

c Facts found in the

_____

[4]Facts are also contained in books. Books can teach you how to do certain things, introduce you to a new **dogma**, or **familiarize** you with other people and places. There are so many things you can learn from books and other reading matter. The **acquisition** of facts, therefore, is one of the benefits of reading.

d And in _____

_____

[5]Reading exposes you to **opinions**, which give varying points of view. As you consider different viewpoints, you can weigh your own opinions and ideas against what others think and, in this way, refine your own ideas. As you read, you will come across opinions you agree with, opinions you disagree with, and some about which you remain undecided.

Second Reason:

e Reading also gives

_____

_____

[6]An opinion should not be judged wrong simply because it does not agree with your own. There can be many different ways of looking at the same thing. As you become curious about why certain people hold certain opinions, you will learn more about people. At the same time, you can learn more about yourself and your opinions. Ask yourself how you came to hold the opinions you have on such subjects as politics, religion, jobs, marriage, and children.

f Opinions let you

_____

_____

[7]It is valuable to form your own opinions on things, but it is also valuable to read and think about other opinions. At the same time, avoid becoming **dogmatically opinionated**. If your mind is too soon closed on a subject, you can be cut off from much of life. Interesting people are open-minded people who have their own ideas, but who are always willing to listen to those of others.

g Don't become _____

_____

[8]Opinions are found in **media** other than books, of course. You can learn about people's opinions by talking to them. The advantage of a book, however, is that it stays with you. A book, unlike a conversation or even a film, can be reread whenever you choose.

[9]Reading can stimulate new ideas. It is fascinating to think about where ideas come from. They can be stimulated by things you see, things you hear, and things you read. Have you noticed how often one idea leads to another? The stimulation of a new idea creates two pleasures: the pleasure of a new idea itself, and the pleasurable possibility that the first idea may give rise to others.

[10]An example of the chain effect of ideas can be seen in the creation of the ice cream cone. Many years ago, a food seller at a fair began to increase his trade by selling ice cream as well as the usual sandwiches. At first, the ice cream was sold in dishes, until he had a new idea. Noticing that people liked cookies with ice cream, he decided to combine the love of cookies with the need for a container. He created the ice cream cone. Needless to say, this also saved the cost of dishes!

[11]New ideas come into the world every day, and all new ideas come from looking at old ideas in a new way or putting several existing ideas together. If you read widely, you will meet new ideas, and these ideas may give rise to further new ideas of your own.

[12]This book presents readings about many things that can affect our everyday lives. Some of these ideas will be quite new to you, while others will already be **familiar**. All the subjects, however, are worth consideration. You may have formed opinions on some of these subjects already, but as you read, you will find even more ideas to consider and discuss.

[13]It is helpful to discuss with other people the ideas you get from reading. Reading is not an activity that should stop when you close the book. Take the ideas you have discovered and developed while reading and explore them in discussion with others. You will notice your own ideas grow and change as you do this.

[14]Reading provides relaxation. A good story can remove you from the everyday cares of the world. The variety of stories to be found in books is endless.

[15]Some readers have a preference for crime stories. They enjoy playing detective and working out the details of how the crime was committed and by whom.

[16]For others, the choice is science fiction. They enjoy the challenge of future worlds and far-away galaxies. Their imagination is stimulated by thoughts of other planets and times.

h Books can be _____ _____

Third Reason:
i Reading stimulates _____

j New inventions come from _____ _____

k Reading new ideas can _____ _____

l This book _____ _____

m Good to _____ _____

Fourth Reason:
n Reading is _____ _____

Types of stories:
o _____ _____

p _____ _____

Why Read?
Article

¹⁷Alternatively, there are readers who like to relax with a good love story. Most of us enjoy the feeling of being particularly special to one other person. So, most of us enjoy a good love story from time to time.

q _____

_____

¹⁸Through the **medium** of a book, you can pretend to be anything you choose. Moreover, you can tackle a book at your own speed. Where a movie or a record will set the pace for you, you can spread a book over many days or weeks if you wish. A book can be read and reread as often as you choose.

r Books can be read

_____

_____

¹⁹A book is easily transported. You can take it on the bus or read it in the doctor's office. You are never really alone if you have something to read.

s Books can be_____

_____

²⁰Reading is a good habit to have. It can be even more enjoyable if you learn to use what you read. Look for ideas as you read, and then share your ideas with other people so that your reading can make your life more interesting and more fun.

t Learn to_____

_____

■ Write in your Finishing Time and subtract to find your Total Reading Time.
■ Record your Total Reading Time on the Development Chart.
■ Check your answers in the Answer Key.
■ Record your score.
■ Look for the correct answers to any you had wrong.

NUMBER CORRECT _____ (Possible 20)
(1 point for each answer)

Why Read?
Summary

Summary

■ A summary is a brief restatement of the main points of an article. Its purpose is to give you a quick review of what you have read. A summary can usually be made from your Paragraph Key notes.
■ Reread your Paragraph Key notes for this article and then complete this summary.

The reasons for reading:

1 From reading you acquire _____

2 Which can be found on _____

3 And in _____

4 And in _____

5 From reading, you also gain _____

6 Which let you _____

7 Reading can stimulate _____

8 Reading also provides _____

9 Three advantages of books are:

    a _____

    b _____

    c _____

10 Reading is more enjoyable if you _____

■ Check with your teacher or with the manual for the correct answers.
■ Record your score.

NUMBER CORRECT _____ (Possible 10)
(1 point for each answer)

Recalling the Details

■ Now that you have read the article, made Paragraph Key notes, and completed the summary, you should have a good understanding of the facts of the article. Check what you know by choosing the ending suggested by the article for each of these statements. Circle the letter of the correct ending in each case.

1 Reading food containers tells us

    a opinions on the contents
    b facts about the contents
    c who uses the contents

2 Facts in newspapers are about

    a news only
    b fiction only
    c news and other things

3 Books can contain

    a facts and opinions
    b facts only
    c opinions only

4 An interesting person

    a avoids other people's ideas
    b believes every new opinion
    c shows interest in other people's ideas

5 Opinions can be found

    a in books only
    b in all media
    c only in books and TV

6 New ideas come from

    a ideas that already exist
    b brilliant people
    c books only

7 After you read, you should

    a keep your ideas to yourself
    b discuss your ideas with other people
    c always come up with new ideas

8 A good story is useful as

    a a reference book
    b a news provider
    c a source of relaxation

9 One advantage of a book is

    a you can reread it as you choose
    b it always contains the truth
    c you look smart when you read

10 You will enjoy reading more if

    a you read several books at once
    b you use what you read
    c you study reading in college

■ Check with your teacher or with the manual for the correct answers.
■ Record your score.

NUMBER CORRECT _____ (Possible 10)
(1 point for each answer)

★ Personal Opinion

■ Here again are the ten words used for special study with this article. Select the correct word to fill in the blank in each of the following sentences, then complete each sentence **in your own words** so it expresses your ideas on the topic.

acquire	dogma	familiar	media	opinion
acquisition	dogmatically	familiarize	medium	opinionated

1 One ability I would like to _____ in life is

. . . .

2 The _____ that I prefer for getting the daily news is

. . . .

3 The newspaper with which I am most _____ is

. . . .

4 One thing I can state quite _____ is

. . . .

5 When you start a new job, it is a good idea to _____ yourself with

. . . .

6 One piece of _____ we are taught in America is

. . . .

7 I would like to see the news _____ improve the way they

. . . .

8 The most _____ person I have ever met had fixed ideas on

. . . .

9 I consider that the _____ of money is

. . . .

10 In my _____ , the best type of story for relaxation is

. . . .

■ Check with your teacher or with the manual for the correct answers.
■ Record your score.

NUMBER CORRECT _____ (Possible 20)
(2 points for each word)

Why Read?

★ Speed Exercise

■ The Speed Exercise will be timed by your teacher. You will be given exactly one minute to read the article or as much of it as you can. You are not asked to answer the questions within that minute, just read the article. Start reading when your teacher says "Start." Stop reading when your teacher says "Stop." Put an X after the last word you read so you can see how far you got. (If you are working alone, you must time one minute for yourself.)

Speed reading   means   reading fast.   It means   moving your eyes quickly
across the page.   Your eyes move   from left to right   when you read.   Learn to see
more than   one word   at a time.   Learn to keep   your eyes moving.
Keep moving forward.   Do not   let your eyes   go back.   Use your finger   or a marker
to keep yourself   on the   right line.   But do not put   your finger   under each word.
Put your finger   or the marker   under the middle   of each line.   Keep your eyes
moving forward   left to right   all the time.   It will soon   become a habit.   (101 words)

1 Your eyes move from _____ to _____ as you read.

2 Your eyes should be always _____ .

3 Keep your place by using _____ or _____ .

NUMBER CORRECT _____ (Possible 20)
You will score 10 points if you read the whole article, and 2 points for each correct answer. Check your answers by looking back at the article. Deduct 1 point for every line you did not read.

SECTION B.
Reading Opens the Door

ARTICLE 4.
Dreams That Came True
Introduction

Using the 5W + H Question Frame

■ Reading opens the door of your mind to new facts and new ideas, so that your world is expanded by what you read. As you gain more interest in life, you allow more of your real self to develop.

■ One way to enhance your reading is to have questions in mind as you read. The 5W + H Question Frame provides a framework of six questions that can help you extract meaning from what you read. These questions are Who, When, Where, What, Why, and How.

■ You can apply the Question Frame to your reading of an article or a story by asking:
WHO is it about?
WHERE and WHEN did it happen?
WHAT happened?
WHY did it happen?
HOW did it happen or HOW could it be changed or stopped?

■ Apply the 5W + H Question Frame to the next article as you read it.

Dreams That Came True
Word Study

Word Study—Synonyms

■ Words are the tools of reading. The more you understand words and how they are used, the easier it will be for you to read.

■ Different words do different work in the sentence. The work done depends on the *part of speech* of the word. This book reviews the work of nouns, adjectives, verbs, and adverbs. If you are not sure what work is done by each of these parts of speech, you can check them in the Glossary.

■ When you look up a word in the dictionary, you will find out what part of speech it is. Look at this line from the dictionary.

glimpse (glimps), *v.* to take a brief look at; to glance.

This line tells us four things:

1 The word, or the "entry" as it is called in a dictionary.

2 The pronunciation. There is a Pronunciation Key inside the front cover of this book to help you understand how to pronounce words.

3 The part of speech (*v.* = verb). The word *glimpse* as it is used in this article is a verb. The parts of speech are abbreviated in the dictionary and are shown after the pronunciation. They are abbreviated as follows: *adj.* = adjective; *adv.* = adverb; *n* = noun; and *v* = verb. See the Grammatical Key inside the front cover of this book for more details.

4 Meanings. The meaning may be given as a phrase (several words) or it may be given as a single word.

■ A single word meaning is called a *synonym*. A synonym is a word that is very similar in meaning to another word.

★ ■ Here is a list of words being used for special study with this article. Use the Dictionary Definitions to find the part of speech of each word and a synonym for each word. Write the abbreviated part of speech in the parentheses and the synonym on the line.

1 amateur (   ) or (   ) _____

2 deference   (   ) _____

3 impact   (   ) _____

4 impending   (   ) _____

5 naturalist   (   ) _____

6 premonition   (   ) _____

7 scornful   (   ) _____

8 subconscious   (   ) _____

9 vain   (   ) _____

10 weigh   (   ) _____

■ Check your answers in the Answer Key.
■ Record your score.
■ Look for the correct answers to any you had wrong.

NUMBER CORRECT _____ (Possible 10)
(½ point for each answer)

Dictionary Definitions

amateur (am' ə chər), *n.* one who engages in a study, science, or sport as a pastime rather than a profession; a non-professional. *-adj.* made or done by amateurs; being an amateur.

deference (def' ər əns), *n.* esteem which is shown to a superior or an elder; respect; high regard for another's wishes.

glimpse (glimps), *v.* to take a brief look at; to glance.

impact (im' pakt), *n.* a striking of one body against another; a collision; a forceful contact.

impending (im pen' ding), *adj.* about to happen; forthcoming; hovering threateningly.

naturalist (nach' ər ə list), *n.* a student of natural history; a scientist; biologist.

premonition (prē' mə nish' ən), *n.* previous notice or warning; knowledge of an event without reason; forewarning.

scornful (skôrn' fəl), *adj.* rejecting with vigorous anger or contempt; sneering; snobby.

subconscious (sub kon' shəs), *adj.* existing in the mind; unconscious; imperfectly or incompletely conscious.

vain (vān), *adj.* having no real value; having undue pride in oneself; worthless.

in vain, expression meaning to no end; without result or success; uselessly.

weigh (wā), *v.* to lie hard upon something; to press down.

Using the Words

■ Choose the right word from the list to put in the blank in each sentence. In each case you will be told what part of speech to use. Notice how the word is used in the sentence. Use each word only once.

1 Dreams can sometimes tell of _____ (adj) disaster.

2 If you dream you bump into something with a heavy _____ (n) you may wake up with a start.

3 A dream might give you a _____ (n) of something that will happen in the future.

4 A _____ (adj) person might say that people who believe in dreams are silly.

5 It might be wise not to talk about your dreams in public, in _____ (n) to those who are afraid of dreams.

6 Dreams often tell us what we are thinking in our _____ (adj) minds.

7 A _____ (n) is usually interested in protecting the environment.

8 Beware of the _____ (n) who pretends to be a professional dream interpreter and will tell you all sorts of things about what your dreams mean.

9 Sometimes we try in _____ (adj) to remember a dream when we wake up.

10 A dream that seems very realistic might _____ (v) upon your mind all day.

■ Check your answers in the Answer Key.
■ Record your score.

NUMBER CORRECT _____ (Possible 10)
(1 point for each answer)

Dreams That Came True
Article

Paragraph Key

■ Fill in the answers to the 5W + H questions as you read the story.

¹Many people have dreams. Many people have nightmares. Some people have dreams that come true! Mary Daughtery (say DAUGHTER-EE) was fond of saying that when she went to sleep, she didn't waste time dreaming. As for nightmares, she never had them. But on the night of November 7th, 1965, Mary had a terrible nightmare. It was one that she and her husband, George, will never forget.

²She tells about it like this, "I was standing on a hill one night. Lightning flashed and thunder rolled overhead. Then a very bright light appeared in the sky. It seemed to rush towards the earth. There was a shattering **impact**, and smoke and screams filled the air."

³Through the smoke, Mary glimpsed a hand lying on the ground. It filled her with a sense of dread. But she moved closer, until she could see first the arm and then the shattered body to which the arm belonged. "Somebody please help," she screamed. Then some men appeared with a large wicker basket. They put the body into the basket and went away.

⁴Mary was still screaming when she woke up. Her husband was bending over her, shaking her. "What is the matter?" he asked.

⁵"I just saw you killed in a plane crash," said Mary. "I saw your body carried away. Oh please, George, cancel your flight to Cincinnati."

⁶"Nonsense," her husband replied. "I've made dozens of flights and nothing ever happens. You just had a nightmare. But if it will make you feel better, I will call you the minute I get to Cincinnati."

⁷Mary begged him to put off his trip, but in **vain**. George only laughed about people who thought they had **premonitions**. But as he drove to the airport, a strange feeling began to **weigh** upon him. When he heard a plane flying overhead, it made his heart thud with fear. At last, he called the airlines and cancelled his seat on Flight 383. Instead, he called Mary, then he drove to the railway station and took a train to Cincinnati.

a Who? _____

_____

b Where? _____

c When? _____

What 5 things did she see?

d _____

e _____

f _____

g _____

h _____

i How did husband react? George thought

it was_____

but he _____

Dreams That Came True
Article

⁸That evening, Flight 383 flew into a heavy thunderstorm while trying to land at the Greater Cincinnati Airport. The plane crashed into a hill. Mary shuddered as she watched scenes of the wreckage on the television news. She closed her eyes as rescue workers began to carry away bodies in wicker baskets.

⁹Thanks to Mary's dream, however, her husband was not among the dead or injured.

¹⁰Another person who had a terrible nightmare was a man called John Bradley. In 1950, he had a dream of **impending** danger. But when he tried to warn others, they laughed at him.

¹¹Bradley was a teacher in a small English town. He was also an **amateur naturalist**. His class liked this because it meant he often took them on field trips into the country.

¹²His terrible dream came to him one week before a planned field trip. Bradley saw himself leading his class along a country lane beside a churchyard. Bradley told the students to take a shortcut through the churchyard. In his dream, he told two of the older boys to lead the way, while he walked at the end of the line to keep the younger stragglers moving.

¹³As they went through the churchyard, Bradley felt the ground tremble. Then he heard a terrible cracking sound. Then something huge and dark rushed towards him, as an immense elm tree crashed down on the line of children.

¹⁴In his dream, Bradley could hear the children's screams quite clearly. He could see their arms and legs sticking out from under the tree.

¹⁵When Bradley told his class about the dream, many of them laughed. Some of the other teachers were even more **scornful**. One of them said the dream was probably really a **subconscious** expression of his dislike for his students.

¹⁶Finally, he agreed that they would go on the field trip anyway. "Only this time," he told his class, "there will be no shortcuts. In **deference** to my dream, we will take the long way round."

¹⁷The children agreed to do what they were told. The older boys, who were leading the group, stopped when they came to a small wooden bridge. "Which way, sir?" they asked. "Shall we cross here or go on till we come to the footpath?"

¹⁸Something about the footpath made Bradley feel uneasy. "Take the bridge!" he ordered. So the children began to walk across it. Then they all heard a terrible cracking sound. They looked back and saw, just where the footpath began, a huge elm crashing to the ground.

---

j What happened to Flight 383? It _____ _____

k George lived because of _____

l Who? _____ _____

m When? _____
n Where? _____

o What fell? _____ _____

p How did his class react?

Class _____

What happened?

q Footpath made him _____

r Ordered them onto _____

s Tree fell on _____

Dreams That Came True
Article

¹⁹The children stared at each other, and then at their teacher. If they had taken the shortcut, they would have reached the footpath just as the tree fell.

t Children were safe because

_____

²⁰After that, no one made any more jokes about Bradley's dream.

- Write in your Finishing Time and subtract to find your Total Reading Time.
- Record your Total Reading Time on the Development Chart.
- Check your answers in the Answer Key.
- Record your score.
- Look again at any you had wrong.

NUMBER CORRECT _____ (Possible 20)
(1 point for each answer)

Summary

■ Your Paragraph Key has given you the important points of the story. If you read through these points, you will see how easy it is to recall the story, using the 5W + H Question Frame.

■ See if you can complete this summary without looking back at the story. Reread the Paragraph Key before you begin if you wish. (The names of the two people have been filled in for you.)

1 Who? <u>Mary Daughtery</u>
had a nightmare.

2 She dreamed she was

Where? _____

3 When? _____

4 George changed his plans

Why? _____

5 Mary saved her husband's life

How? _____

6 Who? <u>John Bradley</u>
had a nightmare.

7 It happened

When? _____

8 He saw his class

Where? _____

9 The students obeyed him

Why? _____

10 His students were saved

How? _____

■ Check with your teacher or with the manual for the correct answers.
■ Record your score.

NUMBER CORRECT _____ (Possible 10)
(1 point for each answer; numbers 1 and 6 are free points)

Dreams That Came True
Recalling the Details

Recalling the Details

- If you learn to remember as you read, you will recall more and more details. This will make reading easier and more interesting to you for two reasons. First, you will not have to reread several times to get the point. Second, you will be able to share your reading and your ideas about it with other people.
- See what you can recall of this article without looking back. Circle the letter of the right ending to each sentence, according to what you read in the article.

1 Mary's husband was going on a journey to

   a Cincinnati
   b New York
   c Chicago

2 In her dream, Mary saw men put the body in

   a a sack
   b a wooden box
   c a wicker basket

3 Mary's husband canceled his flight and

   a stayed at home
   b went by train
   c drove his car all the way

4 The plane crashed

   a at the end of the runway
   b into a hangar
   c into a hill

5 Mary's husband was

   a killed instantly
   b severely injured
   c neither injured nor killed

6 John Bradley's dream of impending danger at first

   a made his students afraid
   b made him give up teaching
   c made everyone laugh at him

7 In his dream, Bradley saw his students taking a shortcut

   a through a churchyard
   b across a bridge
   c down a footpath

8 In real life, the tree fell

   a on the bridge
   b on the footpath
   c in the churchyard

9 In deference to his dream, Bradley asked his students to

   a give up the field trip
   b go with another teacher
   c take the long way around

10 The tree that crashed was

   a an apple tree
   b an oak tree
   c an elm tree

Inference Question

- As well as giving particular information, an article makes some overall suggestions. When you finish reading, you can *infer*, or gather, some of the author's intentions, even if they are not written down. What do you think was the overall point of this article?

   a Dreams never come true.
   b Dreams sometimes give us premonitions.
   c Only bad dreams come true.

- Check with your teacher or with the manual for the correct answers.
- Record your score.

NUMBER CORRECT _____ (Possible 10)
(1 point for each answer; last question is not graded)

Dreams That Came True
★ Personal Opinion

★ Personal Opinion

■ Here again are the ten words used for special study with this article.
■ Select the correct word to fill in the blank in each of the following sentences, then complete each sentence **in your own words** so it expresses your ideas on the topic.

Nouns		Verb	Adjectives	
amateur	naturalist	weigh	impending	subconscious
deference	premonition		scornful	vain
impact				

1 If I had a _____ of a possible national disaster, I would

....

2 I think it is polite to show _____ to ....

3 Economists try to give us advice about _____ changes in

....

4 Today's media seem to be most critical and _____ of

....

5 One _____ action that we all do without thinking is

....

6 A _____ who works in Alaska would probably study

....

7 Children who feel _____ about something they've done usually show it

by...

8 The difference between a professional and an _____ athlete is

....

9 Many of us _____ more than we should because of

....

10 One person who has had a profound _____ on my life is

....

■ Check with your teacher or with the manual
for the correct answers.
■ Record your score.

NUMBER CORRECT _____ (Possible 20)
(2 points for each word)

Dreams That Came True
★ Speed Exercise

★ Speed Exercise

■ (One minute allowed for reading only. Teacher timed or self-timed.)

Reading uses two things.   Your eyes and your brain.   Both of them   need training.
Train your brain   to work hard.   Do not let your brain   get lazy.   Reading is hard work.
Your brain has to work   on two things.   First it has to understand   what each word is
and what each word means.   And then   your brain has to understand   what all the words
mean together.   So your brain   is very busy   as you read.   You must work hard
to read well.   Train your brain   on one sentence   at a time.   You should be sure
you understand one sentence   before you go on   to the next.   Always read with questions
in your mind.   That will help keep   your brain awake.   (120 words)

1 Reading uses the _____ and the _____ .

2 Brain has to work on _____ things.

3 Brain has to understand _____ .

4 And brain has to understand _____ .

5 So always read with _____ .

NUMBER CORRECT _____ (Possible 20)
Score 10 points if you read the whole article,
and 2 points for each correct answer. Check
your answers by looking back at the article.
Deduct 1 point for every line you did not read.

"DREAMS CAN HELP US SOLVE OUR PROBLEMS"

THAT'S A FACT

IS IT?

Distinguishing Fact from Opinion

■ Reading opens the door of your mind to new information that can be either fact or opinion. It is important for you to be able to distinguish between the two.

■ **fact** (fakt), n. thing known to be true or to have really happened.

■ **opinion** (ə pin′ yən), n. what one thinks; belief not so strong as knowledge.

■ A fact has been proven, so you can accept it and act upon it. An opinion, on the other hand, has not been or perhaps cannot be proven. It is unwise to accept an opinion without examining its basis.

■ When reading an article that claims to be factual, look for these things:

1 Names of those who have done research to find the facts.
2 Names of places or institutions where the research occurred.
3 The authority of those doing the research. (Does his/her academic and professional background indicate grounds for a sound opinion?)
4 Dates when the research was carried out.

■ Use these points as guidelines in reading the next article.

Facts about Dreams
Word Study, Dictionary Definitions

Word Study—Parts of Speech

- If you know how words are used in a sentence, it is easier to understand what they mean and what the sentence means.
- The main work of a sentence is done by nouns, verbs, adjectives, and adverbs. Do you know these parts of speech when you see them in sentences?
- The sentences below use the words that have been chosen for special study with this article. In each sentence, name the part of speech of the underlined word. Put the correct part of speech abbreviation in the parentheses.

1 (   ) Our <u>ascent</u> up the mountain was very slow.

2 (   ) We must try to <u>eliminate</u> crime from our area.

3 (   ) The trees swayed <u>erratically</u> in the strong wind.

4 (   ) It is <u>illogical</u> to expect to be right about all things at all times.

5 (   ) It is said that the heart is less <u>logical</u> than the head.

6 (   ) <u>Paranoia</u> is a disease of the mind.

7 (   ) My grandfather handles all his problems <u>placidly</u>.

8 (   ) A <u>psychologist</u> is a person who tries to understand human behavior.

9 (   ) Democracy is good in <u>theory</u>, but is not always perfect in practice.

10 (   ) Television provides strong <u>visual</u> stimulation for the mind.

- Check your answers in the Answer Key.
- Record your score.
- Look for the correct answers to any you had wrong.

NUMBER CORRECT _____ (Possible 10)
(1 point for each answer)

Dictionary Definitions

ascent (ə sent'), *n.* **1** the act of rising or mounting upward. **2** an advance in social status or reputation.
eliminate (i lim' ə nāt), *v.* **1** to cast out or get rid of. **2** to expel (as waste) from the body.
erratically (ə rat' i kəl lē), *adv.* **1** aimlessly, with no fixed course. **2** without regularity or conformity.
illogical (i loj' ə kəl), *adj.* **1** without reason. **2** not observing the principles of logic.
logical (loj' ə kəl), *adj.* **1** capable of reasoning in an orderly fashion. **2** skilled in logic.
paranoia (par' ə noi' ə), *n.* a type of mental disturbance, marked by being very suspicious of others.
placidly (plas' id lē), *adj.* very calmly, without being ruffled or upset.
psychologist (sī kol' ə jist), *n.* a person who studies and works with problems of the mind and human behavior.
theory (thē' ər ē), *n.* **1** a belief, policy or procedure proposed or followed as the basis of action. **2** a hypothesis assumed for the sake of argument or investigation.
visual (vizh' ü əl), *adj.* **1** of or related to seeing things. **2** producing mental images.

Using the Words

■ Choose the right word from the Dictionary Definitions to fill in the blank in each of the following sentences. Use each word only once.

1 There is a _____ that dreams can tell the future, but so far this has not been proved.

2 A _____ is a person who can discuss people's dreams to help them understand their problems.

3 A _____ message is often easier to understand than a spoken one.

4 Your _____ up the professional ladder of success may be helped by someone you know.

5 Many dreams seem ridiculous and _____ when we think about them after waking up.

6 A person who is drunk will usually walk and talk _____ .

7 It is _____ to think that dreams can help us understand our problems.

8 A nervous state of _____ can be the result of being robbed of sleep and dreams.

9 It would be a very successful society that could _____ poverty all together.

10 If you lie _____ for a few minutes when you wake up, it may help you recall your dreams.

■ Check your answers in the Answer Key.
■ Record your score.

NUMBER CORRECT _____ (Possible 10)
(1 point for each answer)

Facts about Dreams
Article

Paragraph Key

■ Complete the Paragraph Key notes. On the dotted lines, note the names of the people who are quoted as dream authorities.

¹Why do we dream? What do dreams mean? Most of us are interested in dreams. In recent years, there have been many books written about dreams. Some of these books are good; some of them are quite foolish. Some of these books are based on the large amount of new scientific research that is being done on dreams these days.

²In laboratories around the land, research is revealing a lot about dreams. There are many things still not known about dreams. But the researchers almost all agree on one main **theory** about dreams. This theory says that all human beings are information processors who have two ways of dealing with their world.

³One way uses the left side of the brain. And it is here that we process things when we are awake. This is the process that makes us do the things we have to do and put aside the thoughts and ideas which are not really a part of our day's work or activity.

⁴The second process happens in the right side of the brain. It takes all those bits of information we did not use during the day and turns them into dreams at night.

⁵Rosalind Cartwright is a **psychologist**. She is also a dream researcher at the University of Illinois. She says, "This sort of processing of information is our regular night shift work." She says that in our dreams we put together all the leftover pieces of our day so we can go on with the next day when we wake up.

⁶We dream several times each night of our lives. Dogs, cats, and other mammals dream also. And dreaming is a time of great activity in the mind.

⁷About ten minutes after falling asleep, we progress through four stages of sleep. Each stage has its own brainwave pattern. As we go deeper into sleep, it becomes harder and harder for anyone to wake us up. At the end of the fourth stage, we begin to come back to the lighter stage of sleep. The **ascent** takes about ten to twenty minutes.

a New _____
_____

b Theory says that _____
_____

c The left side _____
_____

d The right side _____
_____

. . . .

e We dream _____
_____

f As we sleep deeper,
_____

⁸This time is called the "rousal" period. It is often a time of night terrors, sleepwalking, bed-wetting, or night talking. But instead of waking as we reach this time of lightest sleep, we next enter what researchers call the Rapid Eye Movement phase, or REM phase.

⁹During this phase, sleepers stop tossing and turning **erratically**. Their snoring ends, and their breathing is less regular and may even stop altogether for a few seconds. Both the brain temperature and the blood flow rise. The sleeper's body goes as limp as a rag doll, but the muscles of the arms, legs, and trunk become paralyzed. The eyeballs begin to dart back and forth rapidly.

¹⁰If somebody woke you up at the end of this phase, you would probably report strange dreams. Instead of saying, "I was thinking about going swimming this weekend," you might say, "Wow! I was swimming in a huge, pink, marble bathtub and the water was green." After ten minutes, the rapid eye movements end, and the sleeper gradually descends again through the stages of non-REM sleep.

¹¹We go into the REM stage about four to six times a night, or about once every hour and a half. This ninety-minute rhythm seems to be a basic pulse of human life. More than a hundred different body functions, from stomach contractions to hormone secretions, follow a cycle that repeats itself every ninety minutes.

¹²Another psychologist tells us that "during dreams the **illogical**, highly **visual** right side of the brain is freed from the **logical** left side of the brain." And then we dream. We see images of striking color, because we all dream in color. And we often see strange things that we would not accept **placidly** if we were awake. In this strange world, lofty pine trees can grow in the bottom shelf of the refrigerator, and timid kittens can turn into ten-foot monsters. Moods of great terror and wild happiness are common, even if they have nothing to do with what is happening in the dreams.

¹³We all need dreams. Children need to dream more than adults, and babies spend nearly half their sleep time in the REM stage. Researchers have found that if they **eliminate** the REM stage from a person's sleep, the person will be very disturbed. One person began to show signs of **paranoia** after a few days without dreams. Another man began to cheat waitresses when paying his check in restaurants. When they were allowed to have their REM sleep again, all these people dreamed a lot. They had more periods of REM sleep than usual, and sometimes their dreams lasted a whole night. It seemed they were trying to make up for lost dreams.

¹⁴Too much dreaming can be just as bad as not dreaming at all. "When you doze late on a Sunday morning, often you wake up feeling very tired," says one researcher. "The reason is that the longer you sleep, the longer your dreams become. And dreaming is tiring work."

g "Rousal" is a time of _____

h In REM phase _____ _____

i REM phase lasts _____ _____

j Ninety-minute rhythm is _____

k Dreams occur in _____ _____

l Without REM sleep, _____

m Too much dreaming _____

Facts about Dreams
Article

¹⁵Dreaming seems to be a process that helps you cope with problems. People faced with difficult situations, such as a coming job interview or mastering a new skill, usually spend more time in REM sleep. And dreams do seem to be able to provide answers to problems. Many creative people, like Mozart and Einstein, often used their dreams to solve problems and get new ideas. Train yourself to remember your dreams, and they may help you solve the problems of your day. Researchers suggest that you will remember your dreams better if you try to recall them as soon as you wake up.

n Dreams _____

_____

¹⁶Most dreams follow a standard, organized pattern. The first and shortest dream is usually set in the present. It may have to do with a problem that was on your mind when you fell asleep. The next two dreams usually deal with the past. The fourth dream is often set in the future and may be a wish fulfillment dream. You may dream of what it would be like if your wishes came true. The fifth, and often the last dream of the night, builds onto the material from all the other dreams and makes a sort of grand finale, set in the present.

Four stages of dreams:

o _____

p _____

q _____

r _____

¹⁷Even if you think you do not remember your dreams, it is possible that they affect you during the day. Dr. Milton Kramer* believes your dreams make a big difference to what you are like during the day. He thinks that people with a lot of problems tend to be light sleepers who wake up at the end of their REM stages. This helps their chances of remembering their dreams and using them to solve their problems.

s Dreams affect _____

_____

. . . .

¹⁸Dr. Kramer says, "Maybe it's not a good idea to take a sleeping pill if you're upset. It might be better to dream on it." Research is showing that dreams are an important part of our lives. As the famous dream researcher, Friedrich Kekulé, once said, "Let us learn how to dream . . . and then, perhaps, we will discover the truth."

t Dreams show us _____

_____

. . . .

_____

*Dr. Milton Kramer is former Co-director of the Sleep Laboratory at the Veterans' Administration Hospital in Cincinnati, Ohio.

■ Write in your Finishing Time and subtract to find your Total Reading Time.
■ Record your Total Reading Time on the Development Chart.
■ Check your answers in the Answer Key.
■ Record your score.

NUMBER CORRECT _____ (Possible 20)
(1 point for each answer; the names you wrote on the dotted lines are not graded.)

Summary

■ This is a factual article. You should summarize the facts and the names of the people who proved or researched the facts.

■ Complete this summary by listing the names of the people in the article who have done dream research. Write the facts or ideas they had.

■ Then complete the other main points of the summary.

   1 Psychologist _____ (Name)

   2 Facts/ideas _____

   3 Researcher (Doctor) _____ (Name)

   4 Facts/ideas _____

   5 Dream researcher _____ (Name)

   6 Facts/ideas _____

Make a brief summary note on each of the following points from the article:

   7 Who dreams? _____

   8 How many stages of dreaming? _____

   9 What happens if you don't dream? _____

   10 Why do people dream? _____

■ Check with your teacher or with the manual for the correct answers.

■ Record your score.

NUMBER CORRECT _____ (Possible 10)
(1 point for each answer)

Facts about Dreams
Recalling the Details

Recalling the Details

■ It is often important to remember facts correctly. You will find it easier to recall facts if you use a Paragraph Key to extract the facts from the article and then make a summary of them.

■ See how many of the facts of this article you can remember. Check back with your Paragraph Key if you need to.

1 Research into dreams has found

  a all researchers agree on all points
  b there is still disagreement about many things
  c there is no agreement about anything

2 Dogs, cats, and other mammals

  a do not ever dream
  b dream in black and white
  c dream several times each night

3 Sleepers begin to go through four stages of sleep

  a 10 minutes after falling asleep
  b several hours after falling asleep
  c 90 minutes after falling asleep

4 The "rousal" period can be a time of

  a vivid dreams
  b lightest sleep
  c night terrors

5 During the REM phase, the body

  a gets very cold
  b gets very hot
  c goes as limp as a rag doll

6 The ninety-minute rhythm cycle

  a happens only with dreams
  b is used by more than a hundred body functions
  c is used only by the stomach

7 Dreams

  a are in black and white only
  b can be in color or black and white
  c are always in color

8 Children need dreams

  a more than adults
  b about the same as adults
  c less than adults

9 If you sleep late on Sunday, you may feel more tired because

  a you have dreamed less and slept more
  b you have dreamed more and dreams are tiring
  c you have not had enough sleep

10 Give the names of three researchers who are quoted in this article.

  a _____
  b _____
  c _____

■ Check with your teacher or with the manual for the correct answers.
■ Record your score.

NUMBER CORRECT _____ (Possible 10)
(1 point for each answer)

★ Personal Opinion

■ Here again are the ten words used for special study with this article. Select the correct word to fill in the blank in each of the following sentences, then complete each sentence **in your own words** so it expresses your ideas on the topic.

ascent	erratically	logical	placidly	theory
eliminate	illogical	paranoia	psychologist	visual

1 I have my own _____ about the reasons for dreams, which is

....

2 One of the most _____ and absurd dreams I've ever had was

....

3 I am most likely to dream wildly and _____ when

....

4 One task I would like to _____ from the list of things I have to do every week

is......................................

5 If I were going to talk to a _____ about the thing I fear most in life, it would

be......................................

6 If I want to go to sleep easily and _____ , I find it helpful to

....

7 If I could make the _____ from being a nobody to being world famous, I would

like it to be in the area of......................................

8 The symptoms of the mental disorder known as _____ may include

....

9 It seems reasonable and _____ to me to say that dreams

....

10 Television is a _____ medium that can be most helpful for

....

■ Check with your teacher or with the manual for the correct answers.
■ Record your score.

NUMBER CORRECT _____ (Possible 20)
(2 points for each word)

Facts about Dreams
★ Speed Exercise

★ Speed Exercise

■ (One minute only allowed for reading. Teacher timed or self-timed.)

   There are two types   of reading.   One is reading aloud,   and the other
is silent reading.   They are not the same.   When you read aloud   you move your mouth.
You use your teeth and your tongue and your lips.   When you read aloud
you make the sound of every word   on the page.   When you read silently
you should not make   any sounds.   You should not   have to sound out   every word.
So silent reading   should be much quicker.   When you read silently
try to just look at the words   without saying them.   Do not sound them out
even in your mind.   Keeping your mouth still   will make your reading faster.
Put your finger on your lips   as you read silently.   Do your lips move?   They should not.
(128 words)

1 Two types of reading: _____ and _____ .

2 To read aloud you use _____ and _____ and

_____ .

3 You do not use these for _____ reading.

4 Silent reading should be _____ than reading aloud.

5 During silent reading your lips _____ .

NUMBER CORRECT _____ (Possible 20)
Score 10 points if you read the whole article,
and 2 points for each correct answer. Check
your answers by looking back at the article.
Deduct 1 point for each line you did not read.

ARTICLE 6.
The Meaning of Dreams
Introduction

"YOU CAN FORESEE THE FUTURE IN YOUR DREAMS"

THAT'S AN OPINION!

How to Read Opinions

◼ Much of the material you read consists of opinions rather than facts. Opinions must be handled in a particular way.

◼ **opinion** (ə pin′ yən), n. what one thinks; belief not so strong as knowledge.

◼ An opinion is *not* a fact.

◼ **fact** (fakt), n. thing known to be true or to have really happened.

◼ When you come across an opinion in your reading, ask "What is it based on?" Examine the background of the person giving the opinion. Be sure he/she is sufficiently knowledgeable to be able to have sound opinions on the subject.

◼ Weigh an opinion carefully before you accept it. An opinion is not necessarily wrong if it disagrees with your own viewpoint. It is for you to explore the facts behind the opinion and then determine whether you will or will not accept it.

◼ Examine and discuss the opinions in the next article.

The Meaning of Dreams
Word Study, Dictionary Definitions

Word Study—Homonyms

■ Each word in our language has a different meaning. Some words, however, look and sound like other words. Words that sound exactly the same but have different meanings are called *homonyms*. Example: idle, idol; waste, waist. These words sound the same but are spelled and used differently.

■ Sometimes it is very difficult to remember the meanings of words that sound either exactly alike, or very similar.

■ Often, you can work out the meaning of a word from the way it is used in the sentence (from its *context* in the sentence). Example: The words "faculty" and "facility" sound very alike. Can you tell what each word means from its context in this sentence? We need a strong *faculty* to staff the new sports *facility* at our college.

★ ■ The sentences below make use of some words that appear in this article. When you read the sentences, circle what you believe is the right meaning of the underlined word. Use the sense of the sentence to help you understand the meaning of the word. Then check your choice against the list of Dictionary Definitions. The first one is done for you as an example.

1 The faculty to understand ourselves is something we all need.   (**a** ability   **b** nonsense   **c** joy)

2 We can use our dreams to enhance our understanding of ourselves.   (**a** spoil **b** improve   **c** pretend)

3 Dreams happen when we are asleep, and they are a part of our unconscious, deeper self. (**a** dead   **b** not usually aware   **c** secret)

4 You can use your dreams to gain a greater consciousness of your real self.   (**a** awareness   **b** fear **c** misunderstanding)

5 The bat is a nocturnal animal, which does not like to be out in daylight.   (**a** scary   **b** night **c** cold-blooded)

6 Sometimes it is very hard to decipher a doctor's prescription.   (**a** make out the meaning of **b** follow the requirements of   **c** stick to)

7 When you read a book, you may be able to visualize the characters in your imagination.   (**a** forget **b** make fun of   **c** see)

8 A cane is a device that helps people to walk. (**a** a type of tool   **b** large shoe   **c** vehicle)

9 The younger boxer was a novice in the ring, but he fought like an old pro.   (**a** giant   **b** newcomer **c** wrestler)

10 We had no letters from our son for a long interval, but then three arrived in the same week.   (**a** year **b** month   **c** gap of time)

■ Check your answers in the Answer Key.
■ Record your score.
■ Look for the correct answers to any you had wrong.

NUMBER CORRECT _____ (Possible 10)
(1 point for each answer; the first one is a free point)

Dictionary Definitions

consciousness (kon′ shəs nis), *n*. condition of being conscious; awareness.
decipher (di sī′ fər), *v*. **1** make out the meaning of something that is not clear. **2** interpret (secret writing) by using a key; decode.

device (di vīs′), *n*. **1** something invented, devised, or fitted for a particular use or special purpose. **2** a plan; scheme; trick.

enhance (en hans′), *v.* to make greater in quality, value, or importance; to add to; to heighten.

faculty (fak′ əl tē), *n.* **1** power of the mind or body; capacity; capability. **2** power or ability to do some special thing, especially a power of the mind. **3** the teachers of a school, college, or university. **4** a department of learning in a university.

interval (in′ tər vəl), *n.* **1** a period of time between; pause. **2** space between things; intervening space.

nocturnal (nok tėr′ nl), *adj.* **1** of the night. **2** in the night. **3** active in the night. **4** closed by day—open by night.

novice (nov′ is), *n.* **1** one who is new to what he is doing; beginner. **2** person in the period of preparation before becoming a monk or a nun.

unconscious (un kon′ shəs), *adj.* **1** not conscious; not able to feel or think. **2** not aware. **3** not done deliberately.

visualize (vizh′ ü ə līz), *v.* **1** form a mental picture of. **2** make visible.

Using the Words

■ Choose the right word from the Dictionary Definitions to fill in the blank in each of these sentences. Use each word only once.

1 The high school band played during the _____ in the football game.

2 Some people have a remarkable _____ for interesting dreams.

3 You do not expect professional ability from someone who is a _____ at a sport.

4 Extra training will _____ your chances of getting a better job.

5 A slogan is a _____ used by advertisers to attract the attention of the consumer.

6 Our _____ fears often surface in our dreams.

7 It is sometimes frightening to _____ what our planet may be like in a hundred years.

8 Martin Luther King, Jr., did a great deal to awaken the world's _____ to racial inequality in America.

9 It is sometimes necessary to use a magnifying glass to _____ very small writing.

10 Although many people daydream, dreaming is chiefly thought of as a _____ experience.

■ Check your answers in the Answer Key.
■ Record your score.

NUMBER CORRECT _____ (Possible 10)
(1 point for each answer)

The Meaning of Dreams
Article

Time Key

Finishing Time   _____

Starting Time   _____

Total Reading Time _____ minutes

Paragraph Key

■ Make a brief
Paragraph Key note
to summarize the
main point of each
paragraph.

¹Almost everyone has some interest in dreams, even people who don't
particularly believe in them. The challenging question has always been,
"What do dreams mean?" It is hard to understand why we dream in symbols
and why some people seem to have a greater **faculty** for remembering their
dreams than others.

a Question is _____

_____

²There are many definitions of a dream, and dream researchers and
psychologists do not always agree on a definition. They do, however, agree
that these illusions of our **unconscious** mind can be of real value to us.
In the words of one leading researcher, "A dream is a picture of feeling."

b _____

_____

³Our dreams allow us to **visualize** in **nocturnal** pictures the things we
felt during the day but could not or did not express in words or actions.
There is good reason to suppose, therefore, that if we think about our dreams
and try to understand their meanings, we will have a better chance of
getting in touch with our real feelings.

c _____

_____

⁴The modern world is head oriented rather than heart oriented. We are
encouraged to look at everything with the mind rather than with the
emotions, and not to acknowledge that we have any feelings at all. So
we often find ourselves with the logic of the head telling us one thing,
while the heart may be feeling something else. Our dreams **enhance** our
chances of getting the head and the heart together by showing us what
the heart is feeling.

d _____

_____

⁵According to some dream psychologists, the main function of dreams
is to force us to do some concentrated thinking about our ideas and problems.
If you keep a dream diary, you will indeed find that what you have been
doing or thinking in the day will turn up in your dreams. In a way, your
dreams complete the thinking you started during the day. A dream may
help you find the answer to a problem, or it may let you see something
more clearly or from a different point of view.

e _____

_____

⁶Some people claim they never dream. In fact, everybody dreams. It's
just that not everybody remembers dreams. Research shows that you can
remember your dreams if you work at it. Most people forget their dreams
because they're not really interested in trying to remember them.

f _____

_____

⁷There are many books on the market that give advice on how to
remember dreams, and most of them offer the same suggestions: Take some

time to relax when you go to bed, and remind yourself that you want to remember your dreams. Be ready to record your dreams by having a pencil and paper or a tape recorder by the bed. Try to think about your dreams the minute you wake up. Do not allow even a brief **interval** when you think about anything else.

[8]If you do remember your dreams, how do you know what they mean? How does the **novice** begin to understand dream symbols? There are many books on the market about this, too. Some of them contain long lists of interpretations, telling you what each dream symbol means. This is probably their biggest fault, because the experts say that you create your own dream symbols which no one else can really **decipher** for you.

[9]There are, however, some dream symbols that do seem to have a common meaning for most people.

[10]Dreams about flying: The dream of being able to fly under your own steam gives you the feeling of a "high," and it usually occurs when you are particularly happy or excited about something. Quite clearly, it is a symbol of being able to do anything—even the impossible.

[11]Dreams of nudity: A dream of being caught naked can be a symbol of the fear of being exposed or found out. Take the case of the college professor who often dreamed of arriving in class without his clothes. Beneath his dream lay the fear that his students would find out his lie that the works he said he had written had actually been written by somebody else.

[12]Dreams of discovering a hoard of money: Because this dream is common to many people, it is often interpreted as a wish fulfillment dream. After all, most people would like to be richer than they are. This dream, however, may also have another meaning. Finding stored riches may be a symbolic **device** for reminding you of a hidden personal talent that you have never really used.

[13]Dreams of paralysis: Have you ever had a dream in which you were trying to get away from someone or something and you couldn't move? This can be a dream expression of the fact that your deeper **consciousness** enjoys something that your surface morality tells you is wrong.

[14]Take the case of the young girl brought up under very strict moral rules that forbade her to go on unaccompanied dates. She dreamed of being in a dance hall, pursued by many men. She tried to run away, but she was paralyzed and could not move. The truth of her situation was that she really wanted to attract the attention of the men with whom she was not allowed to associate.

g _____

_____

h _____

_____

i _____

_____

j _____

_____

k _____

_____

l _____

_____

m _____

_____

n _____

_____

The Meaning of Dreams

Article

¹⁵Dreams about wild animals: When you dream about being chased or even attacked by wild animals, it does not necessarily mean that the beast in you is coming out. It may simply mean that you want a chance to show your real power and strength. You want to come out from behind your mask of polite, civilized behavior and have a chance to show what you can really do.

¹⁶The meaning of each of these symbols, however, can be a very individual thing and may be different from the common meanings. It is not always wise to use a ready-made interpretation to help you understand your dreams.

¹⁷You can gradually learn to understand your own symbols if you write down your dreams, study them, and try to understand what they mean. Some people think this is a waste of time, but the dream psychologists say you are wasting a lot of time and a lot of life if you do not understand yourself.

¹⁸They ask the question, "How can you afford not to spend time in understanding your dreams?" Dreams, they believe, can be the key to self-understanding.

o _____

_____

p _____

_____

q _____

_____

(2 points)

r _____

_____

(2 points)

■ Write in your Finishing Time.
■ Subtract to find your Total Reading Time, and record it on the Development Chart.
■ Check your answers in the Answer Key.
■ Record your score.

NUMBER CORRECT _____ (Possible 20)
(2 points for q and r; 1 point for each of the other answers)

Summary

■ A useful summary can be put together with main headings and subpoints.

■ As you read through your Paragraph Key, you will see that any article covers a number of main points, each of which is made up of smaller details.

■ This summary gives you the main headings of this article. Fill in the subpoints to complete the summary.

1 Definition of a dream:

    a A dream is _____

    b It shows you _____

    c It forces you to _____

2 Common dream symbols and meanings:

    a _____

    b _____

    c _____

    d _____

    e _____

3 Understand dreams by:

    a _____

    b _____

■ Check with your teacher or with the manual for the correct answers.

■ Record your score.

NUMBER CORRECT _____ (Possible 10)
(1 point for each answer)

The Meaning of Dreams
Recalling the Details

Recalling the Details

■ See how much of the detail of this article you can recall without looking back at it. You can review the summary and the Paragraph Key notes if you wish and then answer the questions.

1 Almost everybody

   a believes in the importance of dreams
   b has some interest in dreams
   c has the attitude that dreams are a nuisance

2 Dream researchers agree that

   a most dreams are of no value to us
   b the illusions of our unconscious mind can be of real value to us
   c there is only one definition of a dream

3 Dreams help us get together

   a our hands and feet
   b our professional and daily life
   c our head and our heart

4 The people who do not remember their dreams

   a have very bad memories
   b may not be really interested in them
   c are very light sleepers

5 There are many books available on

   a how to remember dreams
   b how to interpret dreams
   c both of these topics

6 The main mistake that people make with dream symbols is

   a trying to interpret them according to someone else's pattern
   b ignoring them
   c thinking they all have the same meaning

7 You can help yourself remember your dreams by

   a drinking something hot before bed
   b being ready to record your dreams
   c eating lightly in the evening

8 Dreams tend to deal mostly with

   a things we have forgotten
   b current problems and happenings
   c possible happenings in the future

9 Dream psychologists think understanding our dreams is not a waste of time because

   a it helps us understand ourselves
   b it gives us something to think about
   c dreams solve all our problems

10 The main purpose of this article is

   a to tell you how to work out what your dreams mean
   b to offer some opinions about the importance of dreams
   c to show how stupid it is to believe in dreams

■ Check with your teacher or with the manual for the correct answers.
■ Record your score.

NUMBER CORRECT _____ (Possible 10)
(1 point for each answer)

★ Personal Opinion

■ Here again are the ten words used for special study with this article. Select the correct word to fill in the blank in each of the following sentences, then complete each sentence **in your own words** so it expresses your ideas on the topic.

consciousness	device	faculty	nocturnal	unconscious
decipher	enhance	interval	novice	visualize

1 I think one way in which each of us can _____ our self-image is by

....

2 Dreams present us with _____ pictures of

....

3 If there is one thing I would like to be able to _____ in my dreams, it would

be..

4 A dream symbol that I would particularly like to be able to _____ is

....

5 If I could choose one particular _____ that I could possess, I would like it to

be the ability to..

6 If I could invent a _____ that would make some aspect of life easier or more

attractive, it would be..

7 If I were ever to lose _____ and wake up in a strange place, I would like to

be in..

8 If I were Rip Van Winkle and fell asleep for an _____ of 20 years, I think the

biggest change I would find when I woke would be..

9 One time in my life when I would really like to have been _____ and not known

what was going on was..

10 One sport in which I can say I am certainly a _____ is

....

■ Check with your teacher or with the manual
for the correct answers.
■ Record your score.

NUMBER CORRECT _____ (Possible 20)
(2 points for each word)

The Meaning of Dreams
★ Speed Exercise

★ Speed Exercise

■ (One minute only allowed for reading. Teacher timed or self-timed.)

Speed reading requires practice.   You can speed up your reading   if you work at it.
Train yourself not to sound out   every word.   If you have the habit   of moving your lips
when you read silently   you must learn not to.   Keep your finger on your lips   as you read.
You do not have to   sound out the words.   Your brain can understand the words
by looking at them.   Train yourself to keep your eyes moving   from left to right
across the page.   Do not let yourself   regress to words you've already read.
Train yourself   to see several words   at one time.   Train your brain   to concentrate.
Train your brain to ask questions   all the time.   Train yourself
to think about what you read.   Train yourself to share   what you read   with other people.
To read well you must practice.   (140 words)

1 Speed reading requires _____ .

2 Train your eyes to _____ .

3 Train your brain to _____ .

4 Train yourself to _____ .

5 And train yourself to _____ .

NUMBER CORRECT _____ (Possible 20)
Score 10 points if you read the whole article,
and 2 points for each correct answer. Check
your answers by looking back at the article.
Deduct 1 point for every line you did not read.

SECTION C.
Reading Enlarges Opportunity

Learning from Examples

■ Do you ever wish you could get more out of life? Perhaps you yearn for a better job opportunity or to be very wealthy.

■ Reading about the success of others can sometimes motivate you to find ways to improve your own life. Reading can enlarge your personal opportunities in life.

■ Examples of other people's success methods can provide guideposts for you.

■ Writers use examples to help their readers understand their message. An example is not necessarily proof that something will work for you, but it shows the writer's theory in practice and gives you something by which to judge it.

■ The next article has some ideas on getting rich. It contains three examples, each demonstrating a different way of getting rich.

■ Read the examples carefully, and examine how each example demonstrates the theory the author puts forward in the first paragraph.

Getting Rich Your Own Way
Word Study, Dictionary Definitions

Word Study—Understanding Words from Context

■ A word you have not seen before may be impossible to understand if you see it by itself. If you see it in the context of a sentence, the words around it may help you understand its meaning. For example, if you have not seen the word *peregrinations* before, you probably have no idea what it means. Now look at it in this sentence: "Their *peregrinations* took them to many strange and interesting places." The other words in the sentence will help you guess that *peregrinations* has something to do with *travels*, which is, in fact, what the word means.

★ ■ The following sentences contain the ten words chosen for special study with the next article. Use the context of the sentence to help you determine the meaning of each word. Circle the letter of the word that gives the best meaning.

1 You can <u>surpass</u> your previous record if you work hard. (**a** forget **b** go beyond)

2 He ran the meeting with a very <u>dictatorial</u> attitude. (**a** friendly **b** domineering)

3 A relaxed, encouraging classroom invites creative thinking and <u>spontaneity</u>. (**a** naturalness **b** rebellion)

4 Her latest record looks as if it will be a big <u>hit</u>. (**a** success **b** strike)

5 The job of doorman in this hotel requires the wearing of special <u>apparel</u>. (**a** facial expression **b** clothes)

6 As president of a large <u>conglomerate</u>, she has to work long hours. (**a** group of corporations **b** rock quarry)

7 Early diagnosis is <u>crucial</u> in the treatment of cancer. (**a** useless **b** critical)

8 Many people enjoy having time to <u>bask</u> in the summer sun. (**a** get burned **b** warm pleasantly)

9 A church is not the place where you would expect to find <u>uninhibited</u> behavior. (**a** unrestrained **b** very religious)

10 An investor always likes to have <u>stock</u> in a sound company. (**a** a job **b** shares)

■ Check your answers in the Answer Key.
■ Record your score.

NUMBER CORRECT _____ (Possible 10)
(1 point for each answer)

Dictionary Definitions

apparel (ə par′ əl), *n.* clothing, dress.
bask (bask), *v.* **1** expose oneself to the warmth of sunshine, the heat of a fire, etc. **2** feel great pleasure.
conglomerate (kən glom′ ər it), *n.* **1** mixture of various materials or elements, clustered together without assimilation. **2** a miscellaneous group of unrelated corporations operating under a single ownership.
crucial (krü′ shəl), *adj.* **1** very important or decisive; critical. **2** very trying; severe.

dictatorial (dik′ tə tôr′ ē əl), *adj.* **1** of or like that of a dictator; **2** domineering; overbearing.
hit (hit), *n.* **1** a blow; strike. **2** getting to what is aimed at. **3** a sharp attack or criticism. **4** a successful attempt, performance, or production.
spontaneity (spon′ tə nē′ ə tē), *n.* **1** quality, condition, or fact of being spontaneous. **2** a natural action or movement.
stock (stok), *n.* the capital of a company or corporation divided into portions or shares. **2** the

shares or portions of one such company or corporation. **3** debt owed, especially by a nation, city, etc. (there are also many other listed meanings for this word).
surpass (sər pas′), *v.* **1** do better than; be greater than; excel. **2** be too much or too great for; go beyond; exceed.
uninhibited (un in hib′ it əd), *adj.* **1** not held back, hindered, restrained; unchecked. **2** not prohibited; not forbidden.

Using the Words

■ Choose the right word from the Dictionary Definitions to complete the blanks in the following sentences. Use each word only once.

1 The words and actions of young children are usually completely _____ .

2 Most of us find there are certain types of _____ we prefer to wear.

3 It is always exciting to _____ your own highest expectations.

4 Most people would like to own _____ in some of our nation's biggest companies.

5 It is not uncommon these days for a corporation to be a _____ of several companies with different interests.

6 The winner of an Olympic gold medal should expect to _____ in the congratulations of the whole world.

7 A singer's career is often turned around by just one _____ .

8 A good education encourages creative thinking and _____ of ideas.

9 A career choice may be the most _____ decision you make in life.

10 A _____ boss who will not listen to other people's ideas can make a job unpleasant.

■ Check your answers in the Answer Key.
■ Record your score.

NUMBER CORRECT _____ (Possible 10)
(1 point for each answer)

Getting Rich Your Own Way
Article

Time Key

Finishing Time   ————

Starting Time   ————

Total Reading Time ———— minutes

Paragraph Key

■ Make brief notes on the main points of each example and on the "lesson" shown by each example.

¹A famous businessman was once asked, "Do you think young people who want to become millionaires should go into business on their own?" He answered, "Absolutely not! They're wrong to think that's the only way they'll become millionaires."

a ——————————
——————————

²Let's look at a few sample cases and see why these people became rich.

b ——————————
——————————

³First—Harvey. In high school and college, he was a shy youngster who loved music. He loved the piano and practiced for three to four hours each day. He did some composing as well. "Rodgers and Hammerstein stuff," he called it. Occasionally, he dreamed of being a concert pianist, but he was aware that although he played well, others played better. Besides, he knew he did not want to devote the time and energy needed to catch up to, much less **surpass** them.

c ——————————
——————————

⁴He was a history major in college because he thought studying music would take the fun out of it. His first few jobs did not amount to much. In one, he was a record reviewer and entertainment columnist for a small town newspaper. Eventually he got a job with a record company. This position allowed a variety of his skills to develop.

d ——————————
——————————

⁵He wasn't a professional composer, but that didn't matter. His supervisors were far more interested in his ability to recognize when someone had a potential **hit**. There were composers, writers, singers, and musicians everywhere. The company needed someone to tell them which ones to spend money on.

e ——————————
——————————

⁶Harvey viewed the position as a very **dictatorial** one. Even after fourteen years in the business, he still wasn't ready to be the one to point the finger and say, "You stay. You go."

f ——————————
——————————

⁷Harvey stayed in the background and made the **crucial** judgments about what would and would not sell. Then his bosses proudly announced these decisions as their own. They would **bask** endlessly in the spotlight that he tried so hard to avoid. It was a good arrangement, and Harvey never thought to ask for a cut of the profits. He did, however, earn substantial increases in pay from time to time.

g _____
_____

⁸And how did Harvey finally make his million? One of his two bosses resigned to form a company of his own. He took Harvey and some of the best salespeople with him. The new company soon prospered. Harvey no longer received his high salary. Instead, he got 33 1/3 percent of the **stock** of the new company. Three years later, when business was booming, the company was bought by a big **conglomerate** for $4 million, and Harvey was rich.

h _____
_____

⁹Second case is Ralph. He got rich a different way. He was a tall, ungainly youth who had little interest in sports. His words and his behavior were carefully planned so that it seemed impossible for Ralph to make a fool of himself. Yet that was what Ralph feared. The rigid grip he had on himself prevented any **spontaneity** in his life.

i _____
_____

¹⁰His mind, however, was not suppressed, and over the years he had some first-rate ideas. For eleven years he worked for a mid-sized supplier of chemicals. One day, one of his fellow workers fell, dropping a case of four-gallon jars of strong acid. The jars shattered, covering the worker's arms, neck, and face with acid. Quick action by a fellow worker prevented blindness, but the man was badly scarred.

j _____
_____

¹¹Ralph determined that such accidents should not happen again. Within three months he had convinced top management to let him design a new line of containers that would be much safer.

k _____
_____

¹²Ralph thoroughly enjoyed the task of designing and constructing the models of the new containers, and then destroying them in order to test their bursting strength. He had been interested in the packaging business for a long time, and he had come to know a great deal about it.

l _____
_____

¹³Now he was free to produce his own ideas. When management saw the price tag for setting up the manufacture of the new containers, however, they would not go ahead.

m _____
_____

¹⁴Rather than lose his opportunity, Ralph suggested going 50–50. He would put up half the money and own half the stock. They would provide the other half. His annual $72,000 salary was to be cut to $30,000. Management agreed.

n _____
_____

¹⁵At first, the company bought all the packaging and storage systems Ralph's outfit could produce. Then he started selling to other companies as well, and soon Ralph's little outfit was no longer little.

o _____
_____

¹⁶Finally the parent company offered to buy Ralph's 50%. He had invested $130,000 of his own money, and he was to get back an amount that promised to bring him $1.1 million to $1.3 million over the next three years.

p _____

_____

¹⁷Our third example is Ellen, who struck many people as being scatterbrained, although she was not really that way at all.

q _____

_____

¹⁸Her interest in designing **apparel** was very strong from an early age. When she graduated from a fashion institute, she got a job as an assistant designer. A year later, she moved to another firm, and two years after that, to a third.

r _____

_____

¹⁹Because of these moves and her **uninhibited** comments, people often thought of her as one who took risks. She wasn't. In fact, she was very tightfisted.

s _____

_____

²⁰Her inclination to save money served her well in her third job, where she became the valued associate of a well-known designer. A few years later her boss died. Because Ellen was the only one who knew every aspect of the firm's operations, she was put in charge. A pay packet was put together guaranteeing her in excess of $160,000 a year. Living simply, but nicely, she had indeed saved her way to a net worth of more than $1 million.

t _____

_____

■ Write in your Finishing Time and subtract to find your Total Reading Time.
■ Record your Total Reading Time on the Development Chart.
■ Check your answers in the Answer Key.
■ Record your score.

NUMBER CORRECT _____ (Possible 20)
(1 point for each answer)

Summary

- This is an article that uses examples to make its point.
- Your summary should include the major facts about each example and the point that the examples illustrate.
- Reread your Paragraph Key notes to remind yourself of the important points, and then write the summary.

Example 1:

1 Name _____

2 Job _____

3 Opportunity that led to wealth _____

_____

Example 2:

4 Name _____

5 Job _____

6 Opportunity that led to wealth _____

_____

Example 3:

7 Name _____

8 Job _____

9 Opportunity that led to wealth _____

_____

10 You can get rich by _____

- Check with your teacher or with the manual for the correct answers.
- Record your score.

NUMBER CORRECT _____ (Possible 10)
(1 point for each answer)

Getting Rich Your Own Way

Recalling the Details

■ Since the examples demonstrate the main point of this article, it is helpful to remember details of the examples and to think about how each example demonstrates the author's point.

■ Reread your Paragraph Key notes and your summary and then complete these statements.

1 Harvey did not become a concert pianist because

    a someone insulted his playing
    b he did not want to work at it
    c he did not have a piano

2 He studied history instead of music because

    a he couldn't afford a music teacher
    b he thought studying music would spoil it
    c he wanted to be a history teacher

3 We know that Harvey's real interest was music because

    a he tells us so
    b he worked with a music company
    c he became a concert pianist

4 Harvey got rich because

    a his boss died
    b he got royalties on the people he recommended
    c he took a third of the stock in the new company instead of salary

5 The second example, Ralph, was

    a good at sports and ideas
    b good at sports only
    c better at ideas than sports

6 His chance to get rich began with

    a an accident
    b a new job offer
    c a college degree

7 Ralph

    a loved working on the new packaging
    b worked on the new packaging because it was part of his job
    c did not want to work on the new packaging

8 Ellen's story shows that

    a a wealthy person must be crazy
    b outward behavior does not always tell you what a person's like
    c women are less likely to get wealthy than men

9 Ellen had a chance to be wealthy because

    a she knew her job well
    b she bribed her boss
    c she was the only employee

10 All these examples demonstrate that

    a you don't have to have your own business to get rich
    b it helps to be friends with the boss
    c success in business depends on luck

■ Check with your teacher or with the manual for the correct answers.

■ Record your score.

NUMBER CORRECT _____ (Possible 10)
(1 point for each answer)

Getting Rich Your Own Way
★ Personal Opinion

★ Personal Opinion

■ Here again are the ten words used for special study with this article. Select the correct word to fill in the blank in each of the following sentences, then complete each sentence **in your own words** so it expresses your ideas on the topic.

apparel   conglomerate   dictatorial   spontaneity   surpass
bask   crucial   hit   stock   uninhibited

1 The type of _____ you wear often indicates

....

2 An area in which I would like to _____ my usual performance is

....

3 The place I would most like to go to _____ in the sun this summer is

....

4 The type of _____ behavior I don't appreciate is

....

5 My favorite _____ record of the year so far is

....

6 If I had to choose between a very _____ boss and no job, I would select

....

7 One of the most _____ factors I consider when making a job choice is

....

8 One job where I would expect _____ and creativity to be encouraged would

be..

9 The company in which I would most like to own _____ is

....

10 If I had the choice of working for a small company or a large _____ I would

prefer .... because ....

■ Check with your teacher or with the manual for the correct answers.
■ Record your score.

NUMBER CORRECT _____ (Possible 20)
(2 points for each word)

Getting Rich Your Own Way
★ Speed Exercise

★ Speed Exercise

■ (One minute only allowed for reading. Teacher timed or self-timed.)

   Are special speed reading courses   any good?   They claim to be able
to teach you to read   as many as two thousand words   a minute.   And they charge you
a lot of money   to teach you.   Is it worth it?   If you have a job
where you need to read a lot   it can be helpful.   But there are two things
you must remember.   You will lose your speed very soon   if you do not practice
every day.   And speed reading is good   only if you do not need   to understand
every word of what you read.   If you read something   at 2,000 words a minute
you might get the general idea of it,   but you will not   fully understand it.
Second, you should know   that reading at that speed   is no good at all   if you are trying
to read something   that's completely new to you.   (147 words)

1 Speed reading is helpful if _____ .

2 Speed reading ability is lost if _____ .

3 Most courses cost _____ .

4 Speed reading is good when _____ .

5 It is no good for _____ .

NUMBER CORRECT _____ (Possible 20)
Score 10 points if you read the whole article,
and 2 points for each correct answer. Check
your answers by looking back at the article.
Deduct 1 point for every line you did not read.

The Man Who Turned *Ebony* into Gold

Reading a Biography

■ We can all learn from other people. Even when it is not possible to meet those who could inspire us, we can know them through reading about them.

■ A *biography* covers the events of a person's life. The word biography comes from two Greek words: *bios* = life and *grapho* = I write. A biography is written by someone about someone else. An *autobiography* tells the story of the author's life.

■ Every biography has a focus—a main point the author wants to make about the subject. You can read and recall a biography more readily if you look for these steps:

STEP 1　　Introduction. This shows why the author thinks the subject is worth writing about.

STEP 2　　Early life. This shows the early influences that shaped the subject's life.

STEP 3　　Events of importance. These suggest turning points that led to the subject's becoming a success.

STEP 4　　Highlight. There is usually one major event that will have made a big difference to this life.

STEP 5　　Conclusion. Here the writer suggests what the reader might learn from this life.

■ Use these steps to guide you as you read the next article.

The Man Who Turned *Ebony* into Gold
Word Study, Dictionary Definitions

Word Study—Verbs

■ Words are the tools of reading. Each word does its own job, just as each tool does. The job that the word does is determined by what part of speech it is.

■ A *verb* is a part of speech that tells you about the *action* of the noun or about the *feeling* or state of being of the noun.
Example: (1) <u>My father *compiles* lists of statistics about baseball players.</u> This verb tells you what the noun (father) does. (2) <u>He *is* a sports fan.</u> Here, the verb does not express an action. Instead it tells you something about his state of being.

★ ■ The following list of verbs is taken from the next article. Some of these verbs are mostly used to express *action*; others to express *thinking* or *feeling*. Some can be used in different contexts to express action or feeling. In the parentheses, write A for those that usually express action and F for those that usually express feeling or thinking. Then fill in the correct synonym for each verb by choosing a word from the synonym list. Two of the words in the list can be used to express both action and feeling.

WORD	SYNONYM	SYNONYM LIST
1 ( ) bombard	_____	begin
2 ( ) compile	_____	collect
3 ( ) conceive	_____	separate
4 ( ) daunt	_____	attack
5 ( ) digest	_____	include
6 ( ) discriminate	_____	think up
7 ( ) dissuade	_____	discourage
8 ( ) encompass	_____	advise against
9 ( ) initiate	_____	summarize
10 ( ) segregate	_____	make distinction

■ Check your answers in the Answer Key.
■ Record your score.

NUMBER CORRECT _____ (Possible 10)
(1 point for each answer)

Dictionary Definitions

bombard (bom bärd'), *v.* **1** to attack with heavy shellfire from artillery, rockets, or naval guns. **2** to drop bombs on; bomb. **3** to keep attacking vigorously; attack. **4** to strike (the nucleus of an atom) with a stream of radioactive rays, etc., to change the structure of the nucleus.
compile (kəm pīl'), *v.* **1** to collect and bring together in one list or account. **2** to make (a book, report, etc.) out of various materials.
conceive (kən sēv'), *v.* **1** to form in the mind; think up. **2** to have (an idea or feeling). **3** to put in words; express. **4** to become pregnant with.
daunt (dônt), *v.* **1** to overcome with fear; frighten; intimidate. **2** to lessen the courage of; discourage; dishearten.
digest (dī jest'), *v.* **1** to change or break down food into materials that the body can assimilate. **2** to promote the digestion of food. **3** to understand and absorb mentally; think over or out; consider. **4** to make a brief statement of; summarize. **5** (in chemistry) to soften or decompose by combinations of heat, moisture, pressure or chemical action.
digest (dī' jest), *n.* a brief statement of what is in a longer book, article, or statement; summary.

The Man Who Turned *Ebony* into Gold

Using the Words

discriminate (dis krim' ə nāt), *v.* **1** to make or see a difference; make a distinction. **2** to accord a particular person, class, etc., distinctive (and usually unfair) treatment.
discrimination (dis krim' ə nā' shən), *n.* **1** the seeing or making of a distinction; noticing a difference between things. **2** a difference in attitude or treatment shown to a particular person,

class, etc.
dissuade (dis swād'), *v.* **1** to persuade not to do something. **2** to advise against.
encompass (en kum' pəs), *v.* **1** to surround completely; encircle. **2** to include; contain.
initiate (i nish' ē āt), *v.* **1** to be the first one to start; get going; begin. **2** to admit (a person) with formal ceremonies into a group or

society. **3** to help to get a first understanding; to introduce into the knowledge of some art or subject.
segregate (seg' rə gāt), *v.* **1** to separate from others; set apart; isolate. **2** to separate or keep apart (one race, people, etc.) from another or from the rest of society by maintaining separate schools, separate public facilities, etc.

Using the Words

■ Use the Word List or the Dictionary Definitions to find the correct word to go in each blank in these sentences. Use each word only once.

1 I have been asked to _____ a file of all the jobs open to people with no college education.

2 Our club plans to _____ a wide range of activities for our members next year.

3 It would be helpful if someone would _____ this textbook to a short summary.

4 It is illegal to _____ against people on the grounds of age, race, or sex.

5 It is hard to _____ of a world where there is neither crime nor violence.

6 It is very hard to _____ young people from smoking.

7 Some people think it is better to _____ handicapped children from other children in the classroom.

8 If you want to succeed in life, you should not let hard work _____ you.

9 Advertisements _____ us with offers that are hard to resist.

10 It is often hard to _____ a conversation with people you have not previously met.

■ Check your answers in the Answer Key.
■ Record your score.

NUMBER CORRECT _____ (Possible 10)
(1 point for each answer)

The Man Who Turned *Ebony* into Gold
Article

Time Key

Finishing Time   ————

Starting Time   ————

Total Reading Time ———— minutes

Paragraph Key

■ Complete the Paragraph Key notes for the indicated paragraphs, so you build up a summary of Johnson's life.

¹Ebony is a magazine for those who like to read about black people. It is written for black people, and it stresses stories of successful black people. This may stem from the fact that the editor of the magazine is a success story himself.

²John Harold Johnson is one of the most powerful black men in the country. His present life-style is a far cry from his early life. He was born in 1918 in Arkansas City, Arkansas, at a time when life was often hard for black people.

³Arkansas City was **segregated** and there was **discrimination** even in the schools. Education was available to black children only up to the eighth grade. Beyond that, schools were closed to them.

⁴Johnson's home life was hard, too. He was six when his father died, and his mother, who had gone only to third grade in school, had to work as a domestic. When he was 15, Johnson and his mother moved to Chicago. Soon after that, his mother lost her job, and they had to live on welfare. Johnson believes it was this experience with poverty that made him want to be rich and powerful one day.

⁵At least in Chicago, young John could go to school. He attended Du Sable High School and set out to do well in his school work. His senior year was outstanding. He was president of his class and of the student council. He was editor of the school newspaper and yearbook. He graduated as one of the school's top students.

⁶To celebrate this achievement, he was asked to attend and speak at a party given by the Chicago Urban League in honor of the top students from city schools. The guest of honor was Harry H. Pace, president of the Supreme Life Insurance Company. Pace was so impressed with the way young Johnson spoke that he offered him a job. It was only a part-time job with the insurance company, but it was enough to help Johnson through college.

Introduction:
a Story of a man who

———————————

b Name ——————

———————————

Born ——————

Early Life:
c Educational situation

———————————

d Father——————

———————————

e Mother——————

———————————

f School——————

———————————

Events of Importance:

g ——————

———————————

h ——————

———————————

The Man Who Turned *Ebony* into Gold

[7]On the job he had to **compile** a **digest** of events in the black community, and it was while he was on this job that Johnson **conceived** the idea for his own magazine, *Negro Digest*.

i _____

_____

[8]His friends told him that others had tried this idea and failed. Johnson, however, could not be **dissuaded**, but in order to **initiate** his idea, he needed money. He went to his mother with the suggestion that they mortgage their furniture for the funds. She "prayed to the Lord" for the strength and then agreed to her son's wishes. The furniture brought them $500.

j _____

_____

[9]The way Johnson used this money is just one sign of his clever business mind. He did not spend the money on paper or printing for advertising. Instead, he sent letters to possible subscribers to his magazine with a special $2 offer. Three thousand people took up this offer, which gave Johnson a starting capital of $6,000.

k Used money to _____

_____

[10]His next task was to find a distributor who would handle his magazine. They all told him the same story, that there was no market for such a magazine. Johnson's business sense saved him again. He got his friends to **bombard** the newsstands with requests for the magazine. It wasn't too long before he found someone willing to distribute the new magazine.

l Got friends to_____

_____

[11]*Negro Digest* did well, but not content with that, Johnson was soon thinking about a new magazine. In November, 1945, his new magazine went on the market. It was called *Ebony*. This time, Johnson had no distribution problems, but he did have other troubles.

m New magazine_____

_____

[12]There were not enough people buying advertising space in the magazine. The usual attempts to sell space were not bearing fruit, so Johnson decided to go right to the top. He wrote to Eugene McDonald, president of Zenith Radio Corporation. McDonald at first refused to see Johnson, but this did not **daunt** him. He kept trying, and when at last McDonald agreed to see him, Johnson was ready for him.

n Trouble with _____

_____

[13]He had read in *Who's Who in America* that McDonald had once been the captain of a ship, the SS *Peary* on an expedition to the North Pole. It just so happened that Johnson's friend, Matthew Henson, had been to the North Pole with the very same Captain Peary for whom the boat was named. Henson had later written a book about this trip, so when Johnson went to meet McDonald, he took with him an autographed copy of the book as a gift.

o Gift was _____

_____

[14]The meeting was a success. The Zenith Corporation began to advertise in *Ebony*, and it was not long before other big corporations did, too.

p Soon_____

_____

[15]*Ebony* is now a big success, but Johnson has not stopped there. His publishing business has grown to **encompass** many other magazines and publications.

Highlight:

q _____

_____

The Man Who Turned *Ebony* into Gold
Article

¹⁶Johnson worked hard, and often stayed at his office as late as 8 p.m. He explains it this way, "People take vacations so they can do just what they want to do. I do what I enjoy all the time; so in a way, I'm always on vacation."

¹⁷For young people who would like to succeed in business, Johnson has some sound advice. He says that too many young people want to start at the top and have instant success. But Johnson says, "You should start small and build up."

¹⁸John Harold Johnson is proof that with hard work, determination, and good ideas, you can reach the top from humble beginnings. Johnson started small, he selected a business he knew and loved, and he put energy, determination and hard work into it. These are important guidelines for all of us who might be interested in starting a business of our own.

r Sees job as _____

_____

Conclusion:

s Advice: _____

_____

t Guidelines: _____

_____

_____

- ■ Write in your Finishing Time and subtract to find your Total Reading Time.
- ■ Record your Total Reading Time on the Development Chart.
- ■ Check your answers in the Answer Key.
- ■ Record your score.

NUMBER CORRECT _____ (Possible 20)
(1 point for each answer)

The Man Who Turned *Ebony* into Gold
Summary

Summary

■ A "thumbnail biography" is one that is short and concise. To make a thumbnail biography of this article, you would include only the essential information in the order in which the events happened.

■ Complete the essential details of this summary without looking back at the article.

Introduction

1 Name and occupation _____

Early life:

2 Born: Where _____

3   When _____

4 Family background: Father _____

5   Mother _____

Important steps/highlights:

6 Schooling: Elementary _____

7   High school and college _____

Professional history:

8 First job _____

9 Now _____

Conclusion:

10 Outstanding characteristics _____

■ Check with your teacher or with the manual for the correct answers.

■ Record your score.

NUMBER CORRECT _____ (Possible 10)
(1 point for each answer)

Recalling the Details

■ If you want to retell a biographical story you have read, it is necessary to remember the important details of it correctly. If you have read carefully, made a Paragraph Key, and made a summary, it should not be difficult to remember the details.

■ See how much of this story you can remember without looking back at either the summary or your Paragraph Key notes.

1 John Harold Johnson was born in

 a Arkansas City
 b Chicago
 c Zenith

2 His education went through

 a eighth grade
 b college
 c high school

3 In high school, he was

 a captain of the football team
 b captain of the debating team
 c president of his class

4 His first job was

 a editing a magazine
 b compiling a distribution list
 c compiling a digest

5 His friends did not encourage him to run his own magazine because

 a he didn't have the money
 b others had tried it and failed
 c he didn't have the experience

6 He found a distributor through

 a bribery
 b the help of his friends
 c classified advertising

7 John Harold Johnson had

 a good ideas
 b lots of money
 c a good partner

8 His most successful magazine is

 a *Ebony*
 b *Negro Digest*
 c *Who's Who in America*

9 Johnson believes a vacation means

 a doing nothing at all
 b traveling overseas
 c doing what you enjoy doing

10 He believes the way to get ahead is

 a to start big
 b to start in a partnership
 c to start small

■ Check with your teacher or with the manual for the correct answers.
■ Record your score.

NUMBER CORRECT _____ (Possible 10)
(1 point for each answer)

The Man Who Turned *Ebony* into Gold

★ Personal Opinion

■ Here again are the ten words used for special study with this biography. Select the correct verb to fill in the blank in each of the following sentences, then complete each sentence **in your own words** so it expresses your ideas on the topic.

bombard	conceive	digest	dissuade	initiate
compile	daunt	discriminate	encompass	segregate

1 If I were to _____ a list of the people I most admire, it would include

.... because ....

2 One thing that might _____ me from starting my own business is

....

3 I think a good way to _____ a conversation with a stranger is

....

4 In business, it seems many employers still _____ against

....

5 I believe a business school curriculum should _____ a number of nonbusiness

subjects such as..

6 A book that I would like someone to _____ into a short form for me is

....

7 Nothing can _____ a person who is determined to

....

8 I cannot _____ of any job worse than

....

9 If we allow television to _____ our children with violent films, we can expect

....

10 I believe it is entirely wrong to _____ people on the grounds of

....

■ Check with your teacher or with the manual
for the correct answers.
■ Record your score.

NUMBER CORRECT _____ (Possible 20)
(2 points for each word)

The Man Who Turned *Ebony* into Gold

★ Speed Exercise

★ **Speed Exercise**

■ (One minute only allowed for reading. Teacher timed or self-timed.)

How fast should you read? There is no right answer to that question. You should read different things at different speeds. You can read quite fast if you're reading something you already know, but you may have to read slowly with new materials. Reading very slowly, however, does not always help you to understand better, because your mind can wander when you read slowly. You'll do much better if you keep your brain and your eyes in gear and moving. Very often you do not have to read every word to understand the message. For example, if you are reading a story or if you are reading about a subject you know very well, you can get the gist without reading every word. But when you read something new you have to read more carefully. Then you should read with questions in mind to help you understand. A good reading speed is about 300 words per minute. (159 words)

1 You should read different things at _____ .

2 Read things you know _____ .

3 Read new materials _____ .

4 Reading too slowly lets _____ .

5 A good reading speed is about _____ .

NUMBER CORRECT _____ (Possible 20)
Score 10 points if you read the whole article, and 2 points for each correct answer. Check your answers by looking back at the article. Deduct 1 point for every line you did not read.

THERE MUST BE AN ANSWER

Problems and Solutions

- All of us face problems from time to time and frequently we are quite sure we are the only person in the world who ever had such a problem.

- When you read, you find that others have faced and indeed dealt with similar problems. Their solutions might be of help to you.

- The next article discusses a common problem and suggests a possible solution. You can strengthen your reading of a problem and solution article by following this method:

- Find and make a note on the problem as the author sees it.

- Find and make a note on the solution(s) the author suggests.

- Consider the suitability of the solution. What is its chance of helping to overcome the problem? Would this solution be appropriate for you if you had the same problem?

- Discuss the problem and the solution with other people to strengthen your understanding of the problem and develop a sound opinion of your own as to the solution.

Flextime
Word Study, Dictionary Definitions

Word Study—Stress on Words

■ The dictionary tells you how to pronounce words with the help of a Pronunciation Key. The dictionary also shows you where to put the accent(s) of stress(es) in a word. In a word of more than one syllable, there is usually more stress on one syllable than on the others. For example: In the word "table," we put more stress on the first syllable "ta" than on the second "ble."

■ In longer words, there may be stress on more than one syllable. Example: In the word "fundamental," there is stress on fun′ and on men′. In many dictionaries, the position of the stress is shown with an accent mark (′) immediately after the syllable on which the stress falls.

★ ■ Here is a list of ten words chosen for special study with this article. Put the stress marks in the correct place(s) in each word and provide a synonym for each word. Use the Dictionary Definitions to help you.

WORD	SYNONYM
1 combat	_____
2 complex	_____
3 critical	_____
4 economy	_____
5 flaw	_____
6 interpret	_____
7 legitimate	_____
8 monitor	_____
9 predictor	_____
10 tradition	_____

■ Check your answers in the Answer Key.
■ Record your score.

NUMBER CORRECT _____ (Possible 10)
(1 point for each answer)

Dictionary Definitions

combat (kom′ bat), *v.* **1** fight against, oppose in battle. **2** struggle against.
complex (kom′ pleks), *adj.* **1** made up of a number of parts. **2** complicated. **3** formed by the union of several or many simpler substances.
critical (krit′ ə kəl), *adj.* **1** inclined to find fault or disapprove. **2** of a crisis; being important to the outcome of a situation; crucial.
economy (i kon′ ə mē), *n.* **1** making the most of what one has; avoiding waste in the use of anything. **2** management of affairs and resources of a country, area, or business. **3** efficient arrangement of parts; organization; system.
flaw (flô), *n.* **1** a defective place; crack. **2** a slight defect; fault; blemish.
interpret (in ter′ prit), *v.* **1** explain the meaning of. **2** bring out the meaning of. **3** understand or construe in a particular way; elucidate.
legitimate (lə jit′ ə mit), *adj.* **1** allowed or admitted by law; rightful; lawful. **2** valid; logical; acceptable. **3** conforming to accepted standards; normal; regular.

monitor (mon′ ə tər), *v.* **1** check in order to control something. **2** check the quality, wave, frequency, etc., of (radio or television transmissions, telephone mes-sages, etc.) by means of a monitor.
predictor (pri dikt′ or), *n.* one who announces or tells of an act beforehand; prophet.
tradition (trə dish′ ən), *n.* that which is handed down by beliefs, opinions, customs, stories, etc., from parents to children; customary.

Using the Words

■ Choose the right word from the Dictionary Definitions to complete the blanks in the following sentences. Use each word only once.

1 It is hard to _____ boredom if you really dislike your job.

2 Laziness may come from a character _____ or it may be the effect of physical illness.

3 Turkey for thanksgiving is an established _____ in America.

4 Education can play a _____ part in preparing a person for a career.

5 Many of us find it difficult to _____ instructions that the IRS supplies.

6 The SAT tests are frequently used as a _____ of a student's ability to succeed in college.

7 Caring parents will _____ their children's growth frequently during the early years.

8 A heavy snowstorm provides people with a _____ reason for arriving late at work.

9 War and drought can both have a dramatic effect on the _____ of a country.

10 The _____ issue of nuclear energy and its uses is constantly debated by thinking people.

■ Check your answers in the Answer Key.
■ Record your score.

NUMBER CORRECT _____ (Possible 10)
(1 point for each answer)

Flextime
Article

[1]On a typical day, between 2 and 4 percent of Americans fail to show up at work. This doesn't seem like a high absentee rate, but in the long run it has a bad effect on the national **economy**. More work time is lost each year from absenteeism than from strikes and lockouts. The direct cost to business is about $30 billion a year. Most cases that go to arbitration when an employee grievance is filed are about absenteeism.

a _____
_____

[2]Absentees, managers, and researchers have very different views on why people miss work. Illness is the excuse most often listed in the personnel files. In reality, we don't know how much absence is because of **legitimate** illness. Personnel reporting systems don't always include reasons.

b _____
_____

[3]People normally explain their absence in terms of sickness. Managers and other fellow employees, however, often have explanations that are less kind: laziness, faking sickness, lack of responsibility, poor attitude to work, or other unusual personality characteristics.

c _____
_____

[4]Psychologist Lee Ross of Stanford University has noted that people tend to blame other people's behavior on their personalities. It seems we do not take into account the effect of situations on people's actions. This is especially true when their behavior is unusual. Since most people don't miss much work, the frequent absentee is likely to be described as "odd."

d _____
_____

[5]It is also possible to **interpret** absenteeism in economic terms. Research shows that when unemployment is high, absenteeism goes down. This is because employees want to protect their jobs. Absenteeism increases when overtime pay is readily available. It also increases when workers, especially low-paid ones, get money easily through sick pay plans. Low-paid workers seem to think it is fair if they work fewer hours.

e _____
_____

[6]A number of firms have tried to **combat** absenteeism with plans that offer cash or other rewards for little or no absence. When these plans are kept simple, they usually reduce absenteeism. It has not been possible, however, to **monitor** these plans over long periods of time.

f _____
_____

⁷There are some complicated plans that provide employees with generous paid sick days and then offer "well pay" if employees don't use them. Since such plans have **complex** psychological effects, it is harder to judge their consequences.

g _____

_____

⁸Reason suggests, however, that to defer well pay benefits for a long time, perhaps until the employee retires, shouldn't work well. The reward is too far removed from the immediate behavior to be effective.

h _____

_____

⁹People who place a high value on their time off are usually absent more than those who value it less. This suggests that flextime is one way to reduce absenteeism. Flextime gives employees some flexibility about the time at which they start work. It allows them to work a full shift and still have to themselves that part of the day that is most valuable to them—usually early morning or late afternoon.

i _____

_____

¹⁰While absentees usually explain their behavior medically, co-workers blame their absence on a personality **flaw** or on economics. Psychologists, on the other hand, often see absenteeism as a form of withdrawal from a dissatisfying job. Of all the possible sources of dissatisfaction, dislike of work itself is the best **predictor** of absenteeism. Unhappiness with supervisors, co-workers or other factors is much less **critical**.

j _____

_____

¹¹Studies also show that a worker's job dissatisfaction can be judged by the number of times he or she is absent rather than by the total number of off days each year. A dissatisfied worker is likely to take frequent one or two day breaks rather than long lay-offs.

k _____

_____

¹²Flextime is a word that covers various ways of giving employees a say in their work hours. Actually, it wasn't developed as a way to reduce absenteeism. It wasn't even an American invention. It was introduced in Germany in 1967 as a way to cut down rush-hour congestion.

l _____

_____

¹³It soon became apparent, however, that flextime could help in other ways. It provided employee satisfaction and less job turnover. Research in the United States also suggests that matching working hours to employee needs has helped cut down absenteeism.

m _____

_____

¹⁴Flextime seems to be particularly helpful to married women and mothers whose family responsibilities, by **tradition**, result in high absenteeism.

n _____

_____

¹⁵Researchers point out that flextime makes it easier for women to meet the needs of their families without taking time off. This flexibility, they say, may also help dual-career families cope with their demands.

o _____

_____

¹⁶Researchers have compared different flextime schedules to see which ones reduce absenteeism most effectively.

p _____

_____

Flextime
Article

[17]One study compared a group of employees who had no choice of working hours (group 1) with three groups that had differing degrees of flexibility. The second group could change its hours four times a year. The third group could change every two weeks, and the fourth group could change daily.

[18]As expected, the group with no choice had the highest absenteeism rate. The researchers had thought that absenteeism among the others would decrease with increasing flexibility. This prediction, however, did not come true.

[19]Differences among the flextime groups were slight. The employees who could change their schedules four times actually had the strongest attendance.

[20]Flexibility plus an extended period of commitment, therefore, "may represent a mixture of the best of both worlds."

q _____
_____

r _____
_____

s _____
_____

t _____
_____

■ Write in your Finishing Time and subtract to find your Total Reading Time.
■ Record your Total Reading Time on the Development Chart.
■ Check your answers in the Answer Key.
■ Record your score.
■ Look for the correct answers to any you had wrong.

NUMBER CORRECT _____ (Possible 20)
(1 point for each answer)

Summary

■ This article outlines a problem and discusses a possible solution to it.
■ Your summary should list the main points of both the problem and the suggested solution.
■ Reread your Paragraph Key notes and then fill in the summary points without looking back at the article.

Problem—absenteeism:

1 Common reason given for it _____

2 Its cost to business _____

3 The usual real reason for it _____

4 People often absent seen as _____

Possible solution—flextime:

5 Flextime means _____

6 It began in _____

7 In the year _____

8 In order to _____

9 It now helps _____

10 And it may also help _____

■ Check with your teacher or with the manual
for the correct answers.
■ Record your score.

NUMBER CORRECT _____ (Possible 10)
(1 point for each answer)

Flextime
Recalling the Details

Recalling the Details

■ This article gave you the outline of a problem and a suggestion for a way to solve it. In order to decide if you agree with the solution, see how much detail of the problem and of the suggested solution you can recall. Reread the Paragraph Key and the Summary notes before you begin if you wish.

1 Each year absenteeism costs business about

   a $30 billion
   b $20 million
   c $300,000

2 The most common excuse for absenteeism is

   a poor attitude
   b job dissatisfaction
   c illness

3 When there is overtime work available

   a absence decreases
   b absence stays the same
   c absence increases

4 The "well pay" system

   a gives extra days off
   b pays bonuses to employees who never get sick
   c pays extra to employees who do not use sick days

5 The best predictor of absenteeism is

   a dislike of work
   b unhappiness with supervisors
   c dislike of the work place

6 Job dissatisfaction can be best seen in

   a total number of days absent each year
   b frequency of absences
   c frequent illness

7 Flextime was begun to

   a control rush-hour traffic
   b reduce absenteeism
   c help working mothers

8 Which of the following flextime plans was not studied?

   a change 4 times a year
   b change every 6 months
   c change every 2 weeks

9 Best attendance came from those who

   a changed every 2 weeks
   b did not change at all
   c changed 4 times a year

10 The aim of this article is

   a to discuss the good and bad points of flextime
   b to show that absenteeism is caused by flextime
   c to suggest that flextime might reduce absenteeism

■ Check with your teacher or with the manual for the correct answers.
■ Record your score.

NUMBER CORRECT _____ (Possible 10)
(1 point for each answer)

★ Personal Opinion

■ Here again are the ten words used for special study with this article. Select the correct word to fill in the blank in each of the following sentences, then complete each sentence **in your own words** so it expresses your ideas on the topic.

combat	critical	flaw	legitimate	predictor
complex	economy	interpret	monitor	tradition

1 One _____ I like to keep every year is

....

2 The most successful weather _____ I know is

....

3 If I admit to any _____ in my character, it is

....

4 My advice to anyone trying to _____ the desire to smoke is

....

5 I think the most _____ and difficult subject I have ever studied is

....

6 A successful way to _____ the number of drunk drivers on the nation's highways

is to..

7 The most extraordinary yet _____ excuse I've every heard for being late is

....

8 I think the most _____ and vulnerable time of growing up is

....

9 I try to keep my personal _____ solvent and stable by

....

10 The strangest set of instructions I ever tried to _____ was

....

■ Check with your teacher or with the manual
for the correct answers.
■ Record your score.

NUMBER CORRECT _____ (Possible 20)
(2 points for each word)

Flextime
★ Speed Exercise

★ Speed Exercise

■ (One minute only allowed for reading. Teacher timed or self-timed.)

To be a fast reader you should learn two tricks.   The first one is   that you do not have to sound out every word.   The second one is   that you do not have to read every word on the page   to get the message.   You can learn to skim. This means skipping over little words   like "the" and "and."   Train your eyes to take in the main nouns and the main verbs first.   The nouns will tell you the main subjects of the article.   The verbs will tell you   what the subject (the main person or thing)   is doing.   So from the nouns and verbs   you can begin to get a good outline of the main ideas.   Try it with this sentence. Read only the words in capital letters   in this next sentence.   "The MURDERER RAN very swiftly on catlike feet   into the ROOM and STABBED the unfortunate, lonely little GIRL   right through the HEART." Do you get the idea?   Try it next time you read.   (166 words)

1 One trick is _____ .

2 The other trick is _____ .

3 Look for the main _____ and _____ .

4 Main nouns tell you about _____ .

5 Main verbs tell you about _____ .

NUMBER CORRECT _____ (Possible 20)
Score 10 points if you read the whole article,
and 2 points for each correct answer. Check
your answers by looking back at the article.
Deduct 1 point for every line you did not read.

The Research Article

■ A research article is one that gives you as much information as possible on a certain topic. It does not express the writer's opinions. Instead, the writer brings together the opinions and ideas of many authorities on the subject. The reader then faces the challenge of deciding what to accept and what to discard.

■ Writers of research articles may start out with a particular point of view. They will then interview as many authorities as possible to back up this point of view.

■ Your job as a reader is to make sure that the authorities quoted are believable. As you read a research article, look for and try to remember these facts:

  1 The authority's name
  2 Job or position
  3 Place of employment
  4 Opinions and reasons for holding such opinions

■ Look, too, for a balanced presentation. The writer who presents only one side of the picture may be too biased to be believable.

■ Use these guidelines as you read the next article. Be prepared to remember the details of each authority.

The Question of Ethics
Word Study, Dictionary Definitions

Word Study—Changing Parts of Speech

■ Some words stay the same even when they function as different parts of speech. For example, *poise* is the same whether it is used as a noun or a verb. The speaker has considerable *poise* (n). If you *poise* the vase on the ledge it will fall (*v*).

■ Most words, however, change form when they change function. For example, the verb *publish* becomes *publication* when it is a noun. Understanding parts of speech changes will help you be a better reader.

★ ■ Ten words from this article are listed in the table below. Each word is placed under its correct part of speech heading. Complete the rest of the table for each word. Refer to the Dictionary Definitions for help. Adverbs are listed at the end of the adjective entries. If a word has no form of a particular part of speech, put an X.

	ADJECTIVE	NOUN	VERB	ADVERB
1	_____	_____	_____	conscientiously
2	_____	concurrence	_____	_____
3	_____	consensus	_____	_____
4	daunting	_____	_____	_____
5	_____	_____	deplore	_____
6	elective	_____	_____	_____
7	ethical	_____	_____	_____
8	_____	forbearance	_____	_____
9	_____	_____	grapple	_____
10	_____	integrity	_____	_____

■ Check your answers in the Answer Key.
■ Record your score.

NUMBER CORRECT _____ (Possible 10)
(1 point for each line)

Dictionary Definitions

conscientious (kon′ shē en′ shəs), *adj.* **1** careful to do what one knows is right; controlled by conscience. **2** done with care to make it right; painstaking.—conscientiously, *adv.*—conscientiousness, *n.*

concur (kən ker′), *v.* -curred; -curring. **1** be of the same opinion; **2** come together; happen at the same time. **3** work together; cooperate.

concurrence (kən ker′ əns), *n.* **1** the holding of the same opinion; agreement. **2** a happening at the same time. **3** a working together; cooperating. **4** GEOMETRY. a coming together; meeting at a point.

concurrent (kən ker′ ənt), *adj.* **1** existing side by side; happening at the same time. **2** agreeing; consistent; harmonious. **3** working together; cooperating. **4** having equal authority or jurisdiction. **5** coming together; meeting in a point.—concurrently, *adv.*

consensual (kən sen′ shu əl), *adj.* existing or done by mutual consent.—consensually, *adv.*

consensus (kən sen′ səs), *n.* general agreement; opinion of all or most of the people consulted.

consent (kən sent′), *v.* give approval or permission; agree.

daunt (dönt; dänt), *v.* **1** overcome with fear; frighten; intimidate. **2** lessen the courage of; discourage; dishearten.—daunting, *adj.*—dauntingly, *adv.*

deplorable (di plor′ ə bəl), *adj.* **1** that is to be deplored; regrettable; lamentable. **2** wretched; miserable.—deplorableness, *n.*—deplorably, *adv.*

The Question of Ethics
Using the Words

deplore (di plor'), **-plored, -ing**, *v.* be very sorry about; regret deeply; lament.
elect (i lekt'), *v.* **1** choose or select (a person) for an office, appointment, etc. **2** choose, select.—*adj.* **1** elected for an office, appointment, etc., but not yet installed. **2** specially chosen; selected.—the elect, *n.* a people selected or chosen by God for salvation and eternal life.
election (i lek' shən), *n.* **1** a choosing or selecting for an office, appointment, etc., by vote. **2** being chosen for an office, appointment, etc., by vote. **3** selection by God for salvation. **4** choice; selection or preference.

elective (i lek' tiv), *adj.* **1** chosen by an election; **2** filled by an election; **3** having the right to vote in an election. **4** based upon principle of electing to an office. **5** open to choice; not required; optional. —*n.* subject or course of study that may be taken but is not required.—**electively**, *adv.*—**electiveness**, *n.*
ethic (eth' ik), *adj.* ethical.—*n.* system of ethics.
ethical (eth' ə cəl), *adj.* **1** having to do with standards of right and wrong; of ethics or morals. **2** morally right. **3** in accordance with formal or professional rules of conduct. **4** (of drugs) that cannot be dispensed by a pharmacist

without a doctor's prescription. —**ethically**, *adv.* **ethicalness**, *n.*
forbear (for ber', for bar'), *v.* **-bore, -borne, -bearing**. **1** hold back; keep from doing, saying, using. **2** be patient; control oneself.
forbearance (for ber' əns), *n.* **1** act of forebearing. **2** patience; self control.
grapple (grap' əl), *v.* **-pled, -pling**. **1** struggle by seizing one another; fight closely. **2** try to overcome, solve, or deal (with) a problem, question, etc.—**grapple**, *n.*
integrity (in teg rə tē), *n.* **1** honesty or sincerity; uprightness. **2** wholeness; completeness. **3** perfect condition; soundness.

Using the Words

■ Choose the best word from the ten words printed in the table to complete the blanks in the following sentences. Use each word only once. Do not use any of the words you added to the table.

1 It is a _____ task to have to work all day and attend school at night.

2 When _____ questions arise, some people will turn to a priest or minister for help.

3 It is doubtful that there is a _____ about the state of morality in America today.

4 We frequently learn a lot when we have difficult problems with which to _____ .

5 Some students find _____ subjects in college more interesting than core courses.

6 Children require considerable _____ for the mistakes they make.

7 Many people _____ the use of animals for scientific experiments.

8 _____ is an important characteristic for someone who is to be entrusted with financial affairs.

9 Students who work _____ throughout the year usually do not experience difficulties at examination time.

10 Democracy requires the _____ of the people in the laws of the land.

■ Check your answers in the Answer Key.
■ Record your score.

NUMBER CORRECT _____ (Possible 10)
(1 point for each answer)

The Question of Ethics
Article

Time Key

Finishing Time _____

Starting Time _____

Total Reading Time _____ minutes

Paragraph Key

■ Note the names of the authorities, their workplaces, and their philosophies on this issue.

¹The success of any civilization depends as much on standards of **ethical** behavior as on its economic stability. It seems, however, that nations often ignore their ethics as long as economic conditions are sound. It is only when society seems to be in trouble that people begin to wonder where the real fault lies.

a _____

_____

²As we near the end of the century and look at America's current standing at home and in the world, it is time to ask ourselves, "What are the ethical standards in America today?" Everywhere we look, we see signs of moral weakness. Politics, religion, education, and business are all guilty of actions and attitudes that are clearly unethical.

b _____

_____

³Perhaps there is nothing that can be done about this. Perhaps there is nothing that should be done. The questions of how a nation "behaves itself" and who sets the standards have always been **daunting** ones. Frequently we hear people complain, "There ought to be a law about . . ." but who sets the law, and with what authority?

c _____

_____

⁴What is the relationship, if any, between morality and public policy? Can a society make laws about morality? We do it all the time. Consider the laws against homicide.

d _____

_____

⁵It is foolish for a government to establish moral laws where there is no **concurrence** among the people themselves. So the question is always with us: "Who establishes the ethical standards of our society?"

e _____

_____

⁶Let us look at the views of several concerned public figures with clear opinions on the subject.

⁷First, Donna Shalala. She is the President of Hunter College in Manhattan and a political scientist. She sees the problem as one that involves us all. "If we want to survive," she says, "we will have to reach a **consensus** about the behavior of individuals."

f _____

_____

⁸The Catholic Church's Father Murray, however, raises the question, "Can we fashion a public consensus to direct and control the purpose and uses of the awesome power of society?"

g _____

_____

[9]In answer to his question, ethical standards have now become the concern of many universities that have begun to include ethical studies in their curriculums.

[10]Professor Stothe Kezios, who teaches engineering at Georgia Tech, has recently included an **elective** in engineering ethics. He uses case studies, such as the tragedy of the space shuttle *Challenger*, to encourage students to face ethical questions.

h _____

_____

[11]Kezios reminds his students that several engineers begged NASA to delay that launch. NASA would not. His own philosophy for such cases is "Raise hell, stand firm," but he acknowledges that it is relatively easy to be strong about such cases in the classroom. It is very different when one must **grapple** with such matters in the real world.

i _____

_____

[12]This same conflict of the real world with the world of theory concerns law professor Michael Josephson of Loyola Marymount University. "It's easy to say you want to make a lot of money and also be ethical, when you're a student," he says. "It is much different in the real world." He has started an institute for ethical studies to try to find answers to this dilemma.

j _____

_____

[13]Business students find themselves in similar difficulties. "There are a lot of pressures in fast track environments," according to Kirk Hanson, teacher of ethics at Stanford's Business School. He sees students afraid of the pressures of Wall Street, but he is encouraged by the fact that some students are at least thinking about whether or not they want to throw away their personal **integrity** for the sake of business success.

k _____

_____

[14]Even professors differ in their views of current American attitudes. At Boston University, President John Silber sees the nation influenced by a strong belief in personal pleasure. He says "the gospel preached during every television show is that you only go around once, so get all you can out of life."

l _____

_____

[15]On the other hand, Professor Coles at Harvard University sees a different picture: "Right now, there are almost 1,000 students doing volunteer work with the elderly or with prisoners, or as tutors for children." This shows, he believes, "decency, compassion, and sensitivity to others," which is a contradiction of the "me first" attitude that several of his colleagues deplore.

m _____

_____

[16]Coles uses examples from literature to teach ethical values, stressing the words "tolerance, kindness, **forbearance**, affection." He then invites class discussion on the questions: "Can such values actually be taught? Should they be taught in universities? Do they help the nation?"

n _____

_____

[17]Some people argue strongly that we will never change human nature from its self-serving approach and that school is not the place for correcting the moral values of our society. Others are working **conscientiously** to include value teaching as part of elementary school teaching.

o _____

_____

[18]One strong supporter of this approach is Georgia Attorney Michael Ratelle. He was deeply concerned that his children were receiving no education in basic civics or morality and that "words like honesty and integrity" were not important to today's children.

p _____

_____

[19]Ratelle did something about his problem. He contacted the American Institute of Character Education in Texas and persuaded his local school board to adopt their curriculum, which includes a "freedom code" that stresses such qualities as citizenship, obligations, tolerance, and kindness.

q _____

_____

[20]Now many other elementary schools with the same concerns have also adopted the curriculum. Since 1969, when the curriculum was introduced, it has been adopted by over 33,000 classrooms in 45 states.

r _____

_____

[21]Some teachers think that teaching moral values as a separate subject is not enough. They believe values should be a part of everything taught in schools. Albert Shanker, president of the American Federation of Teachers, says, "Education holds our society together only as long as what is taught has value and is important. You can't teach reading with comic books and rock-star magazines and expect kids to be educated."

s _____

_____

[22]So the debate continues and the questions remain unanswered. Is there a need for tightening ethical standards in America; for looking for values other than the fast buck; the sexual attraction; the political power? If so by whom will these standards be set and how will they be enforced?

t _____

_____

- ■ Write in your Finishing Time and subtract to find your Total Reading Time.
- ■ Record your Total Reading Time on the Development Chart.
- ■ Check your answers in the Answer Key.
- ■ Record your score.

NUMBER CORRECT _____ (Possible 20)
(1 point for each answer)

The Question of Ethics
Summary

Summary

- This article quotes several sources to back up the argument. A comprehensive summary of this material should include the name of each person quoted, the professional status of each, and the point of view of each.
- Reread your Paragraph Key notes and try to complete the summary table without looking back into the article.

1 Problem (question) _____

AUTHORITIES	POSITION and LOCATION (if given)	POINT MADE
2 Donna Shalala		
3 Father Murray		
4 Stothe Kezios		
5 Michael Josephson		
6 Kirk Hanson		
7 John Silber		
8 Coles		
9 Michael Ratelle		
10 Albert Shanker		

- Check with your teacher or with the manual for the correct answers.
- Record your score.

NUMBER CORRECT _____ (Possible 10)
(1 point for each answer)

The Question of Ethics
Recalling the Details

Recalling the Details

■ This article asks you to recall the names of a number of different people and the ideas they put forward. Now that you have made a Paragraph Key and a summary, see if you can recall these details.

1 The major question discussed in this article is

  a why have American morals collapsed?
  b how can American ethical attitudes be changed?
  c should universities teach ethics?

2 The person who uses the *Challenger* tragedy to teach ethics is:

  a Donna Shalala
  b Michael Josephson
  c Stothe Kezios

3 John Silber says modern ethics are:

  a reflected in our television programs
  b easy to follow when you're a student
  c overlooking four important words

4 The 1,000 students doing volunteer work are at:

  a Harvard University
  b Stanford University
  c Altanta Elementary School

5 The person who said you "can't teach reading through comic books" was

  a Albert Shanker
  b Father Murray
  c Michael Ratelle

6 The key words in the American Institute of Character Education charter are

  a self, society, and law
  b forbearance, affection, tolerance, and kindness
  c citizenship, obligations, tolerance, and kindness

7 The pressures of the fast track environment are a concern of

  a Kirk Hanson
  b Michael Josephson
  c Professor Coles

8 Today's belief in pleasure seeking is criticized by

  a Donna Shalala
  b John Silber
  c Albert Shanker

9 The need for a consensus on ethical behavior is seen by

  a Michael Ratelle
  b Stothe Kezios
  c Donna Shalala

10 The teacher who sees signs of "decency and compassion" in today's young people is

  a Professor Coles
  b Father Murray
  c a Georgia attorney

■ Check with your teacher or with the manual for the correct answers.
■ Record your score.

NUMBER CORRECT _____ (Possible 10)
(1 point for each answer)

★ Personal Opinion

■ Here again are the ten words used for special study with this article. Select the correct word to fill in the blank in each of the following sentences, then complete each sentence **in your own words** so it expresses your ideas on the topic.

concurrence	consensus	deplore	ethical	grapple
conscientiously	daunting	elective	forbearance	integrity

1 I think one of the most _____ tasks facing the American nation today is

....

2 One _____ question I find it hard to decide my views on is

....

3 In a democracy there should be _____ of opinion about

....

4 Today's high school students will have to _____ in the future with the problem

of...

5 One _____ course I would like to study for my own pleasure is

....

6 It takes considerable patience and _____ to deal with

....

7 Some people _____ the way the media recently handled the issue of

....

8 I think concepts like honesty and _____ should be taught to children by

....

9 I find it easier to work _____ at a task if

....

10 One change in ethical behavior to which I would give immediate _____ is

....

■ Check with your teacher or with the manual for the correct answers.
■ Record your score.

NUMBER CORRECT _____ (Possible 20)
(2 points for each word)

The Question of Ethics
★ Speed Exercise

★ Speed Exercise

■ (One minute only allowed for reading. Teacher timed or self-timed.)

    Many people   ignore punctuation marks   when they read.   Good readers, however,
make use of these marks   to help them read faster   and understand more.
Each mark has its own job to do   and its own meaning to the reader.   A comma (,) tells you
there is a slight break   in the flow of the sentence.   A period (.) tells you
the sentence is over.   If you keep your eyes   moving forward
you will see the punctuation marks   before you get to them.   This will give you an idea
of how many words   or groups of words   you have to absorb
to get the meaning of the sentence.   This mark (?) indicates   you are reading a question.
This mark (!) says   you are reading an exclamation.   These parentheses ( )
go around extra information   that has been added   to make an idea   clearer to you.
When you are reading quickly   do not bother with those extra words   in parentheses.
Punctuation marks can help you   know how to read   if you learn to see them
before you get to them.   (172 words)

1 This mark (,) means _____ .

2 This mark (.) means _____ .

3 This mark (?) means _____ .

4 This mark (!) means _____ .

5 These marks ( ) mean _____ .

NUMBER CORRECT _____ (Possible 20)
Score 10 points if you read the whole article,
and 2 points for each correct answer. Check
your answers by looking back at the article.
Deduct 1 point for each line you did not read.

Anecdotes

■ **anecdote** (an′ ik dote), n. a short account of some interesting incident or single event, especially one in the life of a person.

■ Writers use these short, short stories to help their readers understand certain things, or to challenge readers to consider a new point of view. People like reading about other people, so a personal anecdote can do more to influence a reader than impersonal facts and numbers.

■ An anecdote is a form of example. In Article 7, *Getting Rich Your Own Way*, there were three case studies. The author used these to show how it is possible to get rich even while working for someone else. The examples made the author's ideas personal.

■ In this article, an anecdote is used to demonstrate how something works. When you have read the anecdote, you can try out the principle behind it for yourself if you like.

■ If you can recall the plot of anecdotes in an article, it might help you to recall the main ideas of the article.

■ As you read this article, look for the anecdote and see if it persuades you to try the ideas in the article for yourself.

Word Study—Parts of Speech and Misused Words

★ ■ There are two areas of study for this section.
■ First, there are five words listed in the table below. See if you can fill in the rest of the parts of speech so that you will recognize and understand them in the article. Put an X where there is no form for that part of speech.
■ Next is a group of five words that are commonly used in conversation and writing, but that are often incorrectly used. See if you can identify and circle the correct meaning for each of the underlined words.

	ADJECTIVE	NOUN	VERB	ADVERB
1	voluntary	_____	_____	_____
2	_____	exertion	_____	_____
3	_____	_____	intervene	_____
4	_____	reflex	_____	_____
5	_____	affliction	_____	_____

6 There are many <u>physiological</u> diseases for which there are still no cures. (**a** dealing with the mind **b** dealing with functions of the body **c** incurable)

7 The crazy dog <u>literally</u> climbed up the wall. (**a** actually did **b** almost did **c** didn't really)

8 The judge stated <u>categorically</u> that the criminal would spend ten years in prison. (**a** with no exceptions **b** with certain provisions **c** formally)

9 The old age <u>syndrome</u> is something that many people no longer accept. (**a** a group of symptoms **b** a myth **c** a single symptom)

10 When the doctor looked for <u>vital</u> signs in the patient, none could be found. (**a** very important **b** life **c** reported)

■ Check your answers in the Answer Key.
■ Record your score.

NUMBER CORRECT _____ (Possible 10)
(1 point for each correct row in the table or multiple choice answer)

Dictionary Definitions

afflict (ə flikt'), *v.* to cause to suffer severely; trouble greatly; distress. —afflicted, *adj.*
affliction (ə flik' shən), *n.* **1** condition of continued pain or distress; misery. **2** cause of continued pain or distress; misfortune.
categorically (kat' ə gôr' ə kəl lē), *adv.* **1** without conditions or qualifications; positively. **2** of or in a category.
exert (eg zért'), *v.* **1** to put into use

or action; bring into effect; use. **2** to exert oneself; make an effort; try hard; strive.
exertion (eg zér' shən), *n.* **1** strenuous action; effort. **2** a putting into action; active use.
intervene (in' tər vēn'), *v.* **1** to come between; be between. **2** to come between persons or groups to help settle a dispute; act as an intermediary.
intervening (in' tər vēn' ing), *adj.*

coming between; acting as an intermediary.
interveningly (in tər vēn' ing lē), *adv.* done in an interfering or interrupting manner.
intervention (in' tər ven' shən), *n.* **1** a coming between. **2** interference, especially by one nation in the affairs of another.
literally (lit' ər ə lē), *adv.* **1** word for word; without exaggeration or imagination. **2** actually. **3** INFOR-

MAL. in effect though not actually; virtually.

physiological (fiz' ē ə loj' ə kəl), *adj.* having to do with the normal or healthy functions of an organism.

reflex (rē' fleks), *n.* **1** an involuntary action in direct response to a stimulation of some nerve cells. **2** something reflected; an image; reflection. **3** a copy. —*adj.* not voluntary; coming as a direct response to a stimulation of some sensory nerve cells.

syndrome (sin' drōm), *n.* group of signs and symptoms considered together as characteristic of a particular disease.

vital (vī' tl), *adj.* **1** of or having to do with life. **2** necessary to life. **3** very necessary. **4** full of life and spirit; lively.

voluntary (vol' ən ter' ē), *adj.* **1** done, made, given, etc., of one's own free will; not forced or compelled. **2** supported or maintained entirely by gifts. —voluntarily, *adv.*

volunteer (vol' ən tir'), *v.* **1** to offer one's services. **2** to offer of one's own free will. **3** tell or say willingly. —*n.* **1** person who enters military or other service of his own free will; not drafted. **2** person who serves without pay. **3** plant that grows from self-sown seed.

Using the Words

■ The following sentences will make use of the ten words studied in the previous exercise. Use the five words printed in the parts of speech table and the five words underlined in the sentences. Choose the correct word to complete the blanks in the following sentences. Use each word only once.

1 It would not be correct to state _____ that everyone is the same in all respects.

2 There are not too many people who will do a _____ job that is dangerous and unpaid.

3 Food and sleep are both _____ to human life.

4 Some people believe the government should not have the right to _____ in the lives of private citizens.

5 Most of us know very little about the internal _____ functions of our own bodies.

6 It seems to be a normal _____ action to shield the eyes against hurt.

7 The body's usual reaction to extreme _____ and hard work is exhaustion.

8 There are _____ millions of people in this country who feel they cannot cope with the pressures of modern living.

9 A person who suffers a very painful _____ will try almost anything to get relief.

10 When doctors are exploring the cause of a disease, they investigate the whole _____ , not just one symptom.

■ Check your answers in the Answer Key.
■ Record your score.

NUMBER CORRECT _____ (Possible 10)
(1 point for each answer)

Using the Mind to Help the Body
Article

Time Key

Finishing Time _____

Starting Time _____

Total Reading Time _____ minutes

Paragraph Key

■ Read each paragraph carefully and then complete the Paragraph Key note before reading the next paragraph. Do not make notes on the anecdotes used.

---

¹What is biofeedback? The science is still too young for a definition that is agreed on by all who practice it. A working definition, however, is that it is the learning of **voluntary** control over automatic body functions. The word "biofeedback" is a short way to describe how you can feed back **physiological** information to yourself and use it.

a _____
_____
(2 points)

²For many years people have been taught that neither humans nor animals could control the **vital** physiological activities of the body. To many scientists there was no such thing as mind, only brain, and they did not agree with the idea of mind over matter.

b _____
_____
(2 points)

³The average person, however, has always known that the mind exists and that it can do wondrous things. Science was so busy with other ideas that it had little time to work out how the brain and mind can work together. Yet, **literally**, all science had to do was look in the mirror—and wink.

c _____
_____
(2 points)

⁴Winking is a clear example of biofeedback. It seems strange that curiosity about it did not spark off the use of biofeedback a long time ago. Winking is learned by biofeedback. It is the **intervention** of a voluntary action over a **reflex** action. The normal reflex action is blinking.

d _____
_____
(2 points)

⁵We blink both eyes together, and we do it without thought at least a thousand times a day. It is a reflex so vital to the function of the eye that it is difficult not to blink. Yet we learn to control that reflex. Most people learn to wink when young, by working with a mirror or learning from a parent. They get biofeedback information about what the eyelid does and whether or not it does it the right way from what they see in the mirror or hear from a parent.

e _____
_____
(1 point)

From *Stress and the Art of Biofeedback* by Barbara B. Brown. Copyright © 1977 by Barbara B. Brown. Reprinted by permission of Bantam Books, a division of Bantam Doubleday, Dell Publishing Group, Inc.

Using the Mind to Help the Body

⁶Could the same voluntary control work with interior body functions, those that make the heart beat or the blood pressure change, or even those strange electric forces of the brain that reflect the mind? Not long ago, the answer was **categorically** no. After the latest biofeedback research, the answer is categorically yes.

f _____
_____
(1 point)

⁷We know now that people can **exert** voluntary control over skin temperature, heart rate, blood pressure, muscle tension, brain waves, or any other internal function. Also, we know that through biofeedback we can learn to make disturbed body functions normal.

g _____
_____
(1 point)

⁸Take the case of a patient who had Raynaud's **Syndrome**, a very painful constriction of blood vessels in the hand. Neither surgery nor medication had helped. Here is how the biofeedback therapist describes the treatment:

⁹"We explained to the patient that we would use skin temperature treatment and that the aim of the treatment was for him to learn to increase the temperature of his hand so that he could either keep it normal or increase it whenever it might fall due to stress or emotion.

¹⁰"We stressed the fact that trying, by making an effort or by conscious thought about the hand itself, would not help. We wanted him to relax and simply think the temperature of the hand up. His first two attempts failed. In fact, the temperature of the **afflicted** hand fell. He had tried too hard. Finally he learned the important lesson. All he had to do was relax and let it happen.

¹¹In his third biofeedback session, he raised the temperature of his painful hand by several degrees. With more practice he would learn to control the temperature of his hand without even looking at the thermometer for help."

¹²Biofeedback is not something you can teach yourself. You need the help of a trained therapist. The average person, however, can demonstrate the biofeedback principle by using an ordinary thermometer purchased from a drugstore or hardware store. Get one that is six to eight inches long and filled with red fluid. Tape the bulb of the thermometer to the fat pad of your middle finger with masking tape, making sure of good contact but no constriction of blood circulation.

h _____
_____
(1 point)

¹³Sit quietly, preferably with your eyes closed, for about five minutes. Then note the temperature of your finger.

i _____
_____
(1 point)

¹⁴While sitting quietly, repeat a few phrases to yourself slowly, such as "I feel relaxed and warm. My hands feel heavy. My hands feel warm and relaxed." Repeat the phrases slowly, allowing the suggestion to take effect. Every five or ten minutes take a reading of the finger temperature. Most people will show a rise in finger temperature after ten or fifteen

j _____
_____
(1 point)

minutes. Some will increase their finger temperature by as much as ten degrees, others by just a degree or two. Only a few will show no change or a drop in temperature. With repeated practice, everyone can learn to increase finger temperature by using this mental activity.

15The mind can affect the body. Our emotions affect our bodies. Much of the pain we feel comes from muscle tension, which is often the direct result of emotional problems. Biofeedback offers the possibility of controlling muscle tension and thereby relieving the problems that may lead to any of the following symptoms: headache, asthma, insomnia, alcoholism, drug taking, learning problems (in children), and pain of childbirth.

16The study and practice of biofeedback have just begun. Many doctors do not agree with or believe in it. But there are people who have had a great deal of pain for a long time and have learned to control their pain by using their minds. For them, biofeedback is the best thing that ever happened.

k _____

_____

(1 point)

l _____

_____

(1 point)

Which four paragraphs will not be included in your summary because they relate an anecdote?

m _____

n _____

o _____

p _____

(1 point each)

- Write in your Finishing Time and subtract to find your Total Reading Time.
- Record your Total Reading Time on the Development Chart.
- Check your answers in the Answer Key.
- Record your score.

NUMBER CORRECT _____ (Possible 20)
(Points as indicated)

Using the Mind to Help the Body
Summary

Summary

■ There are four main areas of information in this article. They can be summarized under the headings included in this summary outline. Reread your Paragraph Key notes and then complete the summary points.

Biofeedback:

  1 Definition _____

  2 An everyday example of it _____

  3 It works on the principle of _____

Pain:

  4 Much of our pain comes from _____

  5 Which in turn comes from _____

  6 Such pain may be controlled by _____

Biofeedback works with:

  7 _____

  8 _____

Present reactions to it:

  9 From doctors _____

  10 From patients _____

■ Check with your teacher or with the manual for the correct answers.
■ Record your score.

NUMBER CORRECT _____ (Possible 10)
(1 point for each answer)

Recalling the Details

■ From your reading of this article, you will have a brief overview of the meaning and uses of biofeedback. You will not have enough information to make you an expert in the subject, but you will have some introductory facts.

■ See how many of these facts you can now recall. Reread your Paragraph Key notes and your summary, and then complete this page.

1 A good way to test the effectiveness of biofeedback for yourself is

   a Raynaud's Syndrome
   b the finger temperature test
   c winking

2 Winking is

   a an unconscious reflex action
   b the intervention of voluntary action over reflex action
   c involuntary action

3 One important thing to remember in using biofeedback is

   a to concentrate very hard
   b to make your mind a complete blank
   c to relax and let it happen

4 Biofeedback

   a can be self-taught
   b has to be learned in a hospital
   c needs the help of a trained therapist in the learning stages

5 The anecdote used shows

   a how biofeedback works
   b that biofeedback works in every case
   c that biofeedback cures only physical problems

6 During the finger temperature test most people show

   a no change in finger temperature
   b a decrease in finger temperature
   c an increase in finger temperature

7 For a long time scientists were

   a more concerned with the brain than with the mind
   b more concerned with the mind than with the brain
   c equally concerned with both the mind and the brain

8 Much of the pain people feel comes from

   a muscle tension
   b mental attitude
   c biofeedback

9 One thing that is not mentioned as being helped by biofeedback is

   a asthma
   b broken limbs
   c pain of childbirth

10 This article offers the reader

   a absolute proof of the effectiveness of biofeedback
   b some valuable evidence about the effects of biofeedback
   c no usable evidence at all

■ Check with your teacher or with the manual for the correct answers.
■ Record your score.

NUMBER CORRECT _____ (Possible 10)
(1 point for each answer)

Using the Mind to Help the Body

★ Personal Opinion

■ Here again are the ten words used for special study with this article. Select the correct word to fill in the blank in each of the following sentences, then complete each sentence **in your own words** so it expresses your ideas on the topic. Cross out the words in parentheses that do not apply to your viewpoint.

affliction	exert	literally	reflex	vital
categorically	intervention	physiological	syndrome	voluntary

1 I (do/do not) believe that the mind can _____ influence over the internal functions of the body because.....................................

2 One thing I think I could say _____ about biofeedback is that

....

3 I think the experiment with the man who had Raynaud's _____ proved

....

4 I (do/do not) think we should try to alter any of the body's natural _____ functions, because.....................................

5 One thing that is of _____ importance for people to understand about their own bodies is.....................................

6 I (would/would not) offer to take part in a _____ experiment with biofeedback, because.....................................

7 I think the most painful _____ anyone can suffer is

....

8 There are _____ thousands of people who suffer the pain of muscle tension as a direct result of.....................................

9 One of the most obvious bodily _____ actions that most of us are aware of is.....................................

10 One example I can think of that shows the possibility of the _____ of mind over matter is.....................................

■ Check with your teacher or with the manual for the correct answers.
■ Record your score.

NUMBER CORRECT _____ (Possible 20)
(2 points for each word)

Using the Mind to Help the Body
★ Speed Exercise

★ Speed Exercise

■ (One minute only allowed for reading. Teacher timed or self-timed.)

There are 186 words   in this article.   In the first speed article   there were 94 words.
If you can read this whole article in one minute   you have improved   by 92 words per minute.
Your reading is improving   in another way, too.   In the first article   there were no more than
three words in each group.   Now you are reading   as many as ten words in a group.
That means your eye span is improved.   You can take in more words   at one time.
As well as this,   you are learning   to keep your eyes moving   from left to right across the page,
and to avoid regressing   to reread.   Your eyes are beginning to work for you
the way they should.   And how about your brain?   Is that working for you, too?
How many of the questions   do you get right each time?   If you get them all right
then your brain is working, too.   Your eyes and your brain   working together
will make you a better and a faster reader.   By now you should be able
to absorb and understand words   without sounding them out.   (186 words)

1 This article has _____ more words than the first one.

2 Some word groups have as many as _____ words.

3 Getting the right answers means your _____ is working.

4 A good reader has _____ and _____ working together.

5 Learn to take in words by _____ at them.

NUMBER CORRECT _____ (Possible 20)
Score 10 points if you read the whole article,
and 2 points for each correct answer. Check
your answers by looking back at the article.
Deduct 1 point for each line you did not read.

ARTICLE 12.
Is There a Doctor in the Body?
Introduction

IS THERE A DOCTOR IN THE BODY ???

Reading with Questions in Mind

- Reading makes your mind work so that you constantly ask yourself how much you know and you are always seeking more knowledge. As you read, many of your previously held ideas may fade away and you will find yourself with new concepts and new perspectives.

- How can you decide which ideas to get rid of and which to keep? You must have a constantly enquiring mind and approach everything you read with questions.

- Start with the title. Ask yourself what the title means; what it suggests about the content of the article. Answer your own question with a guess. As you read, you will find out if your guess was right or wrong, but at least your guess will have given you something to look for as you read.

- Keep questions in your mind all the time you are reading. Ask about the characters, the events, the outcomes. Keep your mind open and active.

- Practice making up and using questions as you read this article.

Is There a Doctor in the Body?
Word Study, Dictionary Definitions

Word Study—Finding Related Parts of Speech

- When you look up a new word in the dictionary, make it a habit also to look for related parts of speech. This will extend your vocabulary and will help you understand how certain words can be used.

- Remember, a noun is a word that names a person, place, thing, or concept. An adjective adds some descriptive information about nouns and usually goes in front of the noun. A verb is an action word or a word that tells about the state of being. An adverb gives more information about the verb.

- ★ Here is a list of ten words that will be used in this article. Each word is placed in its correct place on the parts of speech table. Complete the rest of the table. Some words will have all parts of speech; one word will have only one part of speech. Place an X where there is no form for that part of speech. Refer to the Dictionary Definitions that follow the table if you need help.

	ADJECTIVE	NOUN	VERB	ADVERB
1	adverse			
2			alleviate	
3				arbitrarily
4	beneficial			
5			contend	
6				implicitly
7			materialize	
8		placebo		
9		prescription		
10		skeptic		

- Check your answers in the Answer Key.
- Record your score.

NUMBER CORRECT _____ (Possible 10)
(1 point for each correct row)

Dictionary Definitions

adverse (ad' vers'), *adj*. **1** unfriendly in purpose or effect; antagonistic; hostile. **2** acting against one's interests; unfavorable; harmful. **3** coming from or acting in a contrary direction; opposing. —adversely, *adv*.

adversity (ad vér' sə tē), *n*. **1** condition of being in unfavorable circumstances, especially unfavorable financial circumstances; misfortune; distress. **2** a particular misfortune or calamity.

alleviate (ə lē' vē āt), *v*. **1** to make easier to endure (suffering of the body or mind); relieve. **2** to lessen or lighten; diminish.

alleviation (ə lē' vē ā' shən), *n*. **1** making lighter or easier. **2** something that alleviates.

arbitrary (är' bə trer' ē), *adj*. **1** based on one's own wishes, notions or will; not going by rule or law. **2** fixed or determined by chance. **3** using or abusing unlimited power; tyrannical; despotic. —arbitrarily, *adv*.

arbitrate (är' bə trāt), *v*. **1** to give a decision in a dispute; act as arbiter; mediate. **2** to settle by arbitration.

arbitration (är' bə trā' shən), *n*. settlement of a dispute by a person or persons to whom the conflicting parties agree to refer it for a decision.

beneficial (ben' ə fish' əl), *adj*. producing good; favorable; helpful. —beneficially, *adv*.

benefit (ben' ə fit), *n*. **1** anything that is for the good of a person or thing; advantage; help. —*v*. **1** to be good for; to give good, help to. **2** to receive good from; profit.

contend (kən tend'), *v*. **1** to work hard against difficulties; fight; struggle. **2** to take part in a contest; compete. **3** to argue; dispute.

contention (kən ten' shən), *n*. **1** statement or point that one has argued for; statement maintained as true. **2** an arguing; disputing; quarreling.

contentious (kən ten' shəs), *adj.* fond of arguing; given to disputing; quarrelsome. —contentiously, *adv.*

implication (im' pli kā' shən), *n.* **1** an implying. **2** a being implied. **3** something implied, indirect suggestion, hint.

implicit (im plis' it), *adj.* **1** meant but not stated clearly; implied. **2** without doubting, hesitating or asking questions. **3** involved as a necessary part or condition.

implicitly (im plis' it lē), *adv.* **1** unquestioningly. **2** by implication.

imply (im plī) **-plied, -plying**. *v.* **1** mean without saying so; express indirectly; suggest. **2** involve as a necessary part or condition. **3** signify; mean.

material (mə tir' ē əl), *n.* **1** what a thing is made from; material from which anything is manufactured

or built. —*adj.* **1** having to do with whatever occupies space; of matter or things. **2** of the body. **3** caring too much for the things of this world and neglecting spiritual needs; worldly. **4** that which matters; important.

materialize (mə tir' ē ə līz), *v.* **1** to become an actual fact; be realized. **2** to appear in material or bodily form.

materially (mə tir' ē ə lē), *adv.* **1** with regard to material things; physically. **2** considerably; greatly; substantially. **3** in matter or substance; not in form.

placebo (plə sē' bō), *n.* pill, preparation, etc., containing no active ingredients, but given as a medicine for psychological effect to satisfy a patient, or used as a control in testing the effectiveness of new medicines.

prescribe (pri skrīb'), *v.* **1** to lay

down as a rule to be followed; order; direct. **2** to order as a remedy or treatment.

prescription (pri skrip' shən), *n.* **1** act of prescribing. **2** order; direction. **3** a written direction or order for preparing and using a medicine. **4** the medicine itself.

prescriptive (pri skrip' tiv), *adj.* **1** prescribing. **2** established by law or custom. —prescriptively, *adv.*

skeptic (skep' tik), *n.* **1** person who questions the truth of theories or apparent facts; doubter. **2** person who doubts or questions the possibility or certainty of our knowledge about anything. **3** person who doubts the truth of religious doctrines.

skeptical (skep' tə kəl), *adj.* **1** inclined to doubt; not believing easily. **2** questioning the truth of theories or apparent facts. —skeptically, *adv.*

Using the Words

■ Choose the right word from the Dictionary Definitions to complete the blanks in the following sentences. Use each word only once.

1 Choosing a career is an important decision and should not be made _____ or lightly.

2 Giving a _____ to people who are not really ill but think they are may be the best way to help them.

3 When you take a new medication, you should watch carefully for signs of an _____ reaction.

4 A _____ is a person who doubts the truth of almost everything.

5 People who eat only "natural" foods _____ that they are healthier as a result.

6 Many advertisements suggest _____ that success in life depends on what you look like.

7 A good doctor will not write a _____ for medication that is not needed.

8 A change of scenery is an excellent way to _____ boredom.

9 It is not _____ for children to be given everything they ask for.

10 Sometimes, through hard work, you can see your dreams _____ into reality.

■ Check your answers in the Answer Key.
■ Record your score.

NUMBER CORRECT _____ (Possible 10)
(1 point for each answer)

Is There a Doctor in the Body?
Article

Paragraph Key

■ Practice making Paragraph Key notes that answer questions. Start your reading with the first question in this column. Then stop at the end of each paragraph, fill in the Key, and read the next question before reading the next paragraph.

---

¹Do you feel cheated if you go to the doctor and are sent home without a **prescription**? Doctors have found that in many cases, the psychological effect of being given something to take does people more good than the medicine itself. For such people, doctors sometimes prescribe a **placebo**.

What is the article about?

a _____

_____

²A placebo is a harmless pill, shot, or capsule that has no curative effects of its own, but that can give patients the mental boost they sometimes need to pull themselves through imaginary or minor illnesses.

What is a placebo?

b _____

_____

³Recent research into the placebo is turning up new knowledge about the body's ability to heal itself. It is as though there were a doctor in the body that will cure many of the body's ills, if we will let it.

How does it work?

c _____

_____

⁴Just how the placebo achieves its remarkable effects is not yet fully understood. **Skeptics** say the human mind is easily fooled. They **contend** that if the mind is fooled into thinking it received medicine, then it will make the body act accordingly.

d Skeptics say _____

_____

⁵Others argue differently. They say the placebo allows the wish for health to **materialize** into a reality. They say that since the placebo will not work if the patient knows it is a placebo, the body must not be fooled by it. The fact that patients believe they have been given medicine gives them hope. Their hope strengthens their desire to get better, and this promotes healing in the body.

What do others say?

e _____

_____

⁶Of course it must be acknowledged that placebos do not always work. It seems that a good deal of their success rests ultimately on the relationship between patient and doctor. If the patient trusts the doctor **implicitly**, and if the doctor sincerely wants to help the patient, the placebo is more likely to work. So in a way, the doctor is the most powerful placebo of all.

⁷Consider the following case as an example of the effect of the placebo. A group of people with bleeding ulcers were divided **arbitrarily** into two groups. The first group were told by the doctor that they had been given a new drug which, it was hoped, would give them some relief. The second group were told by a nurse that they had been given a new drug, but that not much was known about how it would work.

⁸The experiment resulted in about 70 percent of the people in the first group showing great improvement, while only 24 percent of the people in the second group showed any improvement at all. In actual fact, both groups had been given the same thing, a placebo. It was significant that the group who had dealt with the doctor showed a much higher rate of improvement than those to whom the doctor did not speak.

⁹The placebo has been found to be effective in many different cases. It has been known to **alleviate** everything from seasickness, to coughs and colds, to pain following an operation. One notable experiment was done to see if the use of the placebo could even help health and longevity in old people.

¹⁰This test, carried out in Rumania, included 150 people over the age of 60. They were divided into three groups of 50 people each. Those in the first group were given nothing at all. Those in the second group were given a placebo regularly, and they were told it would be **beneficial**. The third group were in fact given a new drug, but it was one that in no way had any effect on old age. They too were told the drug would help them.

¹¹All the people were watched for several years, and the results were very interesting. The first group showed no alteration in behavior or the aging process from the other people in the village. The second group, those who took the placebo, showed better health and a lower death rate. The third group, using a real but ineffective drug, showed very much the same result as the group taking the placebo.

¹²If the placebo has been known to have good results, it has also been known to be harmful. If patients believe they will have **adverse** reactions to a medicine, they are very likely to actually have a bad reaction, even to a placebo.

Does it always work?

f _____

_____

g Best results _____

_____

How does the doctor affect the outcome?

h One group told _____

_____

j Other group told _____

_____

j Results: _____

_____

What else can it cure?

k _____

_____

Details of test:

l Groups: _____

_____

_____

m Results: _____

_____

_____

Are placebos harmless?

n _____

_____

¹³This would seem to suggest that much of our reaction to medication is in our minds. Many doctors, however, are reluctant even to investigate the possibilities of the placebo. They believe that if there is any chance of a bad side effect, the placebo should not be used at all. They would rather wait until considerably more research has been completed.

¹⁴The use of the placebo, however, is not something new. It has been accepted practice for centuries in many countries of the world. In some African countries, tribal doctors base their practice on the knowledge that their patients are very likely to get better if they believe they're going to. Many of the so-called "cures" these doctors employ could not possibly cure a sick person, and yet they frequently have the desired effect.

¹⁵The strange power of the placebo has not yet been fully explored, but what is already known does seem to suggest that the human mind is more powerful than we usually acknowledge. One interesting fact is that even people who state categorically they do not believe in mind over matter have themselves been cured by using a placebo.

¹⁶How would you feel if you found out you had been taking a placebo instead of real medicine? If you recovered from your illness anyway, would you think the doctor had cheated you, or would you be grateful to find that your own mind had the power to heal your body?

o Therefore, some

doctors _____

_____

How long have placebos been known?

p _____

q Example:

_____

Is everything known about them now?

r _____

_____

s Sidelight: _____

_____

What do you think of placebos?
t (own answer)_____

_____

_____

- Write in your Finishing Time and subtract to find your Total Reading Time.
- Record your Total Reading Time on the Development Chart.
- Check your answers in the Answer Key.
- Record your score.

NUMBER CORRECT _____ (Possible 20)
(1 point for each answer)

Summary

■ Working through the Paragraph Key with this article has shown you how using questions will help keep you interested in a reading.

■ You will find, too, that working with questions in your mind will help you recall what you read.

■ Reread the answers to the Paragraph Key questions, and then complete this summary by filling in the correct answers to the questions.

 1 What is a placebo? _____

 2 What has it been found to cure? _____

 3 When do placebos seem to work best? _____

 4 When will placebos not work? _____

 5 How do they work? _____

 6 Why are placebos used? _____

 7 Why do some doctors not use them? _____

 8 Where does the healing take place? _____

 9 Where have placebos been used for centuries? _____

10 What does the effect of the placebo suggest? _____

_____

■ Check with your teacher or with the manual for the correct answers.

■ Record your score.

NUMBER CORRECT _____ (Possible 10)
(1 point for each answer)

Is There a Doctor in the Body?
Recalling the Details

Recalling the Details

■ When you read with questions in mind, you may find yourself better equipped to answer questions on the topic and to recall facts more easily.

■ Reread your answers to the Paragraph Key and summary questions, and then complete this exercise.

1 The study of the placebo is giving new information about

 a African tribal doctors
 b the ability of the human body to heal itself
 c the failure of the medical profession

2 The truth about how the placebo works

 a is not yet fully understood
 b is understood by modern doctors
 c is ignored by the medical profession

3 That the body is not fooled by the placebo is suggested by

 a long term research into the subject
 b the fact that the placebo will not work if the patient knows about it
 c the fact that many doctors will not use them

4 The type of doctor who is most likely to have success with using a placebo is

 a one who has worked with tribal doctors
 b one who is sincere in the effort to help the patient and has the patient's trust
 c one who believes in the power of the placebo

5 The effect of the placebo is

 a more psychological than physical
 b more physical than psychological
 c equally psychological and physical

6 Skeptics say

 a the placebo really contains medicine
 b the placebo works by fooling the mind
 c the placebo doesn't really work at all

7 One possible harmful effect of the placebo is

 a the patient may have an adverse reaction to it
 b the patient won't be getting the medicine that's needed
 c the placebo will make the illness worse

8 This article tries to

 a persuade the reader to ask a doctor for placebos
 b dissuade the reader from trusting doctors
 c present some current information about placebos

9 The strange power of the placebo seems to suggest

 a doctors don't know as much as they pretend to
 b the mind does seem to have some power over the health of the body
 c tribal doctors know more than other doctors

10 The facts of this article

 a are not adequately backed up
 b are adequately backed up
 c do not need to be backed up

■ Check with your teacher or with the manual for the correct answers.
■ Record your score.

NUMBER CORRECT _____ (Possible 10)
(1 point for each answer)

Is There a Doctor in the Body?

★ Personal Opinion

★ Personal Opinion

■ Here again are the ten words used for special study with this article. Select the correct word to fill in the blank in each of the following sentences, then complete each sentence **in your own words** so it expresses your ideas on the topic. Cross out the words in parentheses that do not apply to your opinion.

adverse	arbitrarily	contend	materialize	prescription
alleviate	beneficial	implicitly	placebo	skeptic

1 I (do/do not) believe that the mind has power to _____ bodily pain, because

....

2 I (am/am not) a _____ when it comes to believing in the power of the placebo,

because..

3 I (would/would not) be upset if I found I had been cured by a _____ because

....

4 I (do/do not) believe that you should always trust a doctor _____ , because

....

5 I (do/do not) believe the placebo can be _____ in some cases, because

....

6 I (would/would not) _____ that I believe in mind over matter because

....

7 I think the best _____ a person can be given to aid recovery from an illness

is..

8 In my opinion the best way to make a wish for good health _____ into reality

is..

9 People can survive under the most _____ circumstances if

....

10 It probably would not be wise to decide _____ that a placebo is the answer

to your problems. First you should..

■ Check with your teacher or with the manual for the correct answers.
■ Record your score.

NUMBER CORRECT _____ (Possible 20)
(2 points for each word)

Article 12 ● Is There a Doctor in the Body?

119

Is There a Doctor in the Body?
★ Speed Exercise

★ Speed Exercise

■ (One minute allowed for reading only. Teacher timed or self-timed.)

Up until now,   these speed articles   have been about   how to read faster.
Following this exercise, however,   the subject matter of the speed articles   will change.
By now you have been shown   what you need to know   to help you learn to read faster.
All that is required now is constant practice   on your part.   Efficient reading is a skill
that will quickly disappear   if you do not practice it.   So, you should practice
whenever you read,   not just when you read these exercises.   It is very easy to slip back
into bad habits.   Whenever you read   you should remind yourself of the rules
before you begin.   Effective reading is hard work.   That does not mean
reading has to be unpleasant.   Lots of things we do   are not really easy   but we enjoy them
just the same.   Reading can be enjoyable   because it leads to other things.
Reading is a good way   to find out about   a great variety of things.   It provides ideas
that you can share   with other people,   and it provides you   with starting points
for new ideas of your own.   Reading is of much more use to you   when you know how to do it
well.

(200 words)

1 This is the last article for a while about _____ .

2 Practice fast reading _____ .

3 Reading is hard work, but that does not mean it's _____ .

4 Reading lets you _____ .

5 Reading is easier when _____ .

NUMBER CORRECT _____ (Possible 20)
Score 10 points if you read the whole article,
and 2 points for each correct answer. Check
your answers by looking back at the article.
Deduct 1 point for each line you did not read.

Using Inferences in Reading

■ Life presents us with many opportunities for decision making. Often it is hard to know which decision is the right one. The facts, information, and ideas you can get from reading can stimulate your thinking and help your decision making.

■ Reading provides facts and inferences. An inference is unstated information you assume from stated facts. Example: From the sentence "*Starting on Friday, Jane will have three days' hard work at the office*," you can infer that Jane will not play tennis on Saturday. While this is not stated, it follows that if her three days' work begins on Friday, she will be working on Saturday, and if she is working, she will not be playing tennis.

■ Inferences are as important as facts, so a good reader takes note of the inferences as well as the facts, since these may provide the most stimulation for thought.

■ As you read the next article, think about the inferences it suggests as well as the facts it presents. You will be answering some questions on the inferences it contains in the *Recalling the Details* section.

Cloning
Word Study, Dictionary Definitions

Word Study—Finding Meaning from Context

■ A dictionary is a reference book that gives meanings of words and other related information. It is most commonly used for checking word meanings. Before checking the meaning of a new word in the dictionary, however, attempt to understand the new word by examining it in context. You can pick up clues to the meaning of the new word from the general meaning of the sentence in which it is found.

■ Determining meaning from context always contains some guesswork. It is wise to check the precise meaning with a dictionary if you want to be able to use the word freely in other contexts.

★ ■ These sentences contain the ten words chosen for special study with this article. Read each sentence carefully, then select the word in parentheses that gives the best meaning of the underlined word. Check your choice with the Dictionary Definitions.

1 There is considerable <u>controversy</u> in this country over the use of nuclear energy. (**a** ruling **b** argument **c** decision)

2 A student should be expected not to <u>countermand</u> the orders of a teacher. (**a** obey **b** carry out **c** cancel)

3 Some people drink to the <u>detriment</u> of their health. (**a** damage **b** improvement **c** proportion)

4 <u>Genetic</u> makeup determines much of what we look like. (**a** artificial **b** subtle **c** inherited)

5 Some students with <u>potential</u> ability are never discovered in a big school system. (**a** possible **b** athletic **c** scholarly)

6 Democracy is based on the <u>premise</u> that the majority is always right. (**a** assumption **b** fact **c** opinion)

7 Joseph Kennedy was the <u>progenitor</u> of a family of outstanding politicians. (**a** leader **b** ancestor **c** educator)

8 A cheap <u>replica</u> is never as good as an original work of art. (**a** fake **b** copy **c** photograph)

9 War is a form of <u>reprisal</u> that most countries want to avoid. (**a** entertainment **b** occupation **c** retaliation)

10 A particular <u>trait</u> is often inherited by members of a family. (**a** characteristic **b** disease **c** talent)

■ Check your answers in the Answer Key.
■ Record your score.

NUMBER CORRECT _____ (Possible 10)
(1 point for each answer)

Dictionary Definitions

controversy (kon' trə vėr' sē), *n.* **1** an arguing of a question about which differences of opinion exist. **2** quarrel. **3** wrangle.
countermand (koun' tər mand), *v.* **1** to withdraw or cancel (an order, command, etc.). **2** to recall or stop by a contrary order; order back.
detriment (det' rə mənt), *n.* **1** loss, damage, or injury done, caused to, or sustained by a person or thing; harm. **2** something that causes loss, damage, or injury.

genetic (jə net' ik), *adj.* **1** having to do with origin and natural growth. **2** of or having to do with genetics. **3** of or having to do with genes.
potential (pə ten' shəl), *adj.* possible as opposed to actual; capable of coming into being or action.
premise (prem' is), *n.* (in logic) a statement assumed to be true and used to draw a conclusion.
progenitor (prō jen' ə tər), *n.* ancestor in the direct line; forefather.

replica (rep' lə kə), *n.* **1** a copy, duplicate, or reproduction of a work of art, especially one made by the original artist. **2** a copy or close reproduction.
reprisal (ri prī' zəl), *n.* injury done in return for injury, especially by one nation to another.
trait (trāt), *n.* distinguishing feature or quality of mind, character, etc.; characteristic.

Using the Words

■ Choose the correct word from the Dictionary Definitions to fill in the blank in each of these sentences. Use each word only once.

1 There are times when the _____ that all men and women are created equal does not seem to be true.

2 There has been considerable _____ in America over desegregation of schools.

3 It seems to be a common _____ among redheads that they sunburn easily.

4 Some people sometimes wish they could change their _____ inheritance, but that is something that cannot be changed.

5 A young child with great muscial _____ should be encouraged to develop the talent.

6 A souvenir is very often a _____ of a famous landmark, in miniature.

7 Drinking alcohol during pregnancy can be a _____ to the health of the unborn child.

8 The President has the right to _____ the decision of the Senate.

9 Flying over enemy territory without permission usually leads to some sort of _____ .

10 In Greek mythology, Zeus was the _____ of a large family of gods and goddesses.

■ Check your answers in the Answer Key.
■ Record your score.

NUMBER CORRECT _____ (Possible 10)
(1 point for each answer)

Cloning
Article

Time Key

Finishing Time _____

Starting Time _____

Total Reading Time _____ minutes

Paragraph Key

■ Make brief Paragraph Key notes to remind yourself of the details of the article.

¹Human sex has long been a subject of **controversy**. Many thousands of books have been written about it. Many thousands of opinions have been expressed about what is right and what is wrong in the area of sex. One thing, however, has never been disputed—that two sexes are necessary for human reproduction.

a _____
   _____

²Now, even that basic **premise** is being called into question. Today we are told it is possible for a new human being to begin life without the usual sexual coupling of male and female.

b _____
   _____

³This new method of reproduction is called *cloning* and involves what is, in effect, a single-parent method of reproduction. In the normal method the baby inherits some characteristics of the mother and some of the father, so that it is a mixture of the inherited **traits** of both parents. Cloning is completely different.

c _____
   _____

⁴This is how it works. Every single cell in the human body contains a full set of chromosomes. The nucleus of each cell contains all the **genetic** information that any living thing needs to reproduce itself. In other words, every cell in the body is a **potential** new life. If any one cell can be made to divide and start to grow, the result will be a new human being. Usually the cell will start to divide when it is fertilized by the sperm. But it can also happen if the nucleus is simply replaced with the nucleus of another cell.

d _____
   _____

⁵Because the new being has only one parent, it will be an exact **replica** of that parent. If you think the world is ready for more of you, then cloning could be your answer. Cloning has already been successfully accomplished with plants, fruit flies, and even frogs.

e _____
   _____

⁶In 1968, J.B. Gurdon of Oxford University in England produced a clonal frog. He destroyed the nucleus of an unfertilized egg cell of a frog and implanted the nucleus from the cell of an intestine taken from another frog. Immediately, the egg showed the same behavior as one fertilized in the normal way. It began to grow, and eventually it developed into a tadpole that was the genetic twin of the frog which had been the donor of the intestine cell. The new frog showed none of the mother frog's characteristics, because her chromosomes had been destroyed when the nucleus of her egg cell was destroyed.

f _____
   _____

g _____
   _____

Cloning
Article

⁷Cloning of frogs has been accomplished, but how serious is the possibility of reproducing humans this way? Scientists tell us it is distinctly possible, and that the procedure would be similar to that undertaken with frogs. A healthy egg would be extracted from a woman's body before fertilization. The nucleus of this egg cell would be destroyed and replaced with a donor cell from the parent of the clone. This cell could be taken from anywhere on the donor's body, even from an arm or leg. The egg would then be implanted into a female uterus, and right away new life would begin to develop.

h _____

_____

⁸The parent of this new life would not be the woman in whose body it grew, but the donor of the cell that replaced the destroyed nucleus. The child would be a genetic twin—an exact carbon copy of that donor.

i _____

_____

⁹The institution of cloning would mean that anyone could have a baby. The donor could be male or female. Even those people who have been denied the joys of parenthood in the usual way could become **progenitors** of a whole race of identical human beings without ever being involved in a sexual encounter.

j _____

_____

¹⁰The process of cloning is not yet perfected; but according to many accounts, scientists could clone a human if they wanted to. What apparently holds them back is not lack of scientific knowledge, but the fear of **reprisals** from society.

k _____

_____

¹¹It is obvious that cloning raises many social and moral questions. To begin with, widespread practice of cloning could alter the structure of our present society immeasurably. The family as we know it could cease to exist, and sex could become an indulgence that would have nothing at all to do with reproduction. The concept of parenthood could be completely revised, and we could end up with whole communities, or "clone clans," of identical people.

l _____

_____

¹²It does not require much imagination to consider how cloning could be abused. Any maniac could produce a master race of identical, cruel Hitlers, hell-bent on the domination and destruction of the whole world.

m _____

_____

¹³Criminals could expand their empires of murderers, thieves, and swindlers to create the biggest crime ring in the history of the human race.

n _____

_____

¹⁴And there is always the possibility of even more disastrous results. What if some genetic mistake led to the creation of a race of hideous, malformed monsters that went on cloning themselves indefinitely, to the **detriment** of the present human race?

o _____

_____

¹⁵And there is also the moral question. Is it right for humans to interfere with the natural order of things? Do humans have the right to **countermand** the laws of God?

p _____

_____

q _____

_____

Cloning

Article

¹⁶Those who argue in favor of cloning say its main advantage would be its ability to ensure that the best minds, the best athletes, and the best artists would never be lost. Just as their powers began to wane, they could reproduce themselves and keep their greatness going.

r _____

_____

¹⁷There are a thousand different questions to consider in an issue as controversial as this. The truth remains, however, that whatever you may personally think about cloning, it is a fact. It is not something that has been dreamed up by a fanciful science fiction writer.

s _____

_____

¹⁸So the question becomes, should we stop the further development of cloning? And more importantly, should we try to do something to prevent its use with human beings?

t _____

_____

- Write in your Finishing Time and subtract to find your Total Reading Time.
- Record your Total Reading Time on the Development Chart.
- Check your answers in the Answer Key.
- Record your score.

NUMBER CORRECT _____ (Possible 20)
(1 point for each answer)

Summary

■ In order to be able to draw accurate inferences from something you read, you must be sure you understand the main points of the article.

■ Reread your Paragraph Key notes, and then complete this summary so you can begin to consider the ideas and questions it raises.

1 Cloning:

    a Definition _____

    b Difference from usual reproduction _____

2 How it works:

    a Remove _____

    b Replace it with _____

    c Implant it in _____

3 Results of cloning:

    a Good results (2)

    _____

    _____

    b Bad results (2)

    _____

    _____

4 Biggest problem is:

    _____

■ Check with your teacher or with the manual for the right answers.

■ Record your score.

NUMBER CORRECT _____ (Possible 10)
(1 point for each answer)

Cloning
Recalling the Details

Recalling the Details

■ This article deals with a controversial subject. As you read about it and think about it, you will be aware of a number of possibilities you can infer from the information.

■ Reread your Paragraph Key notes and your summary and then complete this page, which will help you recall some of the details and consider some of the inferences.

1 The chromosomes in every body cell contain

   a a nucleus
   b clones
   c genetic information

2 In making human clones, the nucleus of the female egg would be replaced with the nucleus from

   a another female egg
   b a cell from any other part of the female
   c a cell from any part of the body of the donor, which could be male or female

3 According to the article, cloning of humans

   a has already happened
   b is unlikely ever to happen
   c could very possibly happen

4 The main thing holding back the work of scientists on cloning seems to be

   a fear of producing monsters
   b fear of social reaction
   c lack of evidence on how cloning works

5 According to the article, cloning might cause

   a an increase in crime and destruction
   b society to become all male or all female
   c overpopulation.

6 Those in favor of cloning see its main advantage as

   a allowing single people the chance to have children
   b allowing for the maintenance of certain superior people in the world
   c doing away with the necessity of marriage

Inference Questions

7 The article infers that the whole idea of parenthood would change, because

   a clone babies would be raised by scientists
   b children would have only one parent
   c children would no longer have fathers

8 According to the information in this article, a man using the cloning method could produce

   a male or female children
   b only female children
   c only male children

9 The article's viewpoint on the question of cloning is

   a clearly in favor of cloning
   b in favor of careful considerations of its possible results
   c that cloning is the work of the Devil

10 Overall the article seems to be suggesting that

   a cloning is a foolish science fiction dream
   b cloning of humans is a possibility that requires serious thought
   c cloning is a fact and should not concern us

■ Check with your teacher or with the manual for the correct answers.
■ Record your score.

NUMBER CORRECT _____ (Possible 10)
(1 point for each answer)

Cloning

★ Personal Opinion

★ Personal Opinion

■ Here again are the ten words used for special study with this article. Select the correct word to fill in the blank in each of the following sentences, then complete each sentence **in your own words** so it expresses your ideas on the topic. Cross out the words in parentheses that do not apply to your opinion.

controversy	detriment	potential	progenitor	reprisal
countermand	genetic	premise	replica	trait

1 In my opinion, cloning (would/would not) be a _____ to the moral development of the human race because...

2 If we work on the _____ that God is the Creator, then we must ....

3 I (do/do not) see _____ danger in allowing cloning experiments to continue, because...

4 The main reason I (would/would not) like to have an exact _____ of myself is...

5 One _____ I have that I would like to pass on to my offspring is ....

6 I (do/do not) think fear of social _____ is the main thing cloning experimenters should worry about, because...

7 It seems to me that the main area of _____ about cloning would be ....

8 In the question of whether environment or _____ inheritance has more to do with making us what we are, I think...

9 If I could be the main _____ of a new race of people, I would like them to be...

10 I (do/do not) believe people have the right to _____ the laws of God, because ....

■ Check with your teacher or with the manual for the correct answers.
■ Record your score.

NUMBER CORRECT _____ (Possible 20)
(2 points for each word)

Cloning
★ Speed Exercise

★ Speed Exercise

■ (One minute allowed for reading only. Teacher timed or self-timed.)

In 1978, a book was published   that caused a sensation.   It is called *In His Image*.
It was written by David Rorvik.   The book caused an uproar   because it supposedly proved
that reproduction of humans   through cloning   is a real possibility.
Most people do not believe   the claims of the book,   but even the toughest scientists
are forced to admit   that although the cloning of humans   has not taken place so far,
it could easily become a reality   within the next ten years.   There are many people
who would like the government   to pass a law   compelling publication   of the details
of all experiments   so far undertaken or concluded   in the area of human cloning.
These critics believe   that such experimenting   should not be allowed
to continue in secret.   They stress that these experiments   could threaten the welfare
of all humanity,   present and future.
The question is, of course,   can you really stop something   just by putting   a ban on it?
How can you be sure   that all the experiments   would be reported,   or that they would stop
if the government ordered it?
Throughout history,   people have tried   to stop scientific works,   yet some of them
have turned out to be good.   Maybe this will be so with cloning.   (209 words)

1 The book is called _____ .

2 People were upset because the book suggested _____ .

3 Scientists say human cloning could happen in _____ .

4 People would like to stop cloning by _____ .

5 The big question remains _____ .

NUMBER CORRECT _____ (Possible 20)
Score 10 points if you read the whole article,
and 2 points for each correct answer. Check
your answers by looking back at the article.
Deduct 1 point for each line you did not read.

Examining Questions

■ The word *question* can mean either "an enquiry" or it can mean an "issue about which there are varying opinions." The second meaning is the one being used here. Issues of general importance face us every day, and it is important for us to consider these issues with an informed and open mind. We should avoid the temptation of saying, "It's not my problem."

■ You can learn more about important issues of the day by reading about them, thinking about them, and discussing them with other people. Examine as many ideas and opinions as you can on each issue, before deciding your own point of view.

■ When you read about an important issue, you should:

1 Be sure you understand exactly what the issue is. Make notes on it in your own words to be sure it's clear to you.
2 Look for arguments for the issue.
3 Look for arguments against the issue.
4 Look for unanswered questions about the issue.
5 Consider all points carefully in order to make a rational decision of your own.

New Questions on Human Birth
Word Study, Dictionary Definitions

Word Study—Creating a Glossary

■ When reading an article on a very specific topic, it is often useful to create a *glossary* of words particularly relevant to the topic before you begin to read.

■ This article contains several words and phrases specific to the topic of new developments in the area of human birth.

★ ■ Here is an alphabetical list of these words and phrases. Use the Dictionary Definitions to create working definitions that you can easily understand.

WORD	DEFINITION
1 Alzheimer's disease	_____
2 anencephalic	_____
3 diabetes	_____
4 embryo experimentation	_____
5 fetus	_____
6 genetic engineering	_____
7 in vitro fertilization	_____
8 ovum, ova	_____
9 Parkinson's disease	_____
10 surrogate motherhood	_____

■ Check your answers in the Answer Key.
■ Record your score.

NUMBER CORRECT _____ (Possible 10)
(1 point for each answer)

Dictionary Definitions

Alzheimer's disease (älts' hī mərz), *n.* (After Alois Alzheimer, 1864–1915.) disease occurring in middle-aged or younger persons that is characterized by brain damage of the type associated with senility.
anencephaly (an' ən sef ə le), *n.* congenital absence of all or part of the brain.—anencephalic, *adj.*
diabetes (dī' ə bē' tis), *n.* any of several diseases marked by excessive urination, especially one involving a deficiency of insulin.
embryo (em' brē ō), *n.* **1** animal during the period of its growth from the fertilized egg until three months, until its organs have developed. **2** an undeveloped plant within a seed.
experimentation (ek sper' ə men tā' shən), *n.* the act, process, or practice of experimenting; trying something in order to find out about it; making trials or tests.
fertilization (fér' tl ə zā' shən), *n.* **1** a fertilizing. **2** a being fertilized **3** the union of a male reproductive cell and a female reproductive cell to form a cell that will develop into a new individual.
fetus, also **foetus** (fē' təs), *n.* an animal embryo in the later stages of its development in the womb or in the egg, especially a human embryo from three months until birth.
gene (jēn), *n.* a minute part of a chromosome, containing essentially DNA, that influences the inheritance and development of an organism from a fertilized egg.
genetic engineering, *n.* alteration of the genetic structure or genetic process of an organism or species so as to change inherited features.
in vitro (in vi' trō), *adj.* **1** in an arti-

ficial environment such as a test tube; not in the living animal or plant.
metabolic (met′ ə bol′ ik), *adj.* of or having to do with the sum of the physiological processes by which an organism maintains life.
ovum (ō′ vəm), *n., pl.* **ova.** a

female reproductive cell produced in the ovary; egg. After the ovum is fertilized, a new organism or embryo develops.
Parkinson's disease (pär′ kin sənz), *n.* (After James Parkinson, 1755–1824.) a chronic nervous disease, usually occurring late in

life, characterized by muscular tremor, weakness, and paralysis.
surrogate (sur′ ə git or sur ə gāt), *n.* **1** person or thing that takes place of another; substitute. **2** (in certain states) a judge having charge of the probate of wills, the administration of estates, etc.

Using the Words

■ Select the right word to fill in the blank in each of the following sentences. Use each word only once.

1 Old people who suffer from _____ often do not recognize members of their own families.

2 There is much debate on whether a woman should be paid for _____ services.

3 Sufferers from _____ must take an insulin injection every day.

4 The life of an _____ baby is mercifully very short.

5 An unborn baby is known as a _____ after the eighth week of development.

6 Some people believe that using unborn "babies" for _____ is wrong.

7 _____ concerns altering the structure of the genes.

8 Conception takes place when the sperm and the _____ join.

9 _____ is a form of artificial birth.

10 People with _____ find it impossible to stop the trembling in their bodies.

■ Check your answers in the Answer Key.
■ Record your score.

NUMBER CORRECT _____ (Possible 10)
(1 point for each answer)

New Questions on Human Birth
Article

Time Key

Finishing Time   _____

Starting Time   _____

Total Reading Time _____ minutes

Paragraph Key

■ Make notes on the main issues discussed and the questions raised by each.

¹One of nature's greatest miracles and at the same time one of its deepest mysteries is the creation of human life. While today the miracle remains, much of the mystery is being removed as science investigates new ways to create life. In place of mystery, we now have complex questions.

a _____

_____

²Four recent developments that affect human life are **genetic engineering**, **in vitro fertilization** (IVF), **surrogate motherhood**, and **embryo experimentation**. Each of these offers new hope to long-standing problems but, at the same time, raises a host of legal and ethical questions.

b 1 _____

2 _____

3 _____

4 _____

³Genetic engineering is the process of deliberately altering the natural structure of the genes, either before or after birth, to bring about certain changes in body development.

c _____

_____

⁴Work to date on genetic engineering has produced some positive results. One of these relates to the treatment of **diabetes**. Previously those suffering from this metabolic disorder could be treated only by daily injections of insulin. Now it seems genetic engineering can be used to persuade the body to make its own supplies of insulin.

d _____

_____

⁵Genetic engineering advances also permit doctors to examine a **fetus** in the early stages of development to determine any abnormalities. The potential is also there for the correction of these abnormalities through alteration of the fetal genes.

e _____

_____

⁶Such developments are obviously advantageous, but they also raise questions: What if the detected fetal deformities cannot be corrected? Does the mother then have the right to abort? Does the fetus have rights? Should the fetus be thought of as a living human even before birth?

f 1 _____

2 _____

3 _____

4 _____

⁷The whole debate on the rights of an unborn child is crucial to the question of in vitro fertilization and surrogate motherhood.

g _____

_____

⁸In vitro fertilization (IVF) is used in those cases where a couple is unable to conceive a child in the usual fashion. In this system, sperm from the father and **ova** from the mother are put together in a laboratory dish. If the sperm and an ovum join and a fetus develops, it is implanted in the mother and growth and birth continue as usual.

h _____

_____

⁹The first IVF baby was Louise Brown, who was born in England in 1978. Since then, hundreds of childless couples have tried this method with success.

New Questions on Human Birth
Article

¹⁰Surrogate motherhood involves a woman bearing a child on behalf of others. In cases where a woman is unable to carry a baby to full term, surrogacy may look like a good alternative.

¹¹The "parents" provide the sperm and the ova, which are united outside the body under laboratory conditions. Once the joining has taken place, the resulting fetus is implanted in the surrogate mother artificially. She then carries the baby to term—sometimes for a fee—and relinquishes it to the "parents" after birth.

¹²The obvious advantage of both IVF and surrogate motherhood is that they allow previously infertile couples to know the joy of parenthood.

¹³Yet, neither method is without its share of questions: What if the surrogate mother changes her mind and decides to keep the child? What if the contracting parents have a change of heart before the child is born? What if the baby is born deformed? Does surrogacy amount to the illegal act of selling babies? What about the moral issue of interfering with the natural methods and problems of birth? What does morality dictate about the artificial production of human life?

¹⁴The value of IVF and surrogacy is debated everywhere. Proponents see them as ideal substitutes for adoption, because they allow the couple to have what is, in essence, their own child. Opponents claim surrogacy is baby selling and against the Judeo-Christian ethic. Some see surrogacy as involving three "parents," and they question that this is in the best interests of the child.

¹⁵Many churches criticize IVF as being against the will of God. The Pope has denounced any artificial intervention as morally wrong. He has stated that both surrogate motherhood and IVF are sins in the eyes of the Church.

¹⁶A major question in all these issues is that of public policy and the possible need for government intervention. One side sees laws as providing guidelines and control; the other side maintains that such ethical matters cannot be controlled by law.

i _____
_____

j _____
_____

k _____
_____

1 _____
_____

2 _____
_____

3 _____
_____

4 _____
_____

5 _____
_____

l 1 _____
_____

2 _____
_____

3 _____
_____

m _____
_____

n _____
_____

New Questions on Human Birth
Article

17One constantly difficult issue is the question of when life actually begins. Many arguments exist. Some religious devotees claim life commences as soon as the sperm and ovum join—whether this happens inside the mother's body or in the laboratory. Some scientists claim it begins as soon as the fetus develops a brain; others hold that it begins only after birth has occurred.

18This question is fundamental when it comes to the area of embryo experimentation. In recent years, researchers have learned that human embryo tissue has curative effects in many adult diseases. Tissues from aborted fetuses and anencephalic fetuses have been used to good effect with **Parkinson's disease** and **Alzheimer's disease**.

19Each year, the United States records hundreds of cases of infants born without brains or with only a minimal brain stem. Such infants normally die within a few days.

20If kept alive artificially, however, these infants can provide healthy organs, such as liver and heart, for other ailing children. Is it right to sustain life artificially and then "kill" the infant when organs are needed?

21Since tissue from aborted fetuses is proving so useful, the possibility arises that women may deliberately conceive and abort in order to sell the fetuses. While this seems wrong, what of the ethics of using tissues from fetuses that have aborted naturally?

22Numerous indeed are the problems that have come with these human birth options; only a few are discussed here. England already has legislation to deal with some of these questions. America is still unsure which way to go. Consideration of these problems should concern us all, so that if/when they are put to the vote, we will be ready with sound, considered opinions.

o _____

_____

p 1 _____

_____

2 _____

_____

3 _____

_____

q _____

_____

r _____

_____

s _____

_____

1 _____

_____

t 1 _____

_____

2 _____

_____

■ Write in your Finishing Time and subtract to find your Total Reading Time.
■ Record your Total Reading Time on the Development Chart.
■ Check your answers in the Answer Key.
■ Record your score.

NUMBER CORRECT _____ (Possible 20)
(1 point for each answer)

Summary

▪ This article deals with controversial issues for which there are no clear guidelines as to what is right or wrong.

▪ Your summary should include details of the issues and the questions they·raise.

▪ Reread your paragraph key carefully and then complete the summary.

Four developments in the area of human birth:

Development 1: _____

  1   Definition _____

  2   Advantages **a** _____

                 b _____

  3   Questions   **a** _____

                 b _____

                 c _____

                 d _____

Developments 2 and 3: _____

  4   Definition _____

  5   Definition _____

  6   Advantage _____

  7   Questions   **a** _____

                 b _____

                 c _____

                 d _____

Development 4: _____

  8   Definition _____

  9   Advantages **a** _____

                 b _____

 10   Questions   **a** _____

                 b _____

▪ Check with your teacher or with the manual for the correct answers.

▪ Record your score.

NUMBER CORRECT _____ (Possible 10)
(1 point for each answer)

New Questions on Human Birth
Recalling the Details

Recalling the Details

■ This article concludes with the suggestion that you should be concerned with the issues it raises. You can begin to develop rational opinions of your own by recalling and considering the main issues and the questions raised.

■ Reread your Paragraph Key and your summary and then complete this page.

1 Genetic engineering is

  a the forming of new genes
  b alteration of the genes
  c replacement of the genes

2 Genetic engineering can

  a detect abnormalities before birth
  b detect diabetes and abnormalities
  c cure diabetes

3 Which of the following questions is NOT raised about genetic engineering?

  a does the fetus have rights?
  b does it encourage abortion?
  c is the fetus a human being before birth?

4 In vitro fertilization is used when

  a the baby is likely to be deformed
  b the mother cannot deliver naturally
  c natural conception is unattainable

5 The chief advantage of surrogacy and IVF is

  a they are safe
  b they provide a better alternative than adoption
  c they are morally acceptable

6 One major objection to surrogacy concerns

  a the difficulty of such births
  b the fact that it is against the law
  c the payment of surrogate mothers

7 Embryo experimentation involves

  a fertilization in the laboratory
  b genetic alteration of the fetus
  c using embryo tissues as curatives

8 One question basic to embryo experimentation is

  a who should bear the cost of it?
  b when does life begin?
  c who should benefit from it?

9 The deliberate conception and abortion of fetuses is

  a not at all likely
  b against the law
  c a possibility

10 The creation of public policy on these issues would mean

  a all these developments would be legalized
  b there would be a change in the Pope's opinions
  c providing laws and guidelines

■ Check with your teacher or with the manual for the correct answers.
■ Record your score.

NUMBER CORRECT _____ (Possible 10)
(1 point for each answer)

New Questions on Human Birth

★ Personal Opinion

■ Here again are the ten words used for special study with this article. Select the correct word to fill in the blank in each of the following sentences, then complete each sentence **in your own words** so it expresses your ideas on these topics.

Alzheimer's disease	embryo experimentation	in vitro fertilization	surrogate motherhood
anencephalic	fetus	ova	Parkinson's disease
diabetes	genetic engineering		

1 I believe that the use of _____ babies for organ transplants is

....

2 In my opinion, the use of _____ to find cures for adult diseases is

....

3 If I were a diabetic and found that _____ could help me, I would

....

4 A woman who deliberately aborts a fetus in order to help a relative recover from

_____ should be.......................................

5 To me, the idea of a woman being paid for _____ is

....

6 If I had to vote on whether _____ should be an acceptable birth alternative,

I would vote...

7 To my way of thinking, old people who suffer the tragic memory losses of _____

should be...

8 The fact that genetic engineering might be able to help people who have _____

suggests that.......................................

9 On the question of whether life begins at the moment of conception, after the development of

the _____ , or at birth, my opinion is

....

10 On the question of the morality of joining sperm and _____ artificially, I believe

....

■ Check with your teacher or with the manual
for the correct answers.
■ Record your score.

NUMBER CORRECT _____ (Possible 20)
(2 points for each word)

New Questions on Human Birth
★ Speed Exercise

★ Speed Exercise

■ (One minute allowed for reading only. Teacher timed or self-timed.)

Can abortion ever be right?   Some people maintain it is wrong   under any circumstances. Others claim there are times   when it is allowable,   such as when the mother's life is endangered by the pregnancy.   And then there's a group   who say people should be licensed before they can have a baby.   They claim   this would put an end   to abortion. What do you think   of that idea?

To be eligible for a license,   you would have to undergo   a variety of tests. These would include tests   to find out   about your general health   and how suitable you would be as a parent.   Other tests would determine   your emotional state and your readiness   for the responsibility of parenthood.

The people who are in favor   of such licenses   say that if everyone   underwent tests to determine their suitability   for parenthood,   there would be no need   for abortions. They also say   that if people knew that having a child   without a license would result in a stiff penalty   or even a jail sentence   for both parents,   they would develop a much more responsible attitude   toward parenthood,   and society as a whole would benefit.

What do you think   of this idea?   What are the obvious drawbacks   to it? Do you have ideas of your own   for putting an end   to the need for abortion?   (220 words)

1 Some people say that to have a baby you should first have a _____ .

2 You would get it by _____ .

3 These would find out about _____ .

4 If you did not get a license, _____ .

5 Benefits of this would be felt by _____ .

NUMBER CORRECT _____ (Possible 20)
Score 10 points if you read the whole article,
and 2 points for each correct answer. Check
your answers by looking back at the article.
Deduct 1 point for each line you did not read.

Considering Personal Experience

■ People like to read about people. Many people find it more fascinating to read about other people than to read abstract ideas.

■ You may not always agree with what others do, but the careful reader tries not to judge others too quickly. You may see their actions and attitudes quite differently if you make an effort to understand their motives.

■ When you read about real people, you should be sure that enough information is given. Journalists sometimes select only those bits they think will make a good story. As a thoughtful reader, it is your task to be sure you have all the information. You can use the 5W + H Question Frame as a check.

■ This next article is a true story. Read it thoughtfully and check to see if it gives you all the facts you need to gain a true understanding. Think about and discuss what other facts you would like.

Whose Baby?
Word Study, Dictionary Definitions

Word Study—Precise Definitions

■ With many words we use on an occasional basis, we may be aware of the general meaning but not sure of the precise meaning. Thoughtful readers check the precise meanings of such words when they come across them in articles of importance. Sometimes the precise meaning can be worked out from the context of the word; other times it is necessary to check with a dictionary.

★ ■ The following sentences contain ten words from the next article. Circle the letter of the correct, precise definition for each underlined word. Use the Dictionary Definitions to help you.

1 The mother took her sick child to the pediatrician. (a surgeon b specialist in children's diseases c heart specialist)

2 The obstetrician delivered the twins in the ambulance. (a specialist in delivering babies b specialist in children's diseases c school teacher)

3 The gynecologist assured the woman she would not need an operation. (a specialist in children's diseases b general practitioner c specialist in women's illnesses)

4 The newborn baby was dysmature and sickly. (a overweight b poorly developed c blind)

5 The triplets were nearly a month premature and had to be watched carefully. (a late b early c old)

6 The mother's ill health made it necessary for her baby to be delivered by caesarean section. (a in vitro fertilization b surgical operation c prematurely)

7 Following the recent poll, the mayor seems certain to win. (a public opinion survey b tall stick c scandal)

8 The survey showed the need for a new school in the district. (a physical measurement b book of facts c general inspection)

9 The kangaroo is an animal unique in Australia. (a destructive b found almost nowhere else c only one of its kind)

10 Marriage is an almost universal institution. (a outdated b existing everywhere c very unusual)

■ Check your answers in the Answer Key.
■ Record your score.

NUMBER CORRECT _____ (Possible 10)
(1 point for each answer)

Dictionary Definitions

caesarean section (si zer' ē an), *n.* operation by which a baby is removed from the uterus by cutting through the uterine and abdominal walls (From the belief that Julius *Caesar* was born this way.)

dysmature (dis ma chur') from **dys** bad, abnormal, defective + **mature** ripe or full grown.

gynecologist (gī' nə col ə jist), *n.* doctor who specializes in that branch of medicine that deals with the functions and diseases specific to women, especially those of the reproductive system.

obstetrician (ob' stə trish' ən), *n.* doctor who specializes in that branch of medicine concerned with caring for and treating women before, in, and after childbirth.

pediatrician (pe' de ə trish' ən), *n.* doctor who specializes in that branch of medicine that deals with children's diseases and the care of babies and children.

poll (pōl), *n.* **1** casting or registering of votes as at an election. **2** number of votes cast. **3** the results of these votes. **4** survey of public opinion regarding a particular subject.

premature (prē' mə chur'), *adj.* before the proper time; too soon. A premature baby is one born more than two weeks early or weighing less than 5½ pounds.

survey (ser' vā), *n.* **1** a general

look, view, examination, inspection. **2** a comprehensive literary examination, description, or discussion. **3** a formal or official inspection, poll, study.
unique (yü nēk), *adj.* **1** having no like or equal; being the only one of its kind. **2** INFORMAL. very uncommon or unusual; rare; remarkable.
universal (yü' nə ver' səl), *adj.* **1** of or for all; belonging to all; concerning all; **2** existing everywhere. **3** covering a whole group of persons, cases, things, etc., general. **4** (in logic) asserting or denying something of every member of a class.

Using the Words

■ Select the correct word from the Word List to fill in the blank in each of the following sentences. Use each word only once.

1 When a baby is _____ , doctors usually prescribe extra care and special food until it develops correctly.

2 A recent _____ shows that more than 30 percent of professional parents are likely to have their first child after the age of 35.

3 The love of a mother for a child is a _____ characteristic.

4 A _____ is a doctor who specializes in women's diseases.

5 The _____ operation is said to be named after Julius Caesar, who was born this way.

6 _____ babies must be carefully guarded against too much oxygen, which can cause blindness.

7 Some people prefer to have a midwife instead of an _____ to deliver their baby.

8 The miracle is that each baby is _____ . No two are completely alike, not even identical twins.

9 For specialist medical treatment, a child should be taken to a _____ .

10 A recent _____ indicated that many people believe two children is a good family size these days.

■ Check your answers in the Answer Key.
■ Record your score.

NUMBER CORRECT _____ (Possible 10)
(1 point for each answer)

Whose Baby?
Article

Paragraph Key

■ Make notes on the news report and on the editorial that follows.

---

¹The following true story was reported in *The Johannesburg Star* on October 1, 1987. The story made medical history and at the same time raised serious questions on an issue of **universal** importance.

²"The world's first surrogate grandmother, Mrs. Pat Anthony (48), gave birth to two boys and a girl shortly after 5 A.M. at the Park Lane Clinic in Johannesburg today.

a _____
_____

³"The triplets weighed 2.1 kg, 2.3 kg, and 1.3 kg and were only two weeks **premature**. The smallest baby is apparently **dysmature** and underdeveloped for a newborn baby. There were three **pediatricians** present at the birth.

b _____
_____

⁴"Mrs. Anthony was given an anesthetic which allowed her to remain conscious but feel no pain—and the babies were born by **caesarean section**. This is common in a multiple birth.

c _____
_____

⁵"The operation took about an hour and mother and babies are doing well. An obstetrician said the deliveries appeared to have been 'completely normal.'

d _____
_____

⁶"The birth was filmed by an independent television crew who were seen leaving the theater at 6:30 A.M. clad in green theater garb.

⁷"The Anthony family issued a short statement soon after the birth, announcing that Mrs. Anthony and the babies were well and thanking the clinic and 'the people of South Africa' for their support.

⁸"Mrs. Anthony's daughter, Mrs. Karen Ferreira-Jorge, was present, but neither her husband nor Mr. Anthony was there.

e _____
_____

⁹"A leading **obstetrician** who spoke to *The Star* today said the smallest baby was likely to be put in an incubator and would probably be kept in the hospital until its weight was satisfactory. He said it was not unusual for one baby in a multiple birth to be smaller and weaker than the others. In spite of this, the baby had every chance of doing well.

f _____
_____

Adapted with permission from *The Star*, Johannesburg, October 1st, 1987.

[10]"According to Mrs. Anthony's doctors, she is psychologically well prepared to hand over the babies to their biological mother, Mrs. Ferreira-Jorge (25)."

g _____

_____

[11]The background to this **unique** story was given in an article in the same newspaper on the same day. The article was from a medical reporter—Toni Younghusband.

[12]"It has probably been the most talked about pregnancy in South Africa's history—a pregnancy which turned the attention of the world's media to the sleepy little Transvaal town of Tzaneen and which drastically changed the lives of a soft-spoken mother and her daughter.

h _____

_____

[13]"In April this year, the residents of Tzaneen witnessed an invasion of their town like never before—journalists from all over the world descended in their droves in an attempt to be the first to break the news of the world's first surrogate grandmother.

i _____

_____

[14]"The news had leaked out that a town resident, Mrs. Pat Anthony (48), had agreed to bear her own grandchildren, because her daughter Mrs. Karen Ferreira-Jorge was unable to have any more children. Mrs. Ferreira-Jorge had a hysterectomy three years earlier after giving birth to a son. Mrs. Anthony was three months pregnant when her story hit the headlines.

j _____

_____

[15]"Mrs. Ferreira-Jorge was apparently desperately unhappy when told she could no longer have children and after lengthy discussions with top **gynecologists** and extensive tests, her mother agreed to bear them for her.

[16]"Mrs. Anthony was implanted with her daughter's ova which had been fertilized in vitro by her son-in-law. At first the gynecologists admitted they were a little nervous at the prospect of this surrogacy because of Mrs. Anthony's age, but she appeared healthy and the pregnancy continued without any hitches.

k _____

_____

[17]It was only later that doctors discovered that Mrs. Anthony was to give birth to triplets."

l _____

_____

****

[18]At the time of releasing this story, *The Star* also conducted a **survey** of its readers to find out their reactions to the idea of surrogate motherhood and to this case in particular. They collated the following information:

m _____

_____

Whose Baby?
Article

¹⁹"Surrogate motherhood has been rejected outright by 72% of women interviewed in the recent survey. Twelve in 100 women said they would welcome the opportunity of another woman bearing their husband's child if they were unable to conceive and 15% said they would be happy for their mothers to bear their children. 5% of respondents in the same—35-49 years—age group as Mrs. Anthony and only 2% of women who were 50 years or older said they would accept "without hesitation" the opportunity of bearing another woman's child.

n _____
_____
o _____
_____
p _____
_____
q _____
_____

²⁰"The survey exposed a clear sympathy and understanding for women who cannot conceive and there is a surprisingly high level of acceptance for scientific advances that can now make surrogate motherhood possible.

r _____
_____

²¹"However, the **poll** shows that no matter how fascinating the surrogate grandmother case is, the prevailing view is that it will be a very rare occurrence indeed, with relatively few women at present willing to consider a similar situation. Against the background of news about Mrs. Anthony, 48% of respondents believed that adoption would have been a better course in such circumstances."

s _____
_____

²²That is the story as it happened in 1987. What is the situation today? Is this becoming a commonplace story? What is the world attitude to surrogacy? What is your opinion of what Mrs. Anthony did?

t _____
_____

■ Write in your Finishing Time and subtract to find your Total Reading Time.
■ Record your Total Reading Time on the Development Chart.
■ Check your answers in the Answer Key.
■ Record your score.

NUMBER CORRECT _____ (Possible 20)
(1 point for each answer)

Summary

■ There are three parts to this article: the news story, the background story, and the survey results. Your summary should cover all three. You can use the 5W + H frame for your summary of the two stories:

■ Reread your Paragraph Key, taking careful note of these three parts, and then complete the summary.

News Story:

1 Who? (grandmother's name) _____

2 What? (did she do) _____

3 Where? _____

4 When? _____

Background:

5 Why? _____

6 How? _____

Survey:

7 72% _____

8 12% _____

9 15% _____

10 7% _____

■ Check with your teacher or with the manual for the correct answers.

■ Record your score.

NUMBER CORRECT _____ (Possible 10)
(1 point for each answer)

Whose Baby?
Recalling the Details

Recalling the Details

■ At the end of this article, you are asked to compare the 1987 reactions to surrogacy with today's attitudes. You must recall details of the news story and of the 1987 attitudes clearly before you can make this comparison.

■ Reread your Paragraph Key and your summary and then complete this page.

1 When she had the triplets, Mrs. Anthony was

  a 38 years old
  b 48 years old
  c 35 years old

2 Mrs. Anthony's daughter's name is

  a Karen Ferrera-Jorge
  b Pat Ferreira-Jorge
  c Karen Ferreira-Jorge

3 The daughter

  a had never been able to have children
  b had one son
  c had two previous children

4 The biological mother of the babies was

  a Mrs. Anthony's daughter
  b Mrs. Anthony
  c a donor mother

5 Mrs. Anthony knew she would have triplets

  a in the first weeks of pregnancy
  b only at the time of the birth
  c only after several months of pregnancy

6 Doctors were unsure about the pregnancy because of

  a Mrs. Anthony's age
  b the difficulties of in vitro fertilization
  c lack of support from her husband

7 The largest percentage of those surveyed were

  a in favor of surrogacy
  b against surrogacy
  c undecided

8 The percentage of women in Mrs. Anthony's age group who would do what she did was

  a 5%
  b 2%
  c 72%

9 In this article, men's attitudes to surrogacy are

  a shown as disinterested
  b not shown at all
  c discussed briefly

10 The choice of adoption in such cases was preferred by

  a nearly half the women
  b nearly a third of the women
  c roughly a quarter of the women

■ Check with your teacher or with the manual for the correct answers.
■ Record your score.

NUMBER CORRECT _____ (Possible 10)
(1 point for each answer)

★ Personal Opinion

■ Here again are the ten words used for special study with this article. Select the correct word to fill in the blank in each of the following sentences, then complete each sentence **in your own words** so it expresses your ideas on the topic.

caesarean section	gynecologist	pediatrician	poll	universal
dysmature	obstetrician	premature	unique	survey

1 It is usual for a baby to be born by _____ rather than naturally when

....

2 It is usual for a woman to visit a _____ when

....

3 One danger for a baby born several weeks _____ is

....

4 If I had to choose between a midwife and an _____ to deliver my baby, I would

prefer.....................................

5 If a _____ were conducted on men's attitudes to surrogate motherhood, I believe

they would....................................

6 One big danger for a baby who is _____ and underdeveloped is

....

7 One _____ question facing parents everywhere is

....

8 When it comes to a choice between a family doctor and a _____ for taking

care of children, I prefer....................................

9 I think if a _____ were taken today, the attitudes to surrogacy as compared

with 1987 would show....................................

10 The _____ aspect of the Anthony story that attracted world attention was

....

■ Check with your teacher or with the manual for the correct answers.
■ Record your score.

NUMBER CORRECT _____ (Possible 20)
(2 points for each word)

Whose Baby?
★ Speed Exercise

★ Speed Exercise

■ (One minute allowed for reading only. Teacher timed or self-timed.)

How do people become parents   if they cannot have a child of their own?
One answer is adoption.   But there always seems to be   more people who want babies
than there are babies   to be adopted.   Some people get tired of waiting
or being turned down   for any number of reasons.   When people are desperate,
they will pay good money   to get a baby.   There are people all over the country
who run baby markets.   You can pay someone,   often a lawyer,   a large sum of money
as a down payment.   The lawyer calls you   when he knows of a baby
who will soon be up for adoption.   Then you must have the rest of the money ready.
You do not get the baby   until you pay the money.   Sometimes this can be as much as $10,000;
sometimes it is even more.   What happens to this money?   Some of it goes
to the woman who had the baby.   But usually much more of it   goes to the person
who arranged the adoption.   Some people who go to baby markets   have been turned down
by other adoption agencies,   because they would not be   good parents.   Through the markets,
they can get a baby anyway.   But even for people   who would make good parents,
the baby market   is sometimes the only place to go   to find a child to adopt.   (228 words)

1 People who cannot have their own children may go to _____ .

2 A baby can cost as much as _____ .

3 Most of this money goes to _____ .

4 Some people go to baby markets because _____ .

5 Others go because _____ .

NUMBER CORRECT _____ (Possible 20)
Score 10 points if you read the whole article,
and 2 points for each correct answer. Check
your answers by looking back at the article.
Deduct 1 point for each line you did not read.

First Half Review

■ So far in this book you have practiced:

1 Using new vocabulary
2 Using the dictionary to find:
pronunciation
definitions
synonyms
parts of speech
3 Reading:
a story
to distinguish fact from opinion
for inference
with questions in mind
an instructional article
a biography
a textbook
4 Increasing reading speed

■ To be sure you understand all these skills, the next few pages will offer you some review exercises.
■ See how many of the questions you can answer without looking back. The number of the article in which the answer can be found is listed for you, so you can review anything you are unsure of.

A. General Questions about Reading

■ Circle the letter of the right answer for each of the following. The article number where the answer can be found is listed after the last answer choice.

1 Reading is

a a talent that comes naturally
b a skill that can be improved with practice
c something that is no longer useful in the modern world   (1)

2 When you read a story you should

a have no questions in mind at all
b make up your own questions about things you'd like to know
c use the 5W + H Question Frame to help you recall the important details   (4)

3 An inference is

a an example
b a conclusion drawn from what you read
c factual authority   (13)

4 When reading a factual article, you should look for which three of the following points?

a the names of the people giving the facts
b opinions
c the position of authority of the person giving the facts
d the dates when the research was done   (5)

5 The main reason for using a Paragraph Key is to

a help you understand new words
b be sure you comprehend what you read as you read
c have practice with writing about what you're reading   (1)

6 Making a summary when you have finished reading will show that you

a can recall every specific detail of the article
b understand the main points of the article
c have improved your reading speed   (1)

7 It is good to be able to recall the details of an article so you

a can make use of the information contained in the article
b can outsmart other people with your knowledge
c can make a brief summary outline of the article   (1)

8 One very important thing to remember about the skill of reading is

  a it gives you something to do when you're bored
  b it is easier when you know how to read different types of articles
  c it is something that only highly intelligent people can do well   (1)

9 An important fact you should remember about reading is

  a it is a skill that needs constant practice
  b it is a natural talent that you either have or do not have
  c it is something that is really only useful while you're in school   (1)

10 When you come across a new word when you're reading, you should

  a look it up in a dictionary right away
  b ignore it until you've finished reading and then go back and look for it again
  c underline it and look it up when you've finished reading, if you cannot work it out from context   (1)

B. Review of Reading a Textbook

■ If you do not remember the information about reading a textbook, review the material that begins on page 14, Article 2.

1 The preface to a textbook should tell you which three of the following things?

  a the scope of the subject the book will cover
  b where you will find the index, glossary, and contents page
  c the author's main purpose in writing the book
  d the best way to use the book

2 The glossary in a textbook is

  a a list of the chapter names and what each one of them contains
  b a list of special words and meanings that belong to that subject particularly
  c a list of other books and writings on the same subject
  d an alphabetized list of all the subject matter the book contains

3 A bibliography is

  a a list of other books and writings on the same subject
  b a list of the chapter titles and contents
  c a list of special words and their meanings that are particularly related to the subject
  d a list of other writings by the same author

4 A subtitle

  a tells you more about the title
  b tells you what is in each chapter of the book
  c tells you where to find the index, glossary, and contents page
  d tells you the author's main purpose in writing the book

5 The index of a textbook is found

  a at the front of the book and lists the chapter titles
  b at the back of the book and gives an alphabetical list of all topics covered in the book
  c at the end of each chapter and contains a list of other books on the same topic
  d at the beginning of the chapter and gives a summary of the chapter contents

C. Practice with Synonyms

■ The first column in this exercise contains words from the articles and stories you have read so far. The second column contains synonyms for those words. See if you can match the correct synonym to each list word. Put the corresponding numbers in the parentheses beside the list words. For any words that you have forgotten, check with a dictionary or with the number in the third column, which will tell you the article where the list word was introduced.

WORD	SYNONYM	ARTICLE NUMBER
1 ( ) amateur	1 advise against	4
2 ( ) illogical	2 critical	5
3 ( ) crucial	3 contrary	7
4 ( ) segregate	4 helpful	8
5 ( ) dissuade	5 novice	8
6 ( ) adverse	6 start	12
7 ( ) unique	7 one of a kind	15
8 ( ) beneficial	8 unreasonable	12
9 ( ) daunt	9 discourage	8
10 ( ) initiate	10 separate	8

D. Practice with Parts of Speech

■ Here are ten words that were used in some of the exercises in the first half of this book. See if you can complete the parts of speech table below, putting an X where there is no form for that part of speech. For any word you cannot remember, review the Word Study exercise in which it was used. The article numbers are in parentheses at the end of each line.

ADJECTIVE	NOUN	VERB	ADVERB	
1 ethical	_____	_____	_____	(10)
2 _____	concurrence	_____	_____	(10)
3 _____	_____	volunteer	_____	(11)
4 _____	reflex	_____	_____	(11)
5 beneficial	_____	_____	_____	(12)
6 _____	prescription	_____	_____	(12)
7 _____	_____	afflict	_____	(11)
8 _____	_____	_____	materially	(12)
9 _____	_____	arbitrate	_____	(12)
10 _____	_____	grapple	_____	(10)

E. Practice with Pronunciation

■ The words in this list are all from articles in the first part of this book. In the space provided, write the word with its correct spelling and then write in the meaning.

PRONUNCIATION	WORD	MEANING
1 kon' shəs nis	_____	_____ (6)
2 krü' shəl	_____	_____ (7)
3 fiz' ē ə loj' ə kəl	_____	_____ (11)
4 plə sē' bō	_____	_____ (12)
5 gi' nə kol' ə jist	_____	_____ (15)
6 prō jen' ə tər	_____	_____ (13)
7 sī kol' ə jist	_____	_____ (5)
8 skep' tik	_____	_____ (12)
9 lə jit' ə mit	_____	_____ (9)
10 sin' drōm	_____	_____ (11)

F. Practice with Definitions

■ The following sentences contain 20 words that were used in various dictionary exercises in the first half of this book. Choose and circle the definition that is the right one for the underlined word as it is used in the context of the sentence.

1 It is always a pleasure to watch the spontaneity with which children approach life. (**a** innocence **b** naturalness **c** foolishness) (7)

2 In some cultures, old people are treated with great respect out of deference for their experience and wisdom. (**a** respect **b** fear **c** awareness) (4)

3 If a person possesses the faculty of extra sensory perception, it can be either a valuable or a frightening thing. (**a** supernatural **b** spirit **c** ability) (6)

4 Many people enjoy being able to bask in the reflected glory of someone greater than themselves. (**a** boast **b** feel pleasure **c** tell lies about) (7)

5 The premature disclosure of a secret can cause a lot of trouble. (**a** unkind **b** careless **c** ahead of time) (15)

6 The potential of an athlete is not always apparent in a child. (**a** stature **b** possibilities **c** greatness) (13)

7 The birth of an anencephalic baby is always tragic. (**a** without a brain **b** without parents **c** in vitro) (14)

8 The injured boy was taken to a pediatrician. (**a** children's doctor **b** women's doctor **c** bone specialist) (15)

9 English is commonly regarded as the universal language. (**a** oldest **b** worldwide **c** easiest) (15)

10 James Earl Ray stated <u>categorically</u> that he did not kill Martin Luther King. (**a** under oath **b** frequently **c** without qualification) (11)

11 People should have the right to do what they please in life as long as it is not to the <u>detriment</u> of others. (**a** unfair advantage **b** total destruction **c** damage or injury) (13)

12 According to most doctors, there is very little that can be done to <u>alleviate</u> the distress of serious depression. (**a** ease **b** increase **c** explain) (12)

13 Color-blindness is a <u>trait</u> that is transmitted from mother to child. (**a** disease **b** nervous disorder **c** characteristic) (13)

14 When a normally stable person begins to behave <u>erratically</u>, it may be a symptom of severe stress (**a** without conscience **b** ridiculously **c** aimlessly) (5)

15 People who are always criticizing themselves may be <u>subconsciously</u> looking for approval from others. (**a** in reality **b** obviously and openly **c** without being aware) (4)

16 It is not uncommon for a good student to <u>surpass</u> his or her master. (**a** do better than **b** be jealous of **c** copy) (7)

17 If you operate on the <u>premise</u> that all people are basically honest, you may be in for a few shocks. (**a** mistaken idea **b** foolish belief **c** basic assumption) (13)

18 Some people believe their children should obey them <u>implicitly</u> at all times. (**a** unquestioningly **b** slavishly **c** gratefully) (12)

19 A <u>conscientious</u> student gains more from education. (**a** brilliant **b** hard-working **c** older) (10)

20 Our society says that if you take the law into your own hands, you must expect some sort of <u>reprisal</u>. (**a** injury done in return **b** following **c** official action) (13)

G. Review of Information for Reading Faster

■ Choose the right answer for each of these questions about reading faster. The answers can be found in the article numbered after the last answer choice, if you need to review.

1 Reading quickly involves using

   a both eyes together
   b eyes and brain together
   c eyes and a finger under the line of print (2)

2 It is a fact that the ability to read very fast

   a will stay with you forever once you've learned it
   b is essential for everyone
   c will be lost if you do not practice it constantly (7)

3 In order to read more quickly, you should

   a look for main nouns and verbs
   b look for main nouns and adjectives
   c look for main verbs and adverbs (9)

4 Words should be read

    a one by one
    b in groups
    c slowly and carefully (6)

5 When you read, your eyes should move

    a backwards and forwards over each line
    b from left to right without going back
    c from word to word slowly and carefully (6)

■ Check your answers to all of the First Half Review exercises in the Answer Key.

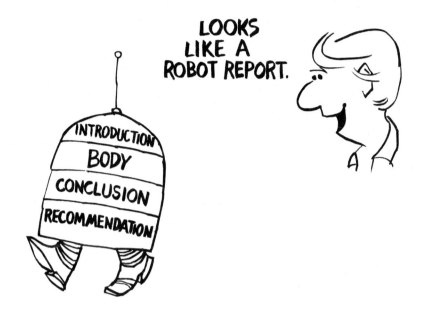

Reading a Report

■ Sometimes you read to get facts and facts alone—not ideas, not opinions, just facts. A *report* is a form of writing that presents the facts on a particular matter.

■ Many jobs require the reading and using of reports. A *report* is a formal, written account. It is written in a special style, which, when you understand it, will make report reading easier.

1 INTRODUCTION. There are 3 parts to the introduction:
   a The Problem, which states the topic of the report.
   b The Purpose, which explains the reason for the report.
   c The Scope, which tells for whom the report was written, which aspects of the subject are covered, and perhaps which aspects are not covered.
2 BODY. This gives the main information, such as:
   a The facts known to date.
   b Tests completed so far.
   c Work completed so far.
   d Costs to date.
   e Any other necessary information.
3 CONCLUSION. This shows what conclusions can be drawn from the facts presented.
4 RECOMMENDATIONS. These are suggestions as to what can be undertaken as a result of the facts presented.

High Blood Pressure

Introduction

■ Four hints for reading a report are:

1 Read the title carefully.

2 Find out who wrote the report. (These two hints will help you know what the report is going to be about.)

3 Use the 5W + H Question Frame on each part of the report as you read.

4 Make a Paragraph Key note (or notes) on each part of the report. Then, reread your Paragraph Key notes to be sure you have covered all parts of the report.

■ This next article is a report. Follow the instructions on these pages to read and understand the report.

High Blood Pressure
Word Study, Dictionary Definitions

Word Study—Choosing the Right Meaning

■ A dictionary gives meanings of words. Many words have more than one meaning. It is up to you to choose the best meaning for the word in the context in which it is used.

■ Many words whose common meanings you know also have less common meanings. You will extend your knowledge of words if you learn the less common, as well as the common, meanings.

★ ■ Here is the list of ten words chosen for special study with this article. Most of these words have more than one meaning. Beside the words is a list of synonyms. Some of the synonyms are the less common meanings of these words. See if you can write the number of the correct synonym in the parentheses beside each word. Use the Dictionary Definitions to help you.

WORD	SYNONYM
1 ( ) broadcast	1 pressure
2 ( ) conclusive	2 nonprofessional
3 ( ) current	3 a raising
4 ( ) elevation	4 opposition
5 ( ) field	5 scatter
6 ( ) lay	6 sort
7 ( ) resistance	7 present
8 ( ) screen	8 seizure
9 ( ) stroke	9 convincing
10 ( ) tension	10 background

■ Check your answers in the Answer Key.
■ Record your score.

NUMBER CORRECT _____ (Possible 10)
(1 point for each answer)

Dictionary Definitions

broadcast (brôd' kast'), v. 1 to transmit (a message, news, music, etc.) by radio or television. 2 to scatter or spread widely. 3 to disseminate widely; make generally known.
conclusive (kən klü' siv), adj. decisive, convincing; final.
current (kėr' ənt), n. 1 a flow of water, air, or any liquid; running stream. 2 flow of electricity through a wire, etc. 3 rate or amount of such a flow. 4 course or movement (of events or of opinions); general direction. —adj. 1 of

the present time. 2 generally used or accepted; commonly occurring. 3 generally known and talked about; prevalent.
elevation (el' ə vā' shən), n. 1 a raised place; a high place. 2 height above the earth's surface. 3 height above sea level. 4 dignity; loftiness; nobility. 5 a raising; lifting up.
field (fēld), n. 1 land with few or no trees. 2 piece of cleared land used for crops or pasture. 3 region where certain military or other operations are carried on. 4 sur-

face on which something is pictured or painted. 5 area where contests in jumping, throwing, etc., are held. 6 all those in game, contest, or outdoor sport. 7 range of opportunity or interest; sphere of activity or operation; background.
lay (lā), adj. 1 of the people of a church not belonging to the clergy. 2 of the people who do not belong to a particular profession.
resistance (ri zis' təns), n. 1 act of resisting. 2 power to resist. 3 thing or act that resists; opposing

High Blood Pressure
Using the Words

force; opposition.
screen (skrēn), v. **1** to shelter, protect or hide with, or as with, a screen. **2** to show (motion picture) on a screen. **3** to photograph with a motion picture camera. **4** to sift with a screen (sand, etc.). **5** to classify, sort, or eliminate by some test.

stroke (strōk), n. **1** act of striking; blow. **2** sound made by striking. **3** piece of luck, fortune, etc. **4** movement or mark made by a pen, pencil, brush, etc. **5** sudden attack or illness, especially of apoplexy; a seizure.

tension (ten' shən), n. **1** a stretching. **2** a stretched condition. **3** a strained condition; pressure. **4** the pressure of a gas. **5** electromotive force.

Using the Words

▪ Choose the correct word from the Dictionary Definitions to complete the blanks in the following sentences. In the parentheses at the beginning of each sentence, write the number of the definition that you use.

1 (   ) The artist applied one last brush _____ to the picture.

2 (   ) Some people believe a radio station has the right to _____ anything it wants to, without any censorship.

3 (   ) It is a custom in some churches to have a _____ preacher give the sermon from time to time.

4 (   ) One can gain a great sense of _____ from personal success.

5 (   ) A person who has been under a lot of _____ may become physically ill.

6 (   ) It is easy to get swept along by the _____ of popular opinion, if you do not learn to think for yourself.

7 (   ) Movie theaters think they should have the right to _____ controversial movies, provided they warn the public ahead of time.

8 (   ) So far there is no _____ evidence about the effects of saccharin on humans.

9 (   ) A champion is one who outstrips the rest of the _____ even under adverse conditions.

10 (   ) A person who is about to be wrongfully imprisoned may put up a strong show of _____ .

▪ Check your answers in the Answer Key.
▪ Record your score.

NUMBER CORRECT _____ (Possible 10)
(½ point for each answer)

High Blood Pressure
Article

Time Key

Finishing Time _____

Starting Time _____

Total Reading Time _____ minutes

Paragraph Key

■ Fill in the key points of the report as you read, under the headings provided. The first one has been done for you.

¹Everyone needs blood pressure to move blood through the circulatory system. Blood pressure is created by contractions of the heart muscles, and by the **resistance** of the walls of the arteries. With each beat of the heart, blood pressure goes up and down within a limited range. When it goes up and stays up, it is called high blood pressure, also known as hyper**tension**.

Introduction:
a Problem: high blood
pressure

²To date, researchers have not found the causes of high blood pressure, or a real cure for it. The research goes on all the time, however, and it is the purpose of this report to summarize some of the **current** work.

Introduction:
b Purpose: _____

_____
(2 points)

³It should be pointed out that this report is prepared and presented for **lay** persons; it is not meant for those in the medical or biological **fields**.

Introduction:
c Scope: _____

_____
(2 points)

⁴High blood pressure is a silent, mysterious killer—silent because it has no characteristic symptoms; mysterious because in more than 90 percent of the cases, there is no known cause or cure. If hypertension is not controlled, it can result in a **stroke**, heart failure, or kidney failure, and it can be a major risk factor in many other heart problems.

Body:
d _____

_____
(2 points)

⁵Surveys conducted throughout the nation with various population groups indicate that one in every six adults has some **elevation** of blood pressure, and about one-half of these do not know they have it. Currently, only 10 to 20 percent of hypertension patients receive any treatment at all.

Body:
e _____

_____
(2 points)

⁶One survey showed that of the people in the U.S. who are over 20 years of age, black females make up the biggest group of high blood pressure sufferers, 28 percent of the total number. Black males make up 26 percent of all high blood pressure sufferers, while white females make up 17 percent, and white males account for only 13 percent. So far there has been no **conclusive** evidence found to explain these figures.

Body:
f _____

_____
(2 points)

High Blood Pressure
Article

[7]High blood pressure can be found by a simple test. Once it has been diagnosed, there is effective treatment which can be given by the doctor, specially trained nurses, or other health personnel under the direction of a doctor. Treatment of even slight high blood pressure can prevent dangerous end results—stroke or heart and kidney failure—and reduce the risk of heart attack.

Body:

g _____

_____

(2 points)

[8]The American Heart Association has set up two big programs to **screen** people for possible signs of hypertension. One program looks at blood pressure readings to uncover hypertension patients. The other uses several methods: a blood test, a blood sugar tolerance test, and an electrocardiogram to find irregular heart rhythms. Height, weight, and smoking history are also often recorded as part of the overall picture of a likely high blood pressure victim.

Body:

h _____

_____

(2 points)

[9]The conclusions that can be drawn from present information about high blood pressure are clear. Far too many people know far too little about it, for one thing. Another clear-cut conclusion is that it is a disease suffered more by black people than by white people. The third conclusion is that there is still room for more screening programs to allow early detection for everyone.

Conclusions:

i _____

j _____

k _____

(3 points)

[10]The American Heart Associaton wants to extend public information and education programs and bring new knowledge to the public on all aspects of heart disease. They stress the importance of early recognition, diagnosis, and treatment, and they urge heart patients and their families to insist on treatment that includes the modern advances of heart treatment. The American Heart Association prints pamphlets, makes films, and provides expert speakers for any group that wants to bring up-to-date information to its members.

[11]The American Heart Association strongly recommends that all people over the age of 20, especially black people, make the effort to have a regular blood pressure checkup, preferably once a year. It is also recommended that more testing centers be set up and more information be **broadcast** among the public about high blood pressure and what can be done to prevent it.

Recommendations:

l _____

m _____

n _____

(3 points)

- Write in your Finishing Time and subtract to find your Total Reading Time.
- Record your Total Reading Time on the Development Chart.
- Check your answers in the Answer Key.
- Record your score.

NUMBER CORRECT _____ (Possible 20)
(Points as indicated)

Summary

■ When you make a summary of a report, it is not necessary to summarize it under all the various headings. You will find, for example, that it is usually not necessary to summarize the conclusions, because that material has already been given in the body of the report. Your aim should be to restate the main facts of the report as briefly as possible. This also means that you can usually reduce the introduction to one or two sentences.

■ See if you can complete the summary of this report.

1 Introduction:

   a The report is about _____

   b The report is for _____

2 Facts:

   a _____

   b _____

   c _____

   d _____

   e _____

3 Recommendations:

   a _____

   b _____

   c _____

■ Check with your teacher or with the manual for the correct answers.

■ Record your score.

NUMBER CORRECT _____ (Possible 10)
(1 point for each answer)

High Blood Pressure
Recalling the Details

Recalling the Details

■ The information in a report such as this can be useful to you only if you remember it, and this particular subject is one that should be important to everyone. See if you can remember these details without looking back at the article.

1 High blood pressure is called a silent killer because

    a nobody likes to talk about it
    b it has no characteristic symptoms
    c there is very little known about it

2 If hypertension is not controlled

    a it will eventually go away
    b it can cause almost immediate death
    c it can lead to heart or kidney failure

3 The number of adults who have high blood pressure is

    a 1 in 6
    b 1 in 100
    c 1 in 20

4 Those who are most likely to suffer from it are

    a black females
    b white females
    c white males

5 The real cause of high blood pressure

    a is of genetic origin
    b is so far not known
    c is dietary

6 The detection of high blood pressure

    a is very difficult
    b can be done by a simple test
    c is twice as difficult in older people as in children

7 An electrocardiogram is

    a a cure for high blood pressure
    b a screen program
    c a device for detecting irregular heartbeats

8 To overcome hypertension it is important

    a to do research into finding cures for cancer
    b to spread information about hypertension more widely among the public
    c to teach people how to survive a heart attack

9 This report was written

    a for people in the American Heart Association
    b to bring doctors up to date on latest developments
    c for the information of the general population

10 The main aim of this article seems to be

    a to inform
    b to scare
    c to mislead

■ Check with your teacher or with the manual for the correct answers.
■ Record your score.

NUMBER CORRECT _____ (Possible 10)
(1 point for each answer)

★ Personal Opinion

■ Here again are the ten words used for special study with this article. Select the correct word to fill in the blank in each of the following sentences, then complete each sentence **in your own words** so it expresses your ideas on the topic.

broadcast   current   field   resistance   stroke
conclusive   elevation   lay   screen   tension

1 I think most of us could use a lot more education in the _____ of ....

2 It should be the job of scientists to help _____ people understand scientific research so that.....................................

3 A good time to _____ people for high blood pressure symptoms would be ....

4 One thing that I like to know about hyper _____ is ....

5 One disease that we definitely need more _____ information about is ....

6 I think one good way to build up _____ to high blood pressure might be ....

7 I think the first important thing to do for the victim of a _____ is ....

8 _____ research into heart diseases suggests it is not good for the heart to ....

9 A message that I would like to have _____ more widely among the public is ....

10 One thing that is most likely to bring about an _____ of my blood pressure is.......................................

■ Check with your teacher or with the manual for the correct answers.
■ Record your score.

NUMBER CORRECT _____ (Possible 20)
(2 points for each word)

High Blood Pressure
★ Speed Exercise

★ Speed Exercise

■ (One minute allowed for reading only. Teacher timed or self-timed.)

You may have heard the saying, "You are what you eat." But did you ever think about how that applies to you? Research indicates that most Americans have very bad eating habits. What are the favorite foods of most Americans? Hamburgers and french fries; sugar-filled drinks; pie and whipped cream; malts and ice cream. All these things are bad for us. Some experts say that all the fast foods we eat lead to only one thing— a faster death. The meat in the hamburger and the milk in the malts may be good for you, but many other things we eat along with the hamburger and all the sugar we have in the malt spoil any possible good effect. Many fast foods are fried in fat, and that is bad for us. Fats and sugars are both bad, and yet that is what many of us eat almost all the time. And what about frozen foods and canned foods? Experts claim they are not good either. They say we do not eat enough fresh vegetables and fruit.

And what about the way we eat? Most of us eat far too fast. Too often we eat on the run. We do not chew our food enough. And we wash it down with great gulps of pop. The experts tell us we must change these habits. But do we listen to the experts? (231 words)

1 Two things we eat too much are _____ and _____ .

2 We do not eat enough _____ or _____ .

3 One bad eating habit is _____ .

4 Experts say we must _____ .

5 Eating too much fast food can lead to _____ .

NUMBER CORRECT _____ (Possible 20)
Score 10 points if you read the whole article, and 2 points for each correct answer. Check your answers by looking back at the article. Deduct 1 point for each line you did not read.

The Topic Sentence

■ **paragraph** (pār′ ə graf), n. a group of sentences about the same idea or topic that forms a distinct part of a chapter, letter, or other piece of writing.

■ This is the dictionary definition of a paragraph. From it you can learn that all the sentences in a given paragraph are on the same subject. That subject is introduced in one particular sentence. That sentence is called the *topic sentence*. It indicates the topic of the paragraph.

■ Look for the topic sentence as you read a paragraph. It will guide your reading and make it easier to find the most important facts. Frequently, the topic sentence is the first one in the paragraph. All the other sentences in the paragraph will expand on what the first one has introduced.

■ Sometimes, the topic sentence is the last sentence in the paragraph. In those cases, all the other sentences in the paragraph will build toward the topic sentence. It will serve as the climax or finale of the paragraph.

■ As you have read the articles in this book, you have made Paragraph Key notes for yourself. This has helped you remember what you read. When you read without making notes, you should look for the topic sentence. If you understand the topic sentence, it will help you understand the rest of the paragraph.

■ In this next article, the topic sentences have been underlined to help you locate them. Use them to guide you in making your Paragraph Key notes.

Your Risk of a Heart Attack

Word Study, Dictionary Definitions

Word Study—Inflected Forms and Restrictive Labels

■ *Inflected* forms are changes that are made in the spelling of a word when it is used in different ways. Inflected forms are used for nouns and verbs.

■ INFLECTED FORMS OF NOUNS: The dictionary will show the inflected form of a noun when it has an unusual plural. Usually the plural of a word is formed by adding "s" to the singular form of the word. For example, the word "egg" is in the singular form. The plural form of this word is formed by adding "s" to get "eggs."

■ The plural of some words cannot be formed by adding "s." These words have a different form altogether for the plural. For example, the word "man" is singular. The plural of that word is not "mans," but "men." And the plural form of "child" is "children." There are some even more unusual plurals, like "mice" (plural of "mouse") and "indices" (one plural form of "index").

■ Because these plurals are not formed in the usual way, they are irregular inflected forms. These inflected forms of plural nouns will be shown in the dictionary. If there is no indication of how the plural is formed, you can assume the word has a regular plural form.

■ INFLECTED FORMS OF VERBS: The spelling of some verbs changes when they are used in the past tense. The usual formation of a past tense is the addition of "ed," for example "jump" (present); "jumped" (past). Many verbs in the English language, however, are irregular. For example, "come" (present); "came" (past). When a verb makes such changes in the past tense, these irregular or inflected forms are listed in the dictionary for you. Some verbs that end in "y" will also change when different verb endings are added. For example, "supply" (present); "supplied" (past). Inflected forms like this are also listed in the dictionary.

★ ■ Here is a list of nouns and verbs used for special study with this article. Each of them has an inflected form. Supply the plural form of each noun and the infinitive (to _____) for each verb. Use the Dictionary Definitions for assistance.

NOUNS	PLURAL	VERB	INFINITIVE
1 basis	_____	8 identified	_____
2 coronary	_____	9 quitting	_____
3 diagnosis	_____	10 squeezing	_____
4 emergency	_____		
5 facility	_____		
6 heredity	_____		
7 tendency	_____		

■ Check your answers in the Answer Key.
■ Record your score.

NUMBER CORRECT _____ (Possible 10)
(1 point for each answer)

Dictionary Definitions

basis (ba′ sis), *n., pl.* **-ses. 1** a fundamental principle or set of principles; foundation. **2** the main or supporting part; base. **3** the essential part. **4** a starting point.

coronary (kôr′ ə ner′ ē, kōr′ ə ner′ ē), *adj., n., pl.* **-ies**. *adj.* of or having to do with coronary arteries.— *n.* coronary thrombosis.

diagnosis (dī′ əg nō′ sis), *n., pl.* **-ses. 1** act or process of identifying a disease by careful investigation of its symptoms. **2** a careful study of the facts about something to find out its essential features,

faults, etc. **3** a conclusion reached after a careful study of symptoms or facts. **4** (in biology) a statement of the determining characteristics of a genus, species, etc.
emergency (i mer′ jən sē), *adj., n., pl.* **-cies**. **1** a sudden need for immediate action. **2** situation in which such a need arises.
facility (fə sil′ ə tē), *n., pl.* **-ties**. **1** absence of difficulty; ease. **2** power to do anything easily and quickly; skill in using the hands or mind. **3** a building or space within a building designed, installed, or set aside for a particular function or service. **5** easygoing quality;

tendency to yield to others.
heredity (hə red′ ə tē), *n., pl.* **-ities**. **1** the transmission of physical or mental characteristics from parent to offspring by means of genes. **2** qualities or characteristics of body or mind that have come to offspring from parents. **3** tendency of offspring to be like their parents.
identify (i den′ tə fi), *v.t.* **-fied, -fying**. **1** recognize as being, or show to be, a particular person or thing; prove to be the same. **2** make the same, treat as the same. **3** connect closely, link, associate.
quit (kwit), *v.* **quit** or **quitted, quitting**, *adj. v.t.* **1** stop, cease, or dis-

continue. **2** go away from. leave. **3** give up, let go. **4** pay back, pay off (a debt). **5** ARCHAIC. behave or conduct oneself (acquit).
squeeze (skwēz), *v.* **squeezed, squeezing**. *v.t.* **1** press hard, compress. **2** hug, embrace. **3** force or thrust by pressing. **4** force out or extract by pressure, or effort, extort. **5** INFORMAL. put pressure on or try to influence.
tendency (ten′ dən sē), *n., pl.* **-cies**. **1** a leaning, inclination, propensity. **2** a natural disposition to move, proceed, or act in some direction or toward some point, end, or result.

Using the Words

■ Select from the words you have written in the lists to complete the following sentences.

1 It is dangerous to _____ too many passengers into an automobile.

2 There are no good reasons to start smoking and many good reasons to _____ .

3 In a big city like New York, you find people from a variety of _____ and backgrounds.

4 Most of us have to control our _____ to like too much rich food and too much salt.

5 If you have two or more _____ of possible heart trouble, you would do well to heed the warnings.

6 Continuous research and medical experience form the joint _____ from which we get our current knowledge of heart disease.

7 Heart attacks are often referred to as _____ .

8 Many people find it difficult to remain calm in _____ .

9 A doctor can _____ a possible heart patient, and give guidance on how to adjust life accordingly.

10 In many cities there are special _____ to assist with heart patients.

■ Check your answers in the Answer Key.
■ Record your score.

NUMBER CORRECT _____ (Possible 10)
(1 point for each answer)

Your Risk of a Heart Attack
Article

Time Key

Finishing Time   ———

Starting Time   ———

Total Reading Time ——— minutes

Paragraph Key

■ Use the underlined topic sentences to guide your preparation of your Paragraph Key notes.

¹<u>Extensive clinical and statistical studies form the **basis** of current knowledge about heart problems.</u> These studies have **identified** several factors that increase the risk of heart attack and stroke. The most significant factors are heredity, male sex, increasing age, smoking, high blood pressure and elevated blood cholesterol. Other (contributing) factors are diabetes, obesity and lack of exercise. Stress may also be a contributing factor.

a ———————

²<u>The more risk factors present, the greater the chance a person will develop heart disease.</u> Some risk factors cannot be changed; other factors can be changed under a doctor's direction; and still others can be controlled without a doctor's supervision.

b ———————
   ———————

Major risk factors that cannot be changed:

³**Heredity**—<u>a **tendency** toward heart disease or atherosclerosis appears to be hereditary.</u> Children of parents with cardiovascular disease are more likely to develop it themselves.

c ———————
   ———————

⁴*Race is a consideration, too.* Black Americans have moderate hypertension twice as often as whites and severe hypertension three times as often. Consequently, their risk of heart attack is greater.

d ———————
   ———————

⁵*Male Sex*—<u>Men have a greater risk of heart attack than women.</u> Even after menopause, when women's death rate from heart disease increases, it is not as great as men's.

e ———————
   ———————

Major risk factors that can be changed:

⁶*Cigarette Smoking*—<u>Smokers have more than twice the risk of heart attack as nonsmokers.</u> In fact, cigarette smoking is the biggest risk factor for sudden cardiac death; smokers have two to four times the risk of nonsmokers.

f ———————
   ———————

⁷When people stop smoking, their risk of heart disease rapidly declines. Ten years after **quitting** smoking, the risk of death from heart disease for people who'd smoked a pack a day or less is almost the same as for people who've never smoked.

⁸*High Blood Pressure*—<u>High blood pressure usually has no specific symptoms and no early warning signs.</u> It is truly a silent killer. A simple, quick, painless test can detect it, however.

⁹*Blood Cholesterol Levels*—<u>The risk of **coronary** heart disease rises with increasing levels of blood cholesterol.</u> When other risk factors (such as high blood pressure and smoking) are present, this risk increases even more. A person's cholesterol level is also affected by age, sex, heredity and diet. Blood cholesterol levels should be measured at least once every five years in healthy adults.

Other contributing risk factors:

¹⁰*Diabetes*—<u>Diabetes most often appears during middle age and among people who are overweight.</u> In a mild form, diabetes can go undetected for many years. When a person has diabetes, controlling other risk factors becomes even more important because diabetes can sharply increase the risk of heart attack. This occurs because diabetes affects cholesterol and triglyceride levels.

¹¹*Obesity*—<u>Recent evidence indicates that where fat is located on the body may affect the risk of coronary heart disease.</u> A waist hip ratio greater than 1.0 for men indicates a significantly increased risk. The corresponding value for women is 0.8. This means that a man's waist measurement should not exceed his hip measurement, and a woman's waist measurement should not be more than 80 percent of her hip measurement.

¹²*Physical Inactivity*—<u>Physical inactivity has not been clearly established as a risk factor for heart disease.</u> When lack of exercise is combined with overeating, however, excess weight can result—and excess weight is unquestionably a contributing factor in heart disease. Overweight individuals should consult a doctor to learn which physical activities best suit people of their age and physical condition.

¹³*Stress*—<u>Some scientists have noted a relationship between risk for coronary heart disease and a person's life stress, behavior habits and socioeconomic status.</u> These factors may influence established risk factors. For example, people in stressful situations may start smoking or smoke more than they would otherwise.

¹⁴<u>It's almost impossible to define and measure someone's level of emotional stress.</u> All people feel stress, but they feel it in different amounts and react in different ways. Life would be dull without stress, but excessive amounts of stress over a long period of time may create health problems in some people.

g _____

_____

h _____

_____

i _____

_____

j _____

_____

k _____

_____

l _____

_____

Your Risk of a Heart Attack
Article

Know the warning signals of heart attack:

[15]You can save your own life or someone else's life if you know how to recognize the signs of an imminent heart attack. These signs are:

- Uncomfortable pressure, fullness, **squeezing** or pain in the center of the chest lasting two minutes or longer.

- Pain spreading to the shoulders, neck or arms.

- Severe pain, dizziness, fainting, sweating, nausea or shortness of breath.

[16]Not all these signs occur in a heart attack. If some start to occur, however, don't wait. Get help immediately.

[17]*Know what to do in an* **emergency:**

- Know which hospitals in your area have 24 hour emergency cardiac care.

- Determine in advance the hospital or medical **facility** nearest your home and office and tell your family and friends.

- Keep a list of emergency rescue service numbers next to the telephone and in your purse or pocket.

- Get an expert **diagnosis**. If you have chest discomfort that lasts two minutes or more, call the emergency rescue service, or have someone drive you to the hospital if you can get there quicker that way.

m _____

_____

n _____

_____

o _____

_____

p _____

_____

q _____

_____

r _____

_____

s _____

_____

t _____

_____

- Write in your Finishing Time and subtract to find your Total Reading Time.
- Record your Total Reading Time on the Development Chart.
- Check your answers in the Answer Key.
- Record your score.

NUMBER CORRECT _____ (Possible 20)
(1 point for each answer)

Summary

■ The information in this article was written to help you understand the factors that can increase your risk of a heart attack. This information is valuable to everyone and is contained in the topic sentences that were underlined.

■ Use the information from the topic sentences to help you summarize the risks.

Major risks you cannot change:

1 _____

2 _____

3 _____

Major risks you can change:

4 _____

5 _____

6 _____

Other contributing risk factors:

7 _____

8 _____

9 _____

10 _____

■ Check with your teacher or with the manual for the correct answers.

■ Record your score.

NUMBER CORRECT _____ (Possible 10)
(1 point for each answer)

Your Risk of a Heart Attack

Recalling the Details

Recalling the Details

■ This article provided details of the factors that can contribute to heart problems. It also provided information on how to recognize a heart attack and what advance preparations to make in case of attack.

▧ For your own protection and the protection of your family, you should be able to complete the details on this page.

1 Heart attack warning pain occurs

   a on the right side of the chest
   b on the left side of the chest
   c in the center of the chest

2 Heart attack pain is likely to spread to

   a the shoulders, neck, or arms
   b the arms and legs
   c the head and neck

3 Dizziness

   a always occurs with a heart attack
   b never occurs with a heart attack
   c may be an accompanying symptom of heart attack

4 You should get help if chest pain lasts for

   a five minutes
   b two minutes or more
   c half an hour

■ Check with your teacher or with the manual for the correct answers.
■ Record your score.

5 A heart attack sufferer

   a will get all the symptoms
   b will not necessarily get all the symptoms
   c is immediately aware of what is happening

6 If you suffer a heart attack you should

   a have someone drive you to the hospital if it is quicker than waiting for an ambulance
   b go to the hospital ONLY in an ambulance
   c drive yourself to the hospital

List the four advance preparations you should make as a safeguard in case of a possible heart attack

7 _____

8 _____

9 _____

10 _____

NUMBER CORRECT _____ (Possible 10)
(1 point for each answer)

★ Personal Opinion

■ Here again are the ten words used for special study with this article. Select the correct word to fill in the blank in each of the following sentences, then complete each sentence **in your own words** so it expresses your ideas on the topic.

basis	diagnosis	facility	identified	squeezing
coronary	emergency	heredity	quitting	tendency

1 The one thing I have a _____ to eat too much of is

. . . .

2 The nearest emergency health _____ to where I live is

. . . .

3 If I thought I was a likely candidate for a _____ heart attack, I would

. . . .

4 I believe it is wise to get a second _____ if you

. . . .

5 My advice for dealing with any _____ situation is

. . . .

6 One habit I have difficulty in _____ is

. . . .

7 One factor that has been _____ as contributing to heart problems is

. . . .

8 In my opinion, the _____ of a healthy life is

. . . .

9 One characteristic of mine that I attribute to _____ is

. . . .

10 One place where there is altogether too much pushing and _____ is

. . . .

■ Check with your teacher or with the manual for the correct answers.
■ Record your score.

NUMBER CORRECT _____ (Possible 20)
(2 points for each word)

Your Risk of a Heart Attack
★ Speed Exercise

★ Speed Exercise

■ (One minute allowed for reading only. Teacher timed or self-timed.)

How are you coming with your reading?   Are you getting faster?
Are you able to read these articles   in a minute?   Perhaps right now we should stop awhile
and remind ourselves   of some important things   that help us to read faster.
Check yourself on these points,   and be sure you are doing the right things.
You should always move your eyes   from left to right across the page.
Always keep moving forward.   Do not let your eyes   go back over words
you have already read.   Do not read each word separately.   Learn to see groups of words.
Do not sound out the words   as you read them.   Look for the main nouns
and the main verbs.   If you want to be sure   that you do not lose your place   as you read,
you can keep your finger   under the line.   But do not move your finger
from left to right along with your eyes.   Your finger should be   under the middle of the line.
Keep your eyes moving all the time.   And remember to practice on everything you read.
Another thing to remember is   to exercise your eyes every day.   This might also be a good place
for a reminder about the value   of being a good reader.   Reading is one way
to find information   about many things quickly.   Reading the daily newspaper, for example,
will keep you informed about and interested in   your immediate world.
An interested person is an interesting person.   (243 words)

List five things you should remember to help you read better:

1 _____

2 _____

3 _____

4 _____

5 _____

NUMBER CORRECT _____ (Possible 20)
Score 10 points if you read the whole article,
and 2 points for each correct answer. Check
your answers by looking at the article. Deduct
1 point for each line you did not read.

ARTICLE 18.
They Lived to Tell the Tale
Introduction

Reading a Story with the 5W + H Question Frame

- A story can be true or fiction (not completely factual).

- The main components of a story are the characters, the setting, the plot, and the theme. You will be able to understand and appreciate a story more if you are aware of these components as you read.

- You can use the 5W + H Question Frame to help you identify these components. This table shows how the 5W + H Question Frame is used with a story to help you understand and remember its main facts:

STORY PART	MEANING	5W + H QUESTIONS
characters:	the people in the story	WHO is the story about?
setting:	the place and time in which the story happens	WHERE and WHEN is it happening?
plot:	the sequence of events; the things that happen	WHAT happened? WHY did it happen? HOW did it happen?
theme:	the special aspect of life that the story makes you think about. Love, courage, betrayal, and fear are common story themes.	WHAT is the message of the story? HOW is it shown?

- As you work at improving your reading skills, you can make Paragraph Key notes on the answers to these questions as you find them. When you are more experienced, you will be able to identify and remember the details of what you read without writing anything down.

- This next article is made up of two stories about people who had heart attacks. Read each story using the 5W + H Question Frame to guide you.

They Lived to Tell the Tale
Word Study, Dictionary Definitions

Word Study—Words That Are Similar

■ As explained in Article 6, some words in our language look very similar to other words but have very different meanings.

■ Quick or careless reading may allow you to read one word in place of one that is very similar to it, and this can result in a misunderstanding of what you are reading. Considering the word in its context will help you decide if you have the correct meaning.

★ ■ Here is a list of five pairs of words that are sometimes confused. Following the list are sentences that contain these words. See if you can determine the meaning of each of the underlined words from its context in the sentence. Use the Dictionary Definitions to help you. Write the meaning in the space provided at the end of the sentence.

ambivalent	eminent	evince	invalid (n)	patently
ambulant	imminent	invincible	invalid (adj)	patiently

1 I have <u>ambivalent</u> feelings about whether or not I believe in drafting men and women for military

service. _____

2 As long as he is <u>ambulant</u>, the cut on his leg will not heal. _____

3 Albert Einstein is one of the most <u>eminent</u> physicists of all time. _____

4 The sound of thunder may herald an <u>imminent</u> storm. _____

5 A nervous person may often <u>evince</u> a sense of false calm to steady his or her own nerves.

_____

6 So far, cancer has proved to be an <u>invincible</u> disease. _____

7 An <u>invalid</u> often has to be cared for by someone else. _____

8 A check is <u>invalid</u> if it is not signed. _____

9 It is <u>patently</u> obvious that there will soon be too many people in the world. _____

10 If you apply yourself <u>patiently</u> to a task, you have a better chance of succeeding at it than if you

rush through it. _____

■ Check your answers in the Answer Key.
■ Record your score.

NUMBER CORRECT _____ (Possible 10)
(1 point for each answer)

Dictionary Definitions

ambivalent (am biv′ ə lent), *adj.* acting in opposite ways; having or showing conflicting feelings.

ambulant (am′ byə lent), *adj.* moving about; walking; ambulatory.

eminent (em′ ə nənt), *adj.* **1** above all or most others; outstanding; distinguished. **2** conspicuous; noteworthy. **3** high; lofty. **4** stand-

ing out above other things; prominent.
evince (i vins'), *v.* **1** to show clearly; manifest. **2** to show that one has (a certain quality, characteristic, etc.)
imminent (im' ə nənt), *adj.* likely to

happen soon; about to occur.
invalid (in' və lid), *n.* person who is weak because of sickness or injury; disabled or sickly person.
invalid (in val' id), *adj.* worthless; without force or effect; not valid.
invincible (in vin' sə bel), *adj.*

unable to be conquered; impossible to overcome; unconquerable.
patently (pat' nt lē), *adv.* clearly; obviously; plainly or openly.
patiently (pā' shənt lē), *adv.* persistently; diligently; with steady effort and hard work.

Using the Words

■ Choose the correct word from the Dictionary Definitions to complete the blank in each of the following sentences.

1 Many young people today have _____ feelings about whether or not to go to college.

2 There are many more buildings these days that make allowances for handicapped persons or for an _____ who has to use a wheelchair.

3 There are always some people in the world who preach the _____ destruction of our earth and everything on it.

4 Sometimes it is hard to wait _____ for something you are looking forward to.

5 Some critics say there are not enough _____ politicians in our government these days.

6 _____ people often forget how lucky they are to be able to move about freely.

7 For most of us it is hard to _____ an expression of courage in the face of danger.

8 Environmentalists tell us it is _____ clear that we are destroying the earth through carelessness.

9 Sometimes people will cast an _____ vote, just to confuse an election.

10 It is a good feeling when the home team is apparently _____ .

■ Check your answers in the Answer Key.
■ Record your score.

NUMBER CORRECT _____ (Possible 10)
(1 point for each answer)

They Lived to Tell the Tale
Article

Paragraph Key

■ Make a brief Paragraph Key note about the introductory paragraph. Then fill in details of the 5W + H questions for each story as you find them.

¹Heart attack. The words conjure up a picture of either sudden death or, for the lucky survivors, a lingering half-life, spent crippled and confined. How do men and women who have had heart trouble and recovered from it live the rest of their lives? Here are the stories of two famous people who lived to tell the tale.

²"I have been to the Valley," says Pearl Bailey, "and God has given me another chance." When Pearl talks about "the Valley," she means the Valley of Death, because during a heart attack in 1972, when she was 54 years old, she actually "died for a few seconds."

³After her recovery, she put the whole incident behind her—perhaps too far, because two years later, while preparing for a Christmas show at a Denver nightclub, she collapsed again. As she lay in the hospital during the next few days, it was **patently** clear to her that she would have to alter her future life-style if she wanted to survive.

⁴Pearl wanted to be able to go on working and still have abundant energy left to devote to her religion, her friends, and the international goodwill projects she had undertaken so successfully on behalf of her country. To start with, that meant giving up one of her favorite pasttimes, food. Pearl had been carrying a lot of excess weight, which had to come off and stay off.

⁵As an entertainer, Pearl Bailey is an **eminent** person, and it is important to her to look good, which gives her the motive to keep her weight down. "The minute I get some of that weight back on," she says, "I start huffing and puffing, and I don't think that looks too glamorous."

⁶She was also told to exercise, not in bursts, but on a regular, steady basis. For Pearl, exercise means walking. "Oh, how I walk," she says. "Feet killing me, but I walk. Heart's beating well. And I think it's wonderful."

Introduction:

a _____

    _____

Story 1:

b Who _____

c When _____

d Where _____

e What_____

f Why_____

g How did she recover?

    _____

Adapted from Sally Wendkos Olds, "The Survivors," *Family Health Magazine* (January, 1977), and Judith Ismach, "Halt That Heart Attack!" *American Health* (Jan/Feb, 1988).

⁷Pearl attributes part of her recovery to the fact that she would not let anyone make an **invalid** of her. She insisted on becoming **ambulant** as soon as possible and refused to sit around being sick. Nevertheless, she did retire from the stage, because of the constant pressures and heavy demands it made on her energy and stamina. Her retirement, however, was only partial, for Pearl still makes occasional appearances on stage and more often on television.

⁸Pearl Bailey **evinces** a feeling of strength and confidence. "I think I feel stronger than ever because I live very sensibly," she says. Once, on a health series produced for television, she sang a song that has a very special meaning for her. It is called "Coming Back into the World."

⁹"I got back," says Pearl quietly, "and I'd like to stay back."

¹⁰Today there is new hope for heart attack sufferers, with the introduction of "clot-busting" drugs called thrombolytic agents.

¹¹It was one such drug, tPA, that saved the life of **invincible** television and radio host Larry King.

Story 2:

h Who _____

i When_____

j Where _____

¹²The symptoms had started at 3:30 A.M., King recalls, after he'd returned home from hosting his television and radio shows. The pain ran along the right side of his body, and, although he tried to sleep through it, it grew worse.

¹³King had recognized himself as a heart attack candidate since he first started having chest pains seven years earlier. "I'd been taking medication, but I still continued to smoke three packs a day," he says.

¹⁴At 6 A.M., King called his cardiologist. "We tried Maalox, Mylanta, nitroglycerin . . . the pain seemed to come and go." Finally, at 9:30 A.M.— six hours after the intermittent pain had started—he drove with his producer to the George Washington University Hospital Emergency Room in Washington, D.C.

¹⁵GW cardiologist Richard Katz saw quickly that a heart attack was not only **imminent** for King, it was actually under way. King met the criteria for tPA treatment, and within minutes of taking the drug, he found that his pain disappeared. The next day, balloon therapy widened the still-narrowed blood vessels in his heart.

What treatment?

k _____

l _____

¹⁶King suffered some heart damage, but tPA halted the attack before more muscle was destroyed. His doctor told him that, at age 53, he's "an eight cylinder car with six good cylinders."

They Lived to Tell the Tale
Article

[17]King obeyed orders **patiently** and he was back on the air four weeks after his heart attack. He's stopped smoking, eats a heart-healthy diet, exercises by walking, and takes three different heart medications daily—plus aspirin to help prevent fresh clots.

[18]King is not **ambivalent** about the cause of his recovery. He gives a lot of credit to GW's Emergency Room doctors and claims he's lucky they had a tPA program.

[19]The government advisory panel had not approved widespread use of the drug, indicating a need for further data. Some major university hospitals, however, considered this concern **invalid**, and they were using the drug on an experimental basis.

[20]"Clot-busters" are proving effective in many cases, but it is important to remember that they can be no help unless used within the early hours as a heart attack evolves. This makes it imperative for people to recognize the early symptoms and get help as soon as possible.

How he lives:

m _____

n _____

o _____

p _____

q _____

Why no government approval?

r _____

_____

s _____

t _____

_____

- Write in your Finishing Time and subtract to find your Total Reading Time.
- Record your Total Reading Time on the Development Chart.
- Check your answers in the Answer Key.
- Record your score.

NUMBER CORRECT _____ (Possible 20)
(1 point for each answer)

Summary

■ The best way to summarize a story is to use the 5W + H Question Frame to cover the main details. Reread your Paragraph Key notes and then complete this summary.

Story 1:

1 Who? _____

2 When first stricken? _____

3 What effect on her life? _____

4 Why did the second attack occur? _____

5 Where did it happen? _____

6 How did life change? _____

Story 2:

7 Who? _____

8 When (time of day)? _____

9 Where was pain? _____

10 What treatment? _____

■ Check with your teacher or with the manual
for the right answers.
■ Record your score.

NUMBER CORRECT _____ (Possible 10)
(1 point for each answer)

They Lived to Tell the Tale
Recalling the Details

Recalling the Details

■ This article tells the stories of two brave people. It also provides information that could act as a warning to other people who want to prevent a heart attack in their own lives.

■ Reread your Paragraph Key notes and your summary and then complete this exercise.

1 One common factor that allowed these two people to recover was

   a someone to stand by them
   b their own determination
   c excellent physicians and surgeons

2 One thing that is helpful in recovering from heart trouble is

   a regular moderate exercise
   b large amounts of very hard exercise
   c putting the whole thing out of your mind

3 Many Americans suffer from one of the causes that led to heart trouble for both these people, which is

   a hardening of the arteries
   b smoking
   c too little exercise

4 The important thing to remember about exercise after heart trouble is

   a it must be regular
   b it must be strenuous
   c it must be avoided

5 Larry King is a

   a television and radio talk-show host
   b television host
   c radio host

6 Thrombolytic drugs

   a prevent heart attack
   b break up clots
   c widen the arteries

7 At the time of this attack, Larry King

   a had already had previous chest pains
   b had already had a heart attack
   c had never suffered heart problems

8 King was treated with a combination of

   a aspirin and tPA
   b tPA and "clot-busters"
   c tPA and balloon therapy

9 The government view of tPA is

   a wary, seeking more information
   b totally against it
   c totally in favor of it

10 "Clot-busters" are most effective

   a if used with aspirin
   b if used with balloon therapy
   c if used during the early part of an attack

■ Check with your teacher or with the manual for the correct answers.
■ Record your score.

NUMBER CORRECT _____ (Possible 10)
(1 point for each answer)

They Lived to Tell the Tale
★ Personal Opinion

★ Personal Opinion

■ Here again are the five pairs of similar words used for special study with this article. Select the right word to fill in the blank in each of the following sentences, then complete each sentence **in your own words** so it expresses your ideas on the topic.

ambivalent	eminent	evince	invalid (n)	patently
ambulant	imminent	invincible	invalid (adj)	patiently

1 The articles on heart trouble make it _____ clear that an important factor in

   preventing trouble is. . . . .

2 I (do/do not) think _____ people should allow the press to publish details of

   their illness, because. . . . .

3 I think one of the hardest things about being an _____ must surely be

   . . . .

4 One thing about which I have mixed and _____ feelings is

   . . . .

5 If I could choose the attitude that I would like to _____ for the rest of the

   world to see, it would be. . . . .

6 I think normal, _____ people often forget that people in wheelchairs face daily

   hardships such as. . . . .

7 Many people overcome physical difficulties to gain success in life. One of the

   most _____ people I have ever heard of is

   . . . .

8 I think if most of us were aware of how close we are to the _____ danger of

   heart attack, we might. . . . .

9 In my opinion one of the hardest things to wait for _____ is

   . . . .

10 The idea that a heart problem will ruin your life becomes _____ when you

   look at. . . . .

■ Check with your teacher or with the manual
   for the correct answers.
■ Record your score.

NUMBER CORRECT _____ (Possible 20)
(2 points for each word)

They Lived to Tell the Tale
★ Speed Exercise

★ Speed Exercise

■ (One minute allowed for reading only. Teacher timed or self-timed.)

The last speed exercise offered some reminders about things to do to improve your reading. Mostly they were things about using the eyes. But the eyes are only part of the reading process. Reading uses your eyes and your brain. You can train your eyes to move faster. But you must also keep your mind in gear. Do not try to read everything in the same way, or at the same speed. A story can be read with the 5W + H questions in mind. Other articles should also be read with questions in mind. You can use the 5W + H questions, or you can use other questions of your own.

Your brain should never be at rest when you read. Think about the type of material you are reading. If you are reading a report, use the report pattern to help you read. Remember that there is some sort of pattern to almost everything you read. Know what sort of material you are reading, and you will read it easier and faster. Words are meant to be understood. You can understand them. And you will understand words better if you look for the meaning as you read.

This article and the one before it were just to remind you about some important things you need to remember. Now you can return to speed exercises that give you things to think about. Learn to read quickly and think hard. Try to involve yourself in what you are reading and develop ideas and opinions of your own that you can share with other people. (260 words)

List five things that this article says are important to good reading:

1 _____

2 _____

3 _____

4 _____

5 _____

NUMBER CORRECT _____ (Possible 20)
Score 10 points if you read the whole article, and 2 points for each correct answer. Check your answers by looking back at the article. Deduct 1 point for each line you did not read.

SECTION G.
Reading Assists on the Job

Reading the Memorandum

■ Almost every job requires some reading. A competent employee can read, interpret, and understand all forms of written communications. One of the most common office communications is the *memorandum*.

■ A memorandum (mәm' ә ran' dәm) is a note sent from one department to another within a business or office, giving instructions or information. The word *memorandum* can be shortened to *memo*, and the plural can be either *memoranda* or *memorandums*.

■ A memorandum is usually set out in standard form, which you will see in this article.

■ Hints for reading a memorandum:

1 Check the date. Be sure the memo is recent and does not cover a subject that has already been taken care of.

2 See if the memo is addressed to you alone or if you have to pass it on to others.

3 If the memo gives you several tasks, number them. Check each task as you finish it.

4 If there is any task you cannot carry out, find someone who can help you with it. Do not leave tasks undone.

Interoffice Memorandum
Word Study, Dictionary Definitions

Word Study—Etymology

■ The dictionary provides you with information about words. One piece of information it provides is the history of the word or its *etymology*. Many English words have come from other languages, most particularly from Latin and Greek.

■ Knowing the original language from which the word comes and the meaning of its root can help you determine the meaning of the word. For example, the Latin root *dicere* means "to say," so you can assume that any word with that root in it will have something to do with "saying." The words dictate, abdicate, dictum, dictator, indicate, and dedicate all have some relation to the word "say."

★ ■ Here is a list of the ten words chosen for special study with this article. Beside the word list you will see headings for nouns, verbs, and the etymologies of the list words. If the list word is a noun or can be used in the noun form, mark the space in the second column with an "N." If the list word is a verb or can be used as a verb, mark the space in the third column with a "V." If the word is neither a noun nor a verb and cannot be used as either, leave the noun and verb columns blank. Then write in the language from which each word originated. Use the Dictionary Definitions to help you.

WORD	NOUN	VERB	ETYMOLOGY
1 comply			
2 document			
3 feasibility			
4 gauge			
5 implement			
6 incentive			
7 longevity			
8 paramount			
9 solicit			
10 trivia			

■ Check your answers in the Answer Key.
■ Record your score.

NUMBER CORRECT _____ (Possible 10)
(1 point for each row)

Dictionary Definitions

comply (kəm plīʹ), *v.* **-plied, -plying**. to act in agreement with a request or command. (Latin *complere* fulfill; complete)
document (dokʹ yə mənt), *n.* a written or printed paper or other object that gives information, evidence, etc., on any subject or matter under consideration. Letters, maps, and pictures are docu- ments. —*v.* to prove or support by means of documents or the like. (Latin *docere* to show, teach)
feasibility (fēʹ zə bilʹ ə tē), *n.* something that is possible without too much difficulty; something that is likely or practical. (Latin *facere* to do)
gauge (gāj), *n.* **1** a standard mea- sure or a scale of standard mea- surements used for the measure of such things as the capacity of a barrel, the thickness of sheet iron, the diameter of a wire, etc. **2** instrument for measuring. **3** means of estimating or judging. **4** size; capacity; extent. —*v.* **1** to measure exact measurement of with a gauge. **2** to determine the capacity or content of. **3** to esti-

mate; judge. (Old French *gauger* to measure)

implement (im′ plə mənt), *n.* a useful article of equipment; tool; instrument; utensil. —*v.* **1** to provide with tools or other means. **2** to provide with the power and authority necessary to accomplish or put something into effect. **3** carry out; get done. (Latin *implere* to fill, from *in* + *plere* to fill)

incentive (in sen′ tiv), *n.* thing that urges a person on; cause of action or effort; motive; stimulus. (Latin *incinere* to cause to sound, from *in* on + *canere* sing)

longevity (lon jev′ ə tē), *n.* **1** long life. **2** length or duration of life. (Late Latin *longus* long + *aevum* age)

paramount (par′ ə mount), *adj.* chief in importance; above others; supreme. (Old French *par* by + *amont* up)

solicit (sə lis′ it), *v.* **1** to ask earnestly; to try to get. **2** to influence to do wrong; tempt; entice. (Latin *sollicitare* to disturb)

trivia (triv′ ē ə), *n., pl.* **1** things of little or no importance; trifles; trivialities. **2** pl. of trivium, which in ancient Rome and the Middle Ages was the name given to the first three of the seven liberal arts: grammar, rhetoric, and logic. (Latin *trivium* triple road or way; crossroads)

Using the Words

■ Choose the right word from the Dictionary Definitions to complete the blank in each of these sentences.

1 Doctors tell us that with proper care, good food, and regular exercise, most of us could increase our _____ considerably.

2 Even the possibility of lung cancer does not seem to be a strong enough _____ to stop a number of teenagers from learning to smoke.

3 If cereal manufacturers were to _____ with good nutrition practices, they would not include as much sugar in their products.

4 Health experts know they must _____ the help of parents in training children to appreciate good food.

5 There are several parent organizations around the country that are trying to _____ the effect of television advertising on young children who watch children's programs regularly.

6 Many factories in Europe and Japan are starting to _____ exercise programs as an essential part of the working day.

7 It would be difficult to _____ how many adults in this country are in poor physical shape, but we are told the number is very high.

8 In recent years, interest in _____ has increased because of several new games on the market.

9 When the Food and Drug Administration looked into the _____ of removing saccharin from the market, they found that the public did not want it removed.

10 Good food is of _____ importance to good health, but most of us pay far too little attention to what we eat.

■ Check your answers in the Answer Key.
■ Record your score.

NUMBER CORRECT _____ (Possible 10)
(1 point for each answer)

Interoffice Memorandum
Article

Paragraph Key

■ Stop at the end of each paragraph to make a Paragraph Key note. As you read, be aware of parts of the memo that will require action.

To: Jim Rader   Department: Personnel

From: Barbara Clarke   Department: Medical

Date: June 14, 19--

Subject: General Health of Employees

¹For the past two years we have been engaged in a study of the health of workers in this company. Now that the study is complete, the president of the company plans to read the results to the shareholders at the next general meeting.

²In the meantime, I think it appropriate to share with you some of the changes we plan to suggest as a means of improving the general health of all employees. We would like you to discuss these ideas with the employees, **gauge** their reactions, and let us know the results.

³From the mass of data we have collected, we have extracted the following facts: Each year we **document** a staggering 12,000 work hours in sick days. Most illnesses reported are of the nature of colds, headaches, digestive troubles, and other similar medical **trivia**, which nevertheless combine to result in a heavy loss of production.

⁴More serious, perhaps, is the realization that each year the company is losing an average of five executives to cardiopulmonary troubles, and this represents a serious drain on the top decision-making power of the company.

⁵It is clear, of course, that not all these problems and illnesses are directly work related, but we believe there are several things the company could do to encourage better general health among the employees. We would therefore like to make the following suggestions:

⁶Changes should be made in the type of food sold in the company cafeteria. We propose to cut down on starchy foods such as french fries and rich desserts, and offer instead a greater variety of fresh fruits and dairy products, along with more broiled meats in place of fried foods. We

a To: _____

From: _____

Subject: _____
(3 points)

(1 point for each of the remaining Paragraph Key notes)

b _____

_____

c _____

_____

d _____

_____

e _____

_____

f _____

_____

g _____

_____

also intend to have more fruit juices available and fewer sweetened, carbonated drinks. Right now we are looking into the **feasibility** of providing these goods.

7We would also like to start a strong antismoking campaign, and we are currently looking at the idea of bonus **incentives** for employees who manage to quit smoking. The details of this proposal are not yet complete.

h _____

_____

8Another idea is the provision of several different exercise plans for employees, and we are open to suggestions about the type of programs that employees would most enjoy. Currently we are thinking along the following lines:

i _____

_____

9A regular calisthenics program could be held at 7:30 a.m., 12 noon, 1:00 p.m., and 4:30 p.m. Each session would last about 20 minutes and would be conducted by an exercise expert to be employed by the company. Employees could sign up for the time slots best suited to their work schedules.

j _____

_____

10We could also use the unused land behind Factory Number 2. There is sufficient space there for two basketball courts, two tennis courts, and a track for running. It is our present intention to offer free instruction in tennis, basketball, volleyball, and jogging. We have already asked the Building and Development Department to look into the cost and feasibility of reclaiming this land.

k _____

_____

11The company can also offer group membership in the local YMCA or YWCA. For those employees who would not wish to undertake their exercise at work, we propose to offer family memberships in these clubs at one-third the usual cost; the remainder of the outlay would be picked up by the company. In return for these reduced rates, the company would expect employees to show evidence of regular use of the club facilities.

l _____

_____

12In addition, we are exploring the possibility of presenting a series of lecture-workshops on the subject of "Good Health for the Heart." We plan that these would be given by experts in the cardiopulmonary field, and we would want to give the strongest encouragement to employees to attend all these lectures.

m _____

_____

13Once again we would be interested in considering some type of incentive plan for employees who remain free of heart troubles between annual medical checkups.

n _____

_____

14We believe there is double benefit to be gained from improving the health of the employees of this company. We see an obvious benefit to the individual in terms of better health and **longevity**, and we see an equal benefit to the company in terms of increased production and less turnover of employees.

o _____

_____

Interoffice Memorandum
Article

¹⁵When these changes are approved, we would like to **implement** them as soon as possible. For this reason, I **solicit** your cooperation in circulating these proposals among the employees and arranging for us to receive feedback on their reactions.

p _____

_____

¹⁶For your information, I am enclosing with this memo a brochure containing facts about a similar employee health campaign undertaken at the Swan Company in Illinois. Feel free to circulate this brochure among heads of departments throughout this company, if you feel it necessary.

q _____

_____

¹⁷I realize I am adding considerable extra work to your already overloaded schedule with these requests, but we do feel it is of **paramount** importance at this time. I would be pleased if you would notify me when you have had the chance to **comply** with the requests in this memo.

r _____

_____

■ Write in your Finishing Time and subtract to find your Total Reading Time.
■ Record your Total Reading Time on the Development Chart.
■ Check your answers in the Answer Key.
■ Record your score.

NUMBER CORRECT _____ (Possible 20)
(Points as indicated)

Summary

■ If you were the recipient of this memorandum, there would be two main things you would have to be aware of: the action that you, as the person receiving the memo, should take, and the information that has to be passed on to other employees. These two points, therefore, form the basis of the summary you will make of the information in the memo.

Action to be taken: (List the five things Jim Rader would have to do as a result of receiving this memo.)

1 _____

2 _____

3 _____

4 _____

5 _____

Ideas to be passed on to employees for consideration: (Keep these general; do not list sub-points.)

6 _____

7 _____

8 _____

9 _____

Two main reasons for wanting to improve employees' health:

10 a _____

b _____

■ Check with your teacher or with the manual
for the correct answers.
■ Record your score.

NUMBER CORRECT _____ (Possible 10)
(1 point for each answer; ½ point for each
answer in #10)

Interoffice Memorandum
Recalling the Details

Recalling the Details

■ This is a lengthy memorandum containing many facts. See how much of the detail you can recall without rereading the article. Reread your Paragraph Key notes and your summary if you wish before you complete this page.

1 The information that led to the proposals in this memorandum came from

   a the president's report
   b a special study
   c a brochure from the Swan Company

2 The memorandum claims that the documented sick time was 12,000 hours per

   a month
   b week
   c year

3 Most of these "sick hours" are accounted for by

   a heart ailments
   b minor illnesses
   c accidents on the job

4 The proposed menu changes were designed to cut down

   a protein and salt
   b fats and sugars
   c preservatives

5 The bonus incentive antismoking campaign

   a was already under way at the time of the memo
   b was based on the success of similar plans in other companies
   c had not been fully worked out at the time of the memo

6 The proposed exercise plan

   a would be self-directed by the employees
   b would be under the direction of an expert
   c would be conducted by the local YMCA or YWCA

7 The proposed outdoor exercise program would include

   a jogging, basketball, and soccer
   b tennis, volleyball, and jogging
   c jogging, volleyball, and swimming

8 According to the information in the article, we

   a know that heart disease attacks only executives in this company
   b know that heart disease attacks employees at all levels
   c cannot tell whether heart disease attacks all employees or only executives

9 It is clear from this memo that the company is interested

   a only in increasing productivity
   b in improving employee health and productivity
   c only in improving employee health

10 The tone of this memo would suggest that the company

   a has just begun to look into the health of its employees
   b is anxious to keep up with the Swan Company
   c is serious about wanting to improve employee health standards

■ Check with your teacher or with the manual for the correct answers.
■ Record your score.

NUMBER CORRECT _____ (Possible 10)
(1 point for each answer)

★ Personal Opinion

■ Here again are the ten words used for special study with this article. Select the correct word to fill in the blank in each of the following sentences, then complete each sentence **in your own words** so it expresses your ideas on the topic.

comply	feasibility	implement	longevity	solicit
document	gauge	incentive	paramount	trivia

1 The best way to _____ improved health standards for the nation as a whole might be . . . .

2 I think the best _____ to stop smoking is

. . . .

3 I think it is important that the government _____ all available evidence on the subject of . . . .

4 To avoid getting caught up in the _____ of everyday life and ignoring our health, I think we should . . . .

5 I have heard that one thing that leads to better health and greater _____ is

. . . .

6 As a means of improving the general health of the people in this country, I would like to see a study made of the _____ of . . . .

7 I think when it comes to teaching people about good food, it is of _____ importance to tell them . . . .

8 I think there is one rule that all food manufacturers should have to _____ with, and that is . . . .

9 If I were going to _____ funds to support a particular charity, it would be

. . . .

10 I think the best way to _____ a person's success in life is

. . . .

■ Check with your teacher or with the manual for the correct answers.
■ Record your score.

NUMBER CORRECT _____ (Possible 20)
(2 points for each word)

Interoffice Memorandum
★ Speed Exercise

★ Speed Exercise

■ (One minute allowed for reading only. Teacher timed or self-timed.)

Much has been written lately   on the subject of health.   All sorts of people are suggesting
many different ways of keeping healthy.   There are two main things   to look after
in order to stay healthy.   They are diet and exercise.   It seems that if you eat the right foods
and the right amount of food,   you have a good chance   of keeping a healthy body.
But what about a healthy mind?   Apparently there is no easy shortcut
for making sure you do not suffer   from depression or paranoia
or other forms of mental illness.   There is one interesting book   on the market now
that does try to show   that happiness needs   a healthy body and a healthy mind.
The book is called *Running and Being*.   It was written by George Sheehan.
He was a heart doctor.   He had been very successful as a doctor.   Then, in his fifties,
he began to think that something was wrong   with his life.   So he began to run.
At the age of 59 he became famous   as a long distance runner.
Dr. Sheehan found   that although he had a well-educated mind,
his body was in terrible shape.   He found that running made him feel better physically
and also gave his mind   time and strength to explore more ideas.
He believed that you can only understand yourself properly
when your body is as fit as it can be.   He also believed it is important
to understand your body "type"   in order to understand yourself.
There are three basic body types.   One is the athletic type, or the doers.
Another is the relaxed and easy-going type, or the talkers.
The third is the small-boned, intense type, or the thinkers.   Each reacts to life differently,
and if you understand your type,   you can learn to understand yourself.   (300 words)

1 Many books have been written about _____ .

2 George Sheehan's book is called _____ .

3 Sheehan worked as a _____ .

4 At the age of 59 he became _____ .

5 He believed in the importance of _____ and _____ .

NUMBER CORRECT _____ (Possible 20)
Score 10 points if you read the whole article,
and 2 points for each correct answer. Check
your answers by looking back at the article.
Deduct ½ point for each line you did not read.

Reading Business Letters

■ Letters are frequently used in business. A competent employee can handle all business letters correctly.

■ Business letters generally have one of two purposes:

1 To get information, or
2 To give information.

■ Both types of letters call for action. If you receive a letter *requesting* information, you should respond to the request. If you receive a letter that *provides* information, you should do something with the information received.

■ This next reading is made up of two letters. The first is requesting certain things to be done. You will read it to determine what action or actions should be taken. The second letter is an application from someone wanting a job. He is giving information about himself. You will read that letter to find out what you can about the applicant.

■ Both letters are poorly written and do not employ Standard Business English. *Standard Business English* is the name given to the preferred method of expression in business. It is good to know and be able to use Standard Business English. You will learn more about it as you read these letters.

Standard Business English
Word Study, Standard Business English Preferences

Word Study—Using the Best Words

▣ A dictionary can provide you with information about individual words. It cannot, however, tell you everything you need to know about how to put words together in the most effective or acceptable way.

▣ Good language usage can be learned by listening to and reading what is written by those people who know how to use the language well.

▣ There are many forms of English throughout the world and many different dialects of it in our own country. Businesses use Standard Business English so that people can clearly understand one another. You should know how to use this form of English when you write business letters.

★ ▣ The following sentences contain some phrases that are no longer considered good style in business writing. There are two such phrases in each sentence. Underline the phrases that you think are outdated. Check the list of Standard Business English Preferences that follows if you are not sure what to underline.

1 In re the matter of your order, we shall arrange to ship it as per your instructions.
2 We are deeply grateful for your order and beg your indulgence in allowing us fill it properly.
3 Please find enclosed a duplicate copy of the information we sent you April 25.
4 Thank you for the kind favor of your letter of recent date asking for our latest brochure.
5 We would like to receive information about your line at your earliest convenience.

▣ Check your answers in the Answer Key.
▣ Record your score.

NUMBER CORRECT _____ (Possible 10)
(1 point for each phrase identified)

Standard Business English Preferences

▣ This list replaces the usual Dictionary Definitions list.
▣ The sentences that follow make use of phrases and expressions that are sometimes misused in business letters. Under each sentence, you will see how the same information would be written in the preferred method of Standard Business English. Read the sentences and note how each underlined phrase has been changed.

1 We thank you for the kind favor of your recommendation.
Better: Thank you for your recommendation.
2 Thank you for your letter of recent date.
Better: Thank you for your letter of March 12. (It is better to give the actual date of the letter.)
3 We are forwarding the materials as per your order.
Better: We are forwarding the materials that you ordered.
4 We would appreciate having a chance to show you our line.
Better: We would appreciate having a chance to show you our products (or our copying machines, or whatever goods are being advertised).
5 In re the matter of your nonpayment of our last bill, we must ask for payment by July 7.
Better: Regarding your nonpayment of our last bill, we must ask for payment by July 7.
6 Please return the enclosed forms at your earliest convenience.
Better: Please return the enclosed forms by July 26. (Wherever possible, it is better to give an actual date.)
7 We beg your indulgence for the late return of your materials.
Better: We apologize for the late return of your materials.

8 We are sending you a <u>duplicate copy</u> of our order.
Better: We are sending you a copy of our order. ("Duplicate" means "copy," so there is no need to use both words.)

9 <u>Please find enclosed</u> some samples of the types of paper we produce.
Better: I am enclosing some samples of the types of paper we produce.

10 We <u>are deeply grateful</u> for your interest in our company.
Better: Thank you for your interest in our company.

Using the Words

■ In each of the following sentences change the underlined words to clear, modern English. Use the list of Standard Business English Preferences to help you.

1 Would you please send us a <u>duplicate copy</u> of everything you mail to the Canadian office?

_____

2 <u>I am deeply grateful for your kindness</u> in reading my letter.

_____

3 In your letter <u>of recent date</u>, you asked for a copy of our brochure.

_____

4 I am sending you 17 cans of orange paint, <u>as per your order</u>.

_____

5 <u>We beg your indulgence</u> for the delay caused by the breakdown in our computer.

_____

6 We wish to inform you that <u>the line</u> you ordered will be on special sale next month.

_____

7 I would like to have the report on the work you have done <u>at your earliest convenience</u>.

_____

8 We appreciate <u>your kind favor</u> of viewing our new apartments last week.

_____

9 <u>Please find enclosed</u> the application forms you asked for.

_____

10 <u>In re</u> your application for a position in our record department, would you please call Mrs. Robinson for an appointment? _____

■ Check your answers in the Answer Key.
■ Record your score.

NUMBER CORRECT _____ (Possible 10)
(1 point for each answer)

Standard Business English
Article: The Letter of Request

Time Key

■ Do not record your reading time with this article. You will not be reading the whole article at one time.

Paragraph Key

■ Briefly restate what the letter is requesting in the Paragraph Key. The boldfaced words will be used on the Personal Opinion page. See if you can work out their meanings from the context as you read.

The Rusden Supply Company
Glenway Pike
Boston, Massachusetts 02154-3669

March 17, 19--

Mr. J. Bowen, Production Manager
Michigan Machines
Hancock, Michigan 49930-2730

Dear Mr. Bowen:

Subject: Your Order #3756/21

¹We acknowledge receipt of your letter of recent date. We are deeply grateful for it and regret the delay in filling your order. Naturally, we want to comply with your requests as per your instructions.

²We wish to advise, however, that the original order you sent us has been **mislaid**. The order number is on record as having been received. Without the order itself, however, we have no information about the nature of the line you ordered. Would you do us the kind favor of sending a duplicate copy of this order #3756/21?

a _____

_____

³In re the matter of your other request, please find enclosed a copy of our most recent brochure, giving details of our latest lines. In particular we draw your attention to model #27B. We believe this to be a considerably **superior** model to its **predecessor**. And we believe it is something which could be of value to your company.

b _____

_____

⁴Would you do us the favor of routing this brochure to your various department heads, so that all your key **personnel** can have the opportunity of being informed of our latest?

c _____

_____

⁵There is one last matter we would like to draw to your attention. That is the matter of your **outstanding** account. At this time, we are **engaged** in balancing our books for the annual **audit**. It would assist us greatly if you could do us the favor of sending a **remittance** at your earliest convenience. Would you kindly draw the attention of your accounts department to this matter so they can handle it **forthwith**?

d _____

_____

e _____

_____

⁶Our company has a long reputation of satisfied customers. We do apologize for the confusion over your last order, and we beg your indulgence in this matter. We assure you we will do whatever we can to **expedite** your delivery as soon as we can get your duplicate copy.

⁷We hope we can look forward to a long and satisfying business association between our two companies.

Sincerely,

THE RUSDEN SUPPLY COMPANY

Gloria Washington
General Manager

- Check your answers in the Answer Key.
- Do not record your score for this Paragraph Key until completing the Paragraph Key for the next letter. Then add both scores and record the total score on the Development Chart.
- Look for the right answers to any you had wrong.

NUMBER CORRECT _____ (Possible 10)
(2 points for each answer. Answers do not have to be worded exactly like the Answer Key, but should express the same ideas.)

Summary: The Letter of Request

- Your summary of the Rusden Supply Company letter will consist of an outline of its contents and a list of actions that must be taken. Reread your Paragraph Key notes and complete this summary of the letter.

1 Rusden Supply Company wants _____

2 because _____

3 In return, they will _____

4 They enclosed _____

5 which they want us to _____

6 They are asking about _____

7 They are asking at this time because _____

In order to comply with their requests, we must:

8 _____

9 _____

10 _____

- Check with your teacher or with the manual for the correct answers.
- Do not record your score for this summary until completing the summary for the next letter. Then add both scores and record your total score on the Development Chart.

NUMBER CORRECT _____ (Possible 10)
(1 point for each answer)

Standard Business English
Article: The Letter of Application

The Letter of Application

■ A letter of application should give the following information:

The name and address of the company being applied to.
The date.
The name of the applicant.
The age of the applicant.*
Marital status* (single, married, divorced, widowed).

Job wanted.
Educational background.
Job experience.
Times available for an interview.
Special interests or special qualifications.
References (people who can give personal or professional information about the applicant).

■ Whenever you read a letter of application, you should look for all this information. Make notes on the information as you find it. Make note of any questions you have as you read the application or on any information that has not been provided.

■ Read the following letter of application to find out all you can about the applicant.

---

*According to the law, you cannot be forced to give your age or your marital status. There are some occasions, however, where it can be to your advantage to supply this information.

Time Key

■ Do not record your reading time.

Paragraph Key

■ Fill in the relevant bits of information as you find them. They will not necessarily be in the same order as the Paragraph Key.

Dear Mr. Marlin:

[1] I would like to have a job in your company. I would like to work for your company because I would like to have more opportunity to use the training I've already had. I'd like to talk to you about the job, next week. I've done a lot of work in your type of business, too. While I was at Indiana University, I worked part-time for the Gardenscape Company. I did a lot of pipe laying and general drainage work. When I left the University, I got a full-time job with the Civil Construction Company in Bloomington. There I worked as a builder.

a Name: _____
  _____

b Job wanted: _____
  _____

c Education: _____
  _____

d Experience: _____
  _____

[2] I am a very strong person. When I was in high school I was on the track team. I was also a member of the wrestling team for two years. I got a degree in Business Administration from Indiana University. I was very busy studying, so I did not do too many sports there. But I was on the track team for one year. I think it is good for people in management

e Salary: _____
  _____

to have had experience on the job. So, I don't want to work as a laborer any more. I think I've done enough of that.

³My boss at the Gardenscape Company was John Crawley. He said I was a very good worker. He said anyone who got me to work for them would be lucky.

⁴I made good money as a builder, usually about $550 a week. I'd like to make about that much in a manager's job with your company.

⁵Just now I'm working part-time at a hamburger place. So, I'd have to come and see you some time in the day because I work at night, except Thursday, when I work during the day.

Sincerely,

Terry Morgan
1324 Crescent Street
Falls Church, Virginia 22041-3663

f References: _____

_____

g Interview time: _____

_____

h Qualifications: _____

_____

List the four things missing from this letter. Check the list on page 204 to help you.

i _____

j _____

k _____

l _____

(½ point each)

- Check your answers in the Answer Key.
- Add your scores for both Paragraph Keys and record the total on the Development Chart.

NUMBER CORRECT _____ (Possible 10)
(1 point for a–h; ½ point for i–l)

Summary: The Letter of Application

- Your summary for the letter of application can be made by using the job application form on the next page. Fill in the form using the information supplied in Terry's letter.
- For extra practice, you can rewrite both these letters in more correct Standard Business English.

Standard Business English
Summary

1 Name <u>Terry Morgan</u>

2 Address _____/_____/_____/_____
         Street name & number   City   State   Zip code

3 Home phone _____ Business phone _____

4 Date of application _____

College Record

5 Name of college _____

6 Years of attendance 19 ___ to 19 ___

7 Diploma or degree received _____

8 Extracurricular activities _____

9 College honors _____

High School Record

10 High school attended _____

11 Highest level reached _____

12 Extracurricular sports _____

13 High school honors _____

Work Record

List the last two jobs you held, giving the most recent one first.

14 _____

15 _____

References

List the names, occupations, and addresses of two people who would give a reference for you.

16 _____/_____/_____
      Name   Occupation   Address

17 _____/_____/_____
      Name   Occupation   Address

18 Special interests or other qualifications _____

19 Job you want in this company _____

20 Salary desired _____

21 Times available for interview _____

■ Check with your teacher or with the manual for the correct answers.

■ Add your scores for both summaries and record the total on the Development Chart. (There is no Recalling the Details page for this article.)

NUMBER CORRECT _____ (Possible 10)
(½ point for each answer)

★ Personal Opinion

■ Here again are the ten words that were boldfaced in the letter from the Rusden Supply Company. You were asked to determine their meanings from the context in which you read them. Select the correct word to fill in the blank in each of the following sentences, then complete each sentence **in your own words** so it expresses your ideas on the topic. If you cannot remember the meaning of the word, look back at how it was used in context in the article. The number of the paragraph in which it was used is shown in parentheses after the word.

audit (5)	expedite (6)	mislaid (2)	personnel (4)	remittance (5)
engaged (5)	forthwith (5)	outstanding (5)	predecessor (3)	superior (3)

1 I think that people who are _____ in work they really like will

....

2 When you begin a new job, it might help to find out what happened to your _____ ,

so that.......................................

3 The best way to save important papers from being _____ is to

....

4 I would leave my job _____ if I found out

....

5 A letter asking for payment of an _____ account should always

....

6 A job that I would consider _____ to most that I have heard about would

be.......................................

7 The best way I know to _____ payment of an account that someone owes me

is to.......................................

8 The welfare of the _____ in a business is important because

....

9 The thing most people fear if they have to undergo a tax _____ is

....

10 It is old-fashioned to say "we beg the favor of your _____ ." It is better to

say.......................................

■ Check with your teacher or with the manual for the correct answers.
■ Record your score.

NUMBER CORRECT _____ (Possible 20)
(2 points for each word)

Standard Business English
★ Speed Exercise

★ Speed Exercise

■ (One minute allowed for reading only. Teacher timed or self-timed.)

Finding the right job is probably   one of the most important things   we do in life.
Sometimes, it is also   one of the hardest.   How do you get a good job?
People get jobs in all sorts of ways.   Some people answer an ad in the paper
and get the best job in the world.   Other people write a lot of places   asking for work.
Other people apply from door to door.   And then there are those   who just seem to be
in the right place at the right time.   For example, there was a young man
who wanted to be a sailor.   He used to spend a lot of time   down by the sea
watching the tall ships.   One day he heard the captain of a ship
complaining that he could not sail   because one of his crew was sick.
The lad offered to take his place.   And so his dream came true.   He spent the rest of his life
sailing the ships he loved.

This story also illustrates   the importance of being able   to take an opportunity
when it comes.   If the boy had gone home   to ponder the offer   for a week,
he may never have become a sailor.

And then there are people   who break all the rules   and still get good job offers.
When you apply for a job   you are expected to say nice things   about why you want to work
for that company.   One man got a very good job   by telling the company
everything that was wrong with it.   He did not even want a job there.   He was just fed up
with the way they did business.   So he wrote and told them so.   They liked his ideas so much
they offered him a job.   Within a year he was the general manager.   (303 words)

List five different ways that people can get jobs:

1 _____

2 _____

3 _____

4 _____

5 _____

NUMBER CORRECT _____ (Possible 20)
Score 10 points if you read the whole article,
and 2 points for each correct answer. Check
your answers by looking back at the article.
Deduct ½ point for each line you did not read.

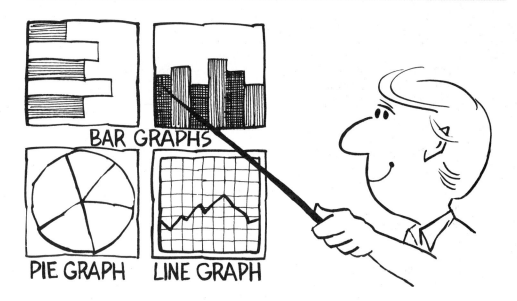

Reading without Words

■ Language does not consist of words alone. We read other things, too, such as pictures and graphs. A *graph* is a diagram that shows how things relate to one another. It provides an immediate view of a number of pieces of information at the same time. Graphs are often used in business.

■ There are different types of graphs: The *line graph* is used to show the progress of something over a period of time. The *bar graph* illustrates something that is not a continuing process. It is usually used to illustrate the differences in related pieces of information. The *pie graph* gets its name from its shape. Its purpose is to show how various parts of a total "picture" fit together.

■ Graphs should be read carefully because they present a number of pieces of information at the same time. You must try to understand the various pieces of information and how they fit together.

■ Your reading of this next article will help you understand how graphs are used and will let you practice using information from graphs.

Jobs of the Future
Word Study, Dictionary Definitions

Word Study—Prefixes

■ Many of the words in our language are derived from Latin and are made up of a Latin prefix with a Latin root, or two Latin roots together. Understanding the meaning of common Latin prefixes can help you work out the meaning of words.

■ Some common Latin prefixes are:

abs = away   *inter* = between
de = from   *re* = back
in = in, on

★ ■ Here is a list of the ten words used for special study with this article. For each word, write the prefix or prefixes it uses (if any) and then write in the meaning of the word in the space provided.

WORD	PREFIX(ES)	MEANING
1 abstract	_____	_____
2 astute	_____	_____
3 customary	_____	_____
4 graphic	_____	_____
5 inference	_____	_____
6 instrumental	_____	_____
7 interdependence	_____	_____
8 prolific	_____	_____
9 recession	_____	_____
10 technical	_____	_____

■ Check your answers in the Answer Key.
■ Record your score.

NUMBER CORRECT _____ (Possible 10)
(1 point for each row)

Dictionary Definitions

abstract (ab′ strakt), *adj.* **1** thought of apart from any particular object or actual instance; not concrete. **2** expressing or naming a quality, idea, etc., rather than a particular object or thing. **3** hard to understand; difficult; abstruse. **4** concerned with ideas or concepts rather than actual particulars or incidents. **5** not representing any actual object or concrete thing. —*n.* **1** a brief statement of the main ideas in an article, book, case in court, etc.; summary. **2 in the abstract**, in theory rather than practice. (Latin *abs* away + *tra-here* to draw)

astute (ə stüt′), *adj.* shrewd, especially with regard to one's own interests; crafty; sagacious. (Latin *astus* sagacity)

astuteness (ə stut′ nis), *n.* shrewdness; sagacity.

custom (kus′ təm), *n.* **1** any usual action or practice. **2** the accepted way of acting in a community or group; convention; tradition. **3** habit maintained for so long that it has almost the force of law. (OF *custume* < Latin *consuescere*

make customary *com* with + *suescere* accustom)

customary (kus′ tə mer′ ē), *adj.* **1** according to custom; as a habit; usual; habitual. **2** holding or held by custom; established by custom.

graphic (graf′ ik), *adj.* **1** producing by words the effect of a picture; lifelike; vivid. **2** of or about graphs and their use. **3** shown by a graph. **4** of or about drawing, painting, engraving, or etching. **5** of or used in handwriting. **6** written; inscribed. (Greek *graphein* to write) —*n.* an etching, drawing, lithograph, etc.; any work of the graphic arts.

inference (in′ fər əns), *n*. **1** process of inferring. **2** that which is inferred; conclusion. (Latin *in* + *ferre* to bring)

inferential (in′ fə ren′ shəl), *adj*. having to do with or depending on inference.

instrument (in′ strə mənt), *n*. **1** a mechanical device that is portable, of simple construction, and usually operated by hand; tool. **2** device for producing musical sounds. **3** device for measuring, recording, or controlling. **4** thing by which or with which something is done; person made use of by another; means. **5** a formal legal document.

instrumental (in′ strə men′ tl), *adj*. **1** acting or serving as a means; useful; helpful. **2** played on or

written for musical instruments. **3** of an instrument; made by a device or tool. (Latin *in* on + *struere* to build)

interdependence (in′ tər di pen′ dəns), *n*. dependence upon each other. (Latin *inter* between + *de* from + *pendere* to hang)

interdependent (in′ tər di pen′ dənt), *adj*. dependent upon each other; mutually dependent.

prolific (prə lif′ ik), *adj*. **1** producing offspring or fruit abundantly. **2** highly productive; fertile. **3** conducive to growth; fruitfulness, etc. (Latin *proles* offspring + *facere* to make)

proliferation (prō lif′ ə rā′ shən), *n*. **1** growth or production by multiplication. **2** multiplication; spreading.

recession (ri sesh′ ən), n. **1** a going backward; moving or slop-

ing backward. **2** withdrawal. **3** period of temporary business reduction, shorter and less extreme than a depression. (Latin *re* back + *cedere* to go)

recessive (ri ses′ iv), *adj*. **1** likely to go back; receding. **2** (biology) having to do with a recessive character.

technical (tek′ nə kəl), adj. **1** of or having to do with a mechanical or industrial art or applied science. **2** of or having to do with the special facts of a science or art. **3** treating a subject technically; using technical terms. **4** of or having to do with technique. **5** judged strictly by the rules; strictly interpreted. (Greek *technikos* art, skill, craft)

technicality (tek′ nə kal′ ə tē), *n*. **1** a technical matter, point, term, detail, expression, etc. **2** technical quality or character.

Using the Words

■ Choose the right word from the Dictionary Definitions to complete the blank in each of these sentences. Then in the parentheses indicate whether the word is used as a noun (n) or an adjective (adj).

1 (　　) The United States is a country that has always had a _____ supply of food.

2 (　　) Some writers are able to give a _____ description of a scene in a few well-chosen words.

3 (　　) Writers work more with _____ ideas than with concrete things.

4 (　　) The availability of work in various career areas can be _____ in helping people make career choices.

5 (　　) Graphs are used to explain the more _____ details of a subject that would be very hard to describe in words.

6 (　　) A serious _____ is marked by an increase in the number of people who are unemployed.

7 (　　) A certain amount of _____ among nations is usually one way of ensuring peace.

8 (　　) In the past, it was _____ for college graduates to be employed only in white-collar jobs.

9 (　　) The _____ business person is always aware of the greatest areas of consumer demand.

10 (　　) One _____ we can draw from the increased use of computers is that schools will include more computer training in their syllabuses.

■ Check your answers in the Answer Key.
■ Record your score.

NUMBER CORRECT _____ (Possible 10)
(½ point for each answer)

Jobs of the Future
Article

Time Key

Finishing Time _____

Starting Time _____

Total Reading Time _____ minutes

Paragraph Key

■ Make notes on the various jobs discussed. Study and make notes on each graph.

[1]When discussing jobs, it is **customary** to divide the economic structure of society into two major groups: One deals with material goods such as apples, coal, refrigerators, and automobiles. The other provides services, such as health care, education, transport, banking, and insurance.

a _____

_____

[2]The growth rate of these two groups has differed markedly in recent years and seems likely to continue that trend. By 1984, 7 out of every 10 jobs were in service industries, while fewer than 3 out of every 10 were in areas such as farming, construction, mining, and manufacturing. The growth of service industries is likely to continue, and jobs in that area will become more **prolific**.

b _____

_____

c Figure 1 shows

_____

d from _____

to _____

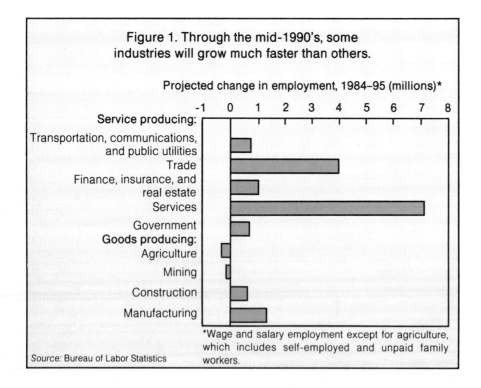

Figure 1. Through the mid-1990's, some industries will grow much faster than others.

Projected change in employment, 1984–95 (millions)*

*Wage and salary employment except for agriculture, which includes self-employed and unpaid family workers.

Source: Bureau of Labor Statistics

Data from Department of Labor and Bureau of Labor Statistics.

³While all service industries require managers, administrators, and clerical staff, there will be a need for these employees to have more specialized training because of the increasingly **technical** nature of service work.

⁴Indeed, the 1970s and 1980s saw an increase in the need for degree training as a prerequisite for many jobs. It seems highly probable that your educational standard will be more and more **instrumental** in determining the type of job you can get in the 1990s. The **graphic** presentation demonstrates this.

e _____

_____

f _____

_____

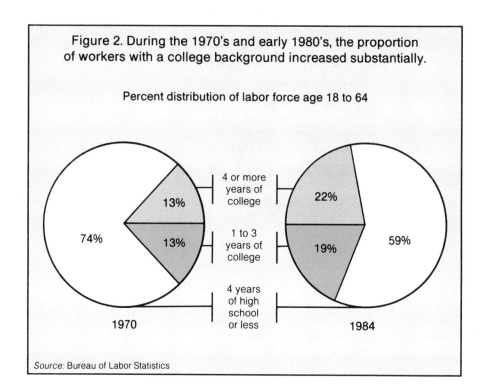

Figure 2. During the 1970's and early 1980's, the proportion of workers with a college background increased substantially.

Percent distribution of labor force age 18 to 64

4 or more years of college

1 to 3 years of college

4 years of high school or less

1970

1984

13% 13% 74%

22% 19% 59%

Source: Bureau of Labor Statistics

g Figure 2 shows

_____

h during_____

and _____

⁵The **interdependence** of technology and service industries will give rise to the demand for engineers and scientists being higher than the overall average employment demand.

⁶With the dramatic rise in the importance of computers to service industries, the demand for all levels of computer workers will increase, with a special emphasis on the need for systems analysts.

⁷Service occupations encompass a wide range of jobs including cleaners, food and beverage processors, household staff, barbers, guards, flight attendants, and health workers.

i _____

_____

j _____

_____

k _____

_____

Jobs of the Future
Article

[8]From the increased growth in numbers of elderly people in our society and the continuing awareness of the importance of health care, we can draw the **inference** that the biggest employment need for service industries will be in the area of health.

l _____

_____

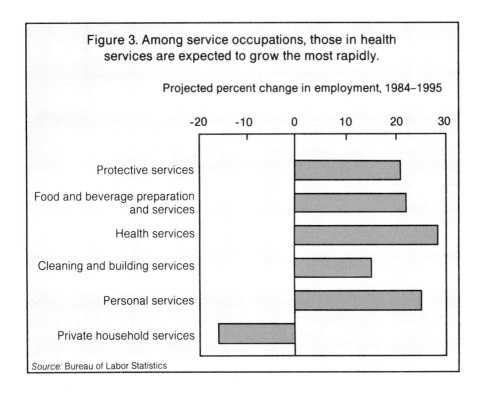

Figure 3. Among service occupations, those in health services are expected to grow the most rapidly.

Projected percent change in employment, 1984–1995

-20   -10   0   10   20   30

- Protective services
- Food and beverage preparation and services
- Health services
- Cleaning and building services
- Personal services
- Private household services

Source: Bureau of Labor Statistics

m Figure 3 shows

_____

n from _____

to _____

[9]Historically, clerical workers have been in steady demand. In 1984, for example, there were about 19 million workers in clerical jobs. The trend is now reversing, however, as computerization is taking over many jobs previously done by people. The **astute** student preparing for the job market might do well to look to fields other than clerical.

o _____

_____

[10]Writers, artists, reporters, and entertainers also come under the umbrella of service industries, and the outlook in this area remains much the same as usual. While they are always in demand, they must constantly face stiff competition and only a few make it to the top.

p _____

_____

[11]The **recession** in the field of secondary teaching, which began in the 1980s, will continue into the 1990s, although there will still be a demand for teachers in the science, mathematics, and computer science subjects.

q _____

_____

[12]Sales work is a service occupation that offers a variety of opportunities. Some sales jobs such as real estate and insurance allow you to be your own boss, while even those where you are under supervision allow you flexibility of hours.

r _____

_____

[13]The majority of sales workers have traditionally learned their skills on the job, but there is now increasing demand for them to have a college degree or other specialized training.

s _____

_____

[14]Employment in sales jobs will rise as fast as or faster than in most other job categories because there are always many replacement jobs in this field as well as the new jobs arising regularly.

t _____

_____

[15]This article presents a brief overview of a very few jobs, but this should be enough to demonstrate that the job market is always changing. It is wise, therefore, to examine society's future needs, rather than planning your career in an **abstract** fashion.

- Write in your Finishing Time and subtract to find your Total Reading Time.
- Record your Total Reading Time on the Development Chart.
- Check your answers in the Answer Key.
- Record your score.

NUMBER CORRECT _____ (Possible 20)
(1 point for each answer)

Summary

- For this article you should summarize the content of each graph, as well as making summary notes on the prospects for each of the jobs mentioned. Reread your Paragraph Key notes and study the graphs again. Then complete the summary.

Graphs:

1 Figure 1 _____

2 Figure 2 _____

3 Figure 3 _____

Prospects for various jobs:

4 Engineers and scientists _____

5 Systems analysts _____

6 Health workers _____

7 Clerical workers _____

8 Writers and entertainers _____

9 Teachers _____

10 Salespeople _____

- Check with your teacher or with the manual for the correct answers.
- Record your score.

NUMBER CORRECT _____ (Possible 10)
(1 point for each answer)

Jobs of the Future
Recalling the Details

Recalling the Details

■ For this exercise, you are required to look for details rather than recall them. You will find the information for your answers in the three graphs.

■ Read the first statement and study the graph to find the correct ending for the statement. Complete each of the following statements in the same way.

Figure 1:

1 The fastest growing industries will be

  a trade
  b services
  c farming

2 A comparison of the growth rate of transportation and manufacturing shows

  a manufacturing is growing faster
  b they are growing at the same rate
  c transportation is growing faster

3 Comparing mining and agriculture suggests there will be

  a less growth in mining
  b less growth in agriculture
  c equal growth in both

Figure 2:

4 Roughly three-quarters of the work force had no college education in

  a 1970
  b 1984
  c 1990

5 In 1984, the percentage of workers with 4 years of college was

  a 5% higher than in 1970
  b 6% lower than in 1970
  c roughly 10% higher than in 1970

6 This graph illustrates that the biggest difference is in the total percentage of people

  a finishing at high school level
  b taking 4 or more years of college
  c taking 1–3 years of college

Figure 3:

7 Those service occupations having an equal growth rate are

  a protective and food and beverage
  b protective and personal
  c personal and food and beverage

8 The need for private household service has dropped by

  a 20%
  b 18.5%
  c between 10% and 20%

9 The second highest rate of growth will occur in

  a personal services
  b cleaning and building services
  c protective services

10 From the article you can infer that

  a you are likely to need college education or specialized training to get a good job
  b there is a decreasing need for college education
  c you must have a college education to get a job

■ Check with your teacher or with the manual for the correct answers.
■ Record your score.

NUMBER CORRECT _____ (Possible 10)
(1 point for each answer)

Jobs of the Future
★ Personal Opinion

★ Personal Opinion

■ Here again are the ten words used for special study with this article. Select the correct word to fill in the blank in each of the following sentences, then complete each sentence **in your own words** so it expresses your ideas on the topic.

| abstract | customary | inference | interdependence | recession |
| astute | graphic | instrumental | prolific | technical |

1 I think one thing that could be _____ in lowering the taxes paid by individuals would be..

2 In my opinion, one of the greatest _____ advances made in this century is
....

3 One sure sign of a severe business _____ is
....

4 One _____ you can draw from the decreased employment needs of the farm industry is that.......................................

5 If I could guarantee a _____ supply of anything for the next ten years, I would like it to be.......................................

6 I think a clever and _____ business person is one who
....

7 In comparing the written descriptions with the _____ presentations in this article, I find it easier to read the.......................................

8 If I had the choice between working with things or with _____ ideas, I would prefer.......................................

9 When applying for a job, it is _____ to
....

10 I believe there should be greater _____ of schools and businesses in the area of.......................................

■ Check with your teacher or with the manual for the correct answers.
■ Record your score.

NUMBER CORRECT _____ (Possible 20)
(2 points for each word)

Jobs of the Future

★ Speed Exercise

★ Speed Exercise

■ (One minute allowed for reading only. Teacher timed or self-timed.)

Work is an important aspect   of our society.   Perhaps this stress on work
began with our Puritan ancestors,   who believed that the best way to serve God
was through hard work.   Or perhaps our worship of work   began when the country was young
and needed people   who believed in hard work   to carry out the business of pioneering.
Whatever the reason,   there is no doubt that work is important to us.
When you want to know more about someone,   you ask, "What do you do?"
which means, "What is your job?"   It is a common question,   and we do not think
there is anything strange about it.   But is it possible   that in the future
we will ask, "What do you play?"
Computers and other machines are making jobs   more automatic and less demanding.
Scientists tell us   that one day   very few people will have to work.
Our society will be run by computers.   So we will all have   a great deal more free time.
And then games may be more important than jobs.
At the beginning of this century,   almost everybody believed in work.
Tomorrow people may think differently.   Tomorrow games and play
may be seen as a very important part of life.   Today people are divided into social classes
because of the type of work they do.   Tomorrow they may be divided
because of the type of games they play.
In the future we may have "fun specialists"   just as we now have
specialists in different types of work.   It would be their job to show us all
how to get the most fun and enjoyment   out of all our spare time.
And our society may be made up of subgroups   such as surfers, skydivers, skiers, etc.
Many of these subgroups   would rely on technology   to provide the equipment
for their games.   (305 words)

1 When we want to get to know someone, we ask, _____.

2 In the future, we might ask, _____.

3 Work became important in our society because _____.

4 In the future, there may be people called _____.

5 Future societal subgroups may be made up of _____.

NUMBER CORRECT _____ (Possible 20)
Score 10 points if you read the whole article,
and 2 points for each correct answer. Check
your answers by looking back at the article.
Deduct ½ point for each line you did not read.

SECTION H.
Reading Brings You the News

ARTICLE 22.
Reading a Newspaper
Introduction

What's in a Newspaper?

■ How often do you read a newspaper? What is your main reason for reading a newspaper? Do you read it for the news or for the comics or for the sports results? Perhaps you read a newspaper only when you need a job or when you're in the market for a particular product.

■ Newspapers are not as widely read as they once were. Many people prefer to watch the news on television, even though television cannot cover the news as fully as a newspaper can. If you want to keep up with what is happening in the world and if you want to acquire an understanding of world affairs, you should develop the habit of reading a good newspaper every day.

■ This next article will give you some advice on how to read a newspaper more effectively. You will learn that there are good newspapers and bad newspapers, and you will learn how to tell the difference.

■ Reading and thinking about the daily news will help you develop a solid base for your opinions. All of the articles in this section about "The Daily News" will help you learn to read and to *think* about the news. When you have read this first article, "Reading a Newspaper," practice the suggestions it gives you each time you read a newspaper.

Reading a Newspaper
Word Study, Dictionary Definitions

Word Study—Restrictive Labels

■ Many words in our language have several meanings. Some words have special meanings that are used only in certain kinds of writing or by members of certain trades or professions. For example, the word "brief" commonly means "very short; concise," but in the legal profession it has the meaning, "the statement of the facts and the points of law in a case to be pleaded in court." This is a special meaning of the word that is used only by people in the field of law.

■ When a word has a special meaning like this, the dictionary indicates it with what is called a *restrictive label*. This label, which is shown in uppercase, italics, or parentheses, introduces the special meaning and tells you the circumstances in which it applies. For example, if you look up the word "pot," you will find the common meaning given as "a container for cooking and other uses." You will also find these entries: "INFORMAL. a large sum of money; INFORMAL. all the money bet at one time; SLANG. marijuana."

★ ■ Several of the words chosen for special study with this article have restrictive label meanings. See if you can match the definitions with the words in the list. Write the number of the correct definition in the parentheses beside the word.

WORD	DEFINITION
1 ( ) authenticity	1 cowardly
2 ( ) chief	2 to cause to be
3 ( ) column	3 falsehood
4 ( ) gist	4 genuineness
5 ( ) invert	5 following
6 ( ) jeopardy	6 the boss
7 ( ) originate	7 the essential part
8 ( ) story	8 a group of soldiers
9 ( ) subsequent	9 danger of being convicted
10 ( ) yellow	10 change by making lowest note higher

■ Check your answers in the Answer Key.
■ Record your score.

NUMBER CORRECT _____ (Possible 10)
(1 point for each answer)

Dictionary Definitions

authenticity (ô′ then tis′ ə tē), *n.* **1** reliability. **2** genuineness.
chief (chēf), *n.* **1** head of a group; person highest in rank or authority; leader. **2** head of a tribe or clan. INFORMAL. the chief = the boss.—*adj.* **1** at the head; highest in rank or authority; leading. **2** most important; main.

column (kol′ əm), *n.* **1** a slender, upright structure; pillar. **2** anything that seems slender and upright like a column. **3** MILITARY. an arrangement of soldiers in several short rows, one behind the other.
4 JOURNALISM. a narrow division of a page reading from top to

bottom, kept separate by lines or blank spaces. **5** JOURNALISM. part of a newspaper or magazine used for a special subject or written by a special writer.
gist (jist), *n.* the essential part; real point; main idea; substance of a longer statement.
invert (in vért′), *v.* **1** to turn upside

down. **2** to turn the other way; reverse. **3** MUSIC. to change by making the lower or lowest note an octave higher or the highest note an octave lower. **4** to turn inside out or outside in.—*adj.* inverted.

jeopardy (jep' ər dē), *n.* **1** risk; danger; peril. **2** LAW. the danger of being convicted and punished

when tried for a crime.
originate (ə rij' ə nāt), *n.* **1** to cause to be; invent. **2** to come into being; begin; arise.
story (stôr' ē), *n.* **1** account of some happening or group of happenings. **2** INFORMAL. falsehood. **3** plot of a play, novel, etc. **4** a newspaper article or material for such an article.

subsequent (sub' sə kwənt), *adj.* coming after; following; later.
yellow (yel' ō), *n.* the color of gold, butter, or ripe lemons.—*adj.* **1** having the color yellow. **2** having a yellowish skin. **3** jealous. **4** INFORMAL. cowardly. **5** characterized by sensational or lurid writing or presentation of the news.

Using the Words

■ Choose the right word from the Dictionary Definitions to complete the blank in each of these sentences. Where there are parentheses at the beginning of the sentence, write the number of the definition you have used.

1 They say that after you make your first parachute jump, the _____ jumps are easier.

2 ( ) It seems that people without a good education today are in _____ when it comes to finding a job.

3 ( ) It is wise to check the _____ of a rumor before you believe it.

4 ( ) A young child can often invent a most surprising _____ to explain disobedient behavior.

5 The _____ of a television show is often outlined in a printed television guide.

6 ( ) "Dear Abby" is a popular newspaper _____ that is read every day by millions of people.

7 ( ) Gossip will often _____ from someone who is jealous.

8 ( ) Football fans say that the game's _____ advantage over baseball is that it is much more active.

9 ( ) Many people in our society still think a person who walks away from a fight is _____ .

10 ( ) If you _____ "You will," you have, "Will you?"

■ Check your answers in the Answer Key.
■ Record your score.

NUMBER CORRECT _____ (Possible 10)
(1 point for each correct word)

Reading a Newspaper
Article

Paragraph Key

■ Stop reading at the end of each paragraph and write a brief Paragraph Key note to summarize the context.

[1]A newspaper is a publication that provides news and information. While it may be true that reading a newspaper every day can make you a more interesting person, you must also remember that there are good newspapers and bad newspapers.

a _____

_____

[2]A newspaper article is called a **story**. It is designed with a special shape, that of an **inverted** pyramid, to make it easy to read and to edit.

b _____

_____

Headline
Lead
Details
of
Story

[3]The shape of the story is a reflection of the way the information is presented, with the most important points first. The opening paragraph of a news story is called the "lead," and it is a summary of the whole article. It presents, in effect, the answers to the 5W + H questions. If you do not have time to read all of a news story, you will get the **gist** of it by reading the lead.

c _____

_____

[4]Each paragraph **subsequent** to the lead is of decreasing importance. There are two reasons for presenting a newspaper story in this shape. One is that it allows for skimming; the other is that it allows for easy editing. When faced with a shortage of page space, the editor has only to start pulling paragraphs from the bottom of the story to make it fit, without placing the content of the story in **jeopardy**.

d _____

_____

[5]A good news story deserves a good headline. The headline is like the title, and it should be brief and accurate. Badly written newspapers often have headlines that make the articles sound more impressive or more horrifying than they really are. A good headline should attract the reader's attention, but it should also reflect the truth.

e _____

_____

[6]Besides the headline, there are some other important things to watch for at the beginning of a news story. One of them is the "dateline."

f _____

_____

[7]In spite of its name, a dateline does not tell you when the story was written; it tells you where the story **originated**, as in this example:

> CHARLOTTESVILLE (UPI)—The
> board of visitors at the University of
> Virginia has abandoned its opposi-

This dateline tells you that the story was reported from Charlottesville, and that it was supplied to the newspaper by the news agency United Press International (UPI).

g _____
_____

[8]Another important feature to watch for is the "by-line," which is, as the name implies, a line of print giving you the name of the reporter who wrote the story. Only the top reporters on any newspaper are allowed to use a by-line, so you will see many less important stories written without by-lines.

h _____
_____

[9]The presence of a by-line, however, does not necessarily mean you can trust the **authenticity** of the story, but at least it shows that the reporter is prepared to acknowledge responsibility for what he or she has written.

i _____
_____

[10]Almost all newspapers make use of news services to provide them with news from outside their immediate vicinities. The names of these news services are shown in initials at the beginning of the story, like the inclusion of "UPI" in the dateline above, or like this:

j _____
_____

> WASHINGTON (AP)—The Presi-
> dent announced Friday night that

[11]The five main news services in the world are: Associated Press (AP) and United Press International (UPI), which are both American agencies; Agence France-Presse in France; Reuters (pronounced roi′ ters) in England; and in Russia the main news service is TASS. These five names have come to be trusted around the world as sources of dependable news information.

k _____
_____

[12]A reliable newspaper will give its readers as much information as possible about the source of the story. If a story is presented without a news agency name, by-line, or dateline, you might well question its reliability. If you also find that the headline of the story is misleading, you can be sure that the paper you are reading is substandard.

l _____
_____

[13]It has been wisely said that a newspaper is only as good as its staff. A good newspaper must have good reporters to go to the scene of the story and report the facts. A news story should contain facts, not opinions, so it is the reporter's duty to be as sure of the facts as possible before the story is printed.

m _____
_____

[14]The editor is the one who decides which stories will be used and where each story will appear in the paper. A large newspaper has several editors, one for each section of the paper and an editor-in-**chief** to coordinate their activities. It is undoubtedly true that every newspaper reflects the philosophy of the editor who is in charge.

n _____
_____

Reading a Newspaper
Article

¹⁵Supposedly, the main purpose of a daily newspaper is to report on current news as it occurs and to give the facts of this news as accurately as possible. Many newspapers, however, also go into the business of interpreting the news for the readers.

o _____

_____

¹⁶Such interpretations are mostly found on the editorial page and are presented in a **column** written by a top reporter or journalist. Their comments are intended to help you understand how the news of the day is likely to affect your personal life. Many people find these interpretations more useful than the actual news stories, which present only the facts.

p _____

_____

¹⁷Unfortunately, there are newspapers that do not adhere to the principles of good news presentation, and even the best newspapers are apt to show a political bias or favor special interest groups in the community. One newspaper, for example, may consistently support the unions, while another may be more apt to present management in a highly favorable light.

q _____

_____

¹⁸Such biases are usually harmless enough. The real danger comes from "**yellow** journalism," a phrase that describes scandal sheets written with the intention of making everything sensational. These publications stoop to any number of unethical practices to attract the reading public.

r _____

_____

¹⁹Many people are attracted to these scandal sheets because they are easy to read, lavishly illustrated, and full of instant excitement. They have little or nothing, however, to do with the news.

s _____

_____

²⁰A good reader learns which newspapers can be trusted and realizes that it is sometimes necessary to read several newspapers to get the facts. If you take the time to read a good newspaper intelligently, you will become a well-informed and more interesting person.

t _____

_____

- Write in your Finishing Time and subtract to find your Total Reading Time.
- Record your Total Reading Time on the Development Chart.
- Check your answers to the Paragraph Key in the Answer Key.
- Record your score.

NUMBER CORRECT _____ (Possible 20)
(1 point for each answer)

Summary

- This article contains information about two main aspects of a newspaper: the news story and the people who work for the newspaper. It could be summarized, therefore, under two main headings.
- Reread your Paragraph Key notes and then fill in the subpoints of this summary.

The news story:

1 _____

2 _____

3 _____

4 _____

5 _____

6 _____

7 _____

8 A well-written news story presents _____

News people:

9 _____

10 _____

- Check with your teacher or with the manual for the correct answers.
- Record your score.

NUMBER CORRECT _____ (Possible 10)
(1 point for each answer)

Reading a Newspaper
Recalling the Details

Recalling the Details

■ Your summary has noted the main points of this article. Now see if you can remember some of the other details as well. Circle the letter of the group of words that would give the right ending to each of these statements:

1 The article says that reading a newspaper can

   a keep you informed and make you more interesting

   b make you more interesting and more intelligent

   c make you more interesting and more powerful

2 The summary of a news story comes

   a at the end

   b in the headlines

   c at the beginning

3 An editor shortens a news story by

   a chopping off the "lead"

   b pulling paragraphs from the end

   c having the reporter rewrite it

4 A dateline tells

   a the date of the story and the name of the reporter

   b the name of the place where the story happened

   c the date and place of the story

5 By-lines are used

   a by all reporters whenever they write stories

   b mostly by top reporters

   c only by good newspapers

6 One of the following is NOT mentioned as being a top news service. Which one?

   a TASS

   b American News Service

   c United Press International

7 A newspaper represents

   a facts only

   b opinions only

   c facts and opinions

8 The main boss of a newspaper is usually called

   a the editor-in-chief

   b the chief editor

   c the manager

9 "Yellow journalism" stresses

   a use of yellow paper

   b sensationalism and good personal reporting

   c sensationalism and scandal

10 The main aim of this article is to

   a encourage people to read newspapers

   b give information about the newspaper

   c outline one person's opinions about newspapers

■ Check with your teacher or with the manual for the correct answers.

■ Record your score.

NUMBER CORRECT _____ (Possible 10)
(1 point for each answer)

★ Personal Opinion

■ Here again are the ten words used for special study with this article. Select the correct word to fill in the blank in each of the following sentences, then complete each sentence **in your own words** so it expresses your ideas on the topic.

authenticity   column   invert   originate   subsequent
chief   gist   jeopardy   story   yellow

1 A recent news _____ I read that I found hard to believe was

....

2 A badly written newspaper that I would say is an example of _____

journalism is...

3 I think the best way to get the _____ of what an article is about is to

....

4 I find myself questioning the _____ of the recent news story about

....

5 One newspaper _____ that I particularly like to read regularly is

....

6 The _____ trouble that I see with many newspapers is

....

7 A good news story and its _____ editorial can

....

8 I think some newspapers put the reputations of certain people in _____

by...

9 I think the most interesting news stories are those that _____ from

....

10 One aspect of our society that I would like to completely _____ is

....

■ Check with your teacher or with the manual for the correct answers.
■ Record your score.

NUMBER CORRECT _____ (Possible 20)
(2 points for each word)

Reading a Newspaper
★ Speed Exercise

★ Speed Exercise

■ (One minute allowed for reading only. Teacher timed or self-timed.)

     Newspapers are not nearly as popular today   as they were in the past.
There are not very many people   who seriously read a newspaper   every day.
Most people read only the sports page,   the advice or gossip columns,   the comics,
and perhaps the classified advertisements.   Most people don't take the time
to read the real news.   Newspaper editors say   that their readers are lazy.
They say nobody really wants to read   a newspaper.   So they say they have to trick people
into reading the news.   They attempt to catch the
reader's interest with pictures and exciting headlines.
These techniques are used on the front page   because it is the first thing you see
when you pick up the paper.   The first page attracts attention
and encourages the reader to look through the rest of the paper.   This is why editors always look
for a good first page story and headlines   that make you stop and look.
If the headline is horrible enough or frightening enough   or wild enough,
perhaps you will go on to read   the rest of the story.   Just the same, there are a lot of people
who do not even read the front page anymore.   They may read the headlines,   but that is all.
Then they turn to the sports page,   or comics,   or advertisements.
It seems that people do not want the news   from a newspaper anymore.
They say they get the news on television now.
     More people watch television news   because it is easier and more
interesting than reading a newspaper.   What about you?   Do you read news from a newspaper?
Do you watch the news on television?   Do you think it is easier   to get the news from television?
Do you listen to the news on the radio?   Or do you even care about news at all?
Would you mind if there were no news?   (311 words)

1 Compared with the past, newspapers _____ .

2 Editors think the most important part of the paper is _____ .

3 Most people read _____ and _____

  and _____ .

4 Most people get news from _____ .

5 Or from _____ .

NUMBER CORRECT _____ (Possible 20)
Score 10 points if you read the whole article,
and 2 points for each correct answer. Check
your answers by looking back at the article.
Deduct ½ point for each line you did not read.

Finding the News Slant

■ All newspapers report the news, but they do not all report it in exactly the same way. Each newspaper has a particular slant on the news. The *slant* is the point of view or the stress that is put on certain aspects of the news. Most newspapers, for example, have a particular political slant.

■ Because of this tendency for each newspaper to slant the news in a certain way, you can gain a more accurate picture of a news event if you read more than one newspaper. Look for the slant in each paper, and then think about all the points of view and decide which seems most acceptable to you.

■ In this article, you will read three news stories. They all discuss the resignation of President Richard M. Nixon. You will read them to find the particular slant of each story.

■ The method of reading this article will be different from the method you have used for other articles. You will do the Word Study and Using the Words exercises as usual. Then you will read an article from the *New York Times* and make Paragraph Key notes as you read. You will then answer questions about this article. Next, you will read an article from the *Washington Post* and make Paragraph Key notes as you read. You will then answer questions about that article. Finally, you will read an article from the *Chicago Tribune*, make Paragraph Key notes for it, and then answer questions about it. There will be no Recalling the Details exercise with this article. You will finish, as usual, with the Personal Opinion and Speed Reading exercises.

■ Read to find the slant of each newspaper, then think about the opinions expressed in it.

The End of a Presidency
Word Study, Dictionary Definitions

Word Study—The Language of a Newspaper

■ A newspaper is designed to be read quickly and to give its readers an immediate understanding of the news. This means that a newspaper is usually written in fairly simple language. There are times, however, when an unusual story requires particular words that may not be commonly used. The resignation of a President is not a common event in the United States, so the words used to describe this event may be words that are less well known.

★ ■ Here are ten words taken from the newspaper articles about the resignation of President Nixon. Use the Dictionary Definitions to find the correct synonym for each word, and write it in the second column. In the third column, write an antonym for each word. An *antonym* is a word having the opposite meaning of the defined word. Choose the correct antonym for each word from the antonym list.

WORD	SYNONYM	ANTONYM	ANTONYM LIST
1 abhorrent	_____	_____	acknowledge
2 arduous	_____	_____	removed
3 combative	_____	_____	easy
4 conciliatory	_____	_____	minority
5 disclaim	_____	_____	hostile
6 impeachment	_____	_____	peaceful
7 landslide (adj)	_____	_____	·likeable
8 misdemeanor	_____	_____	common
9 sworn in	_____	_____	acquittal
10 unprecedented	_____	_____	lawful deed

■ Check your answers in the Answer Key.
■ Record your score.

NUMBER CORRECT _____ (Possible 10)
(½ point for each answer)

Dictionary Definitions

abhorrent (ab hôr′ ənt), *adj.* **1** causing horror and disgust; detestable. **2** contrary or repugnant. **3** having or showing dislike; hateful.
arduous (är′ jü əs), *adj.* hard to do; difficult; using up much energy; requiring much effort.
combative (kəm bat′ iv), *adj.* ready to fight or oppose; fond of fighting; pugnacious; aggressive.
conciliatory (kən sil′ ē ə tôr′ ē), *adj.* tending to win over, soothe or reconcile; peacemaking.

disclaim (dis klām′), *v.* refuse to recognize as one's own; deny (connection with).
impeachment (im pēch′ ment), *n.* accusation of wrong conduct during office before a competent tribunal; accusation.
landslide (land′ slīd′), *n.* **1** sliding down of a mass of soil or rock on a steep slope. **2** an overwhelming majority of votes for one political party or candidate; majority.—*adj.* by an overwhelming majority.

misdemeanor (mis′ di mē ′ nər), *n.* a breaking of the law, not so serious as a felony; misdeed.
sworn in (swôrn in), *v.* having taken an oath; bound by an oath; declared, promised with an oath; admitted (to office).
unprecedented (un pres′ ə den′ tid), *adj.* having no precedent; never done before; never known before; unknown.

Using the Words

■ Choose the right word from the Dictionary Definitions to complete the blank in each of the following sentences.

1 President Nixon was heard to _____ any participation in the Watergate scandal when he resigned.

2 When _____ to office, the President promises to serve the country well.

3 A politician has an _____ job that requires long hours of work and involves lots of responsibility.

4 Every politician dreams of a _____ victory at election time.

5 A politician may make all sorts of _____ promises to the voters in order to win votes.

6 A politician is not likely to win votes by taking a _____ attitude toward the voters.

7 Careless waste of federal tax dollars is _____ to many people.

8 A politician's small _____ can become a crime when it is reported by the media.

9 It is never an easy job to remove a President from office by _____ .

10 The election of our first woman President will be an _____ event in this country.

■ Check your answers in the Answer Key.
■ Record your score.

NUMBER CORRECT _____ (Possible 10)
(1 point for each answer)

The End of a Presidency
Article

Time Key

■ Do not record your reading time
with this article, because you will
not be reading the whole article
through at one time.

Paragraph Key

■ Make your own brief
Paragraph Key notes on
the indicated paragraph
as you read.

The New York Times

**NIXON RESIGNS
HE URGES A TIME OF 'HEALING';
FORD WILL TAKE OFFICE TODAY**

**The 37th President
Is First to Quit Post**

By John Herbers
Special to the *New York Times*

[1]WASHINGTON, Aug. 8—Richard Milhous Nixon, the 37th President of
the United States, announced tonight that he had given up his long and
arduous fight to remain in office and would resign, effective at noon
tomorrow. Gerald Rudolph Ford, whom Mr. Nixon nominated for Vice-
President last Oct. 12, will be **sworn in** tomorrow at the same hour as
the 38th President, to serve out the 895 days remaining in Mr. Nixon's
second term.

a _____

_____

[2]Less than two years after his **landslide** re-election victory, Mr. Nixon,
in a **conciliatory** address on national television, said that he was leaving,
not with a sense of bitterness, but with a hope that his departure would
start a "process of healing that is so desperately needed in America."

b _____

_____

[3]He spoke of regret for any "injuries" done "in the course of the events
that led to this decision." He acknowledged that some of his judgments
had been wrong.

c _____

_____

[4]The 61-year-old Mr. Nixon, appearing calm and resigned to his fate
as a victim of the Watergate scandal, became the first President in the
history of the Republic to resign from office. Only 10 months earlier his
first Vice-President, Spiro T. Agnew, became the first man to resign the
Vice-Presidency.

d _____

_____

[5]Mr. Nixon, speaking from the Oval Office, where his successor will be
sworn in tomorrow, may well have delivered his most effective speech since
the Watergate scandals began to swamp his Administration in early 1973.

⁶In tone and content, the 15-minute address was in sharp contrast to his frequently **combative** language of the past, especially his first "farewell" appearance—that of 1962, when he announced he was retiring from politics after losing the California governorship race and declared that the news media would not have "Nixon to kick around" anymore.

⁷Yet he spoke tonight of how painful it was for him to give up the office. "I have never been a quitter," he said. "To leave office before my term is completed is opposed to every instinct in my body." But he said that he had decided to put "the interests of America first."

e _____
_____

■ Check your answers in the Answer Key.
■ Look for the right answers to any you had wrong.

NUMBER CORRECT _____ (Possible 10)
(2 points for each answer.)

■ Consider the slant taken by the *New York Times* story. Answer the following questions about the news story.

1 Using the information from the first paragraph only, fill in the answers to as many of these 5W + H questions as you can. For those questions that are not answered in the first paragraph, write "no answer."

a Where? _____

b When? _____

c Who? _____

d What? _____

e Why? _____

f How? _____
(½ point each)

2 The *New York Times* story says that the main reason for President Nixon's resignation was (Circle the letter of the correct answer.)

a shame over Watergate scandals
b to help America
c a sense of bitterness

3 The main stress of the *New York Times* story is on

a the wrongs done by Nixon
b the facts of the resignation
c the advantages of having Ford as President

4 The *New York Times* seems to be

a in favor of Mr. Ford and against President Nixon
b in favor of President Nixon and against Mr. Ford
c not making any judgments

5 The headlines of this story

a do not suggest the slant of the story
b do suggest the slant of the story

■ Check with your teacher or with the manual for the correct answers, and write the number correct in the scoring box.
■ Look for the right answers to any you had wrong.

NUMBER CORRECT _____ (Possible 5)
(½ point for each answer)

The End of a Presidency
Article

The Washington Post

■ Read the next story from the *Washington Post* of the same date. Think about the slant of the story as you read. Make Paragraph Key notes as indicated while you read.

NIXON RESIGNS

By Carroll Kilpatrick
Washington Post Staff Writer

¹Richard Milhous Nixon announced last night that he will resign as 37th President of the United States at noon today.

a _____

_____

²Vice-President Gerald R. Ford of Michigan will take the oath as the new President at noon to complete the remaining 2½ years of Nixon's term.

³After two years of bitter public debate over the Watergate scandals, President Nixon bowed to pressures from the public and leaders of his party to become the first President in American history to resign.

b _____

_____

⁴"By taking this action," he said in a subdued yet dramatic television address from the Oval Office, "I hope that I will have hastened the start of the process of healing which is so desperately needed in America."

c _____

_____

⁵Vice-President Ford, who spoke a short time later in front of his Alexandria home, announced that Secretary of State Henry A. Kissinger will remain in his Cabinet. The President-to-be praised Mr. Nixon's sacrifice for the country and called it "one of the very saddest incidents that I've ever witnessed."

d _____

_____

⁶Mr. Nixon said he knew he must resign when he concluded that he no longer had "a strong enough political base in the Congress" to make it possible for him to complete his term of office.

e _____

_____

⁷Declaring that he has never been a quitter, Mr. Nixon said that to leave office before the end of his term "is **abhorrent** to every instinct in my body. But as President, I must put the interests of America first," he said.

f _____

_____

⁸While the President acknowledged that some of his judgments "were wrong," he made no confession of the "high crimes and **misdemeanors**" with which the House Judiciary Committee charged him in its bill of **impeachment**.

g _____

_____

⁹Specifically, he did not refer to Judiciary Committee charges that in the cover-up of Watergate crimes he misused government agencies such as the FBI, the Central Intelligence Agency and the Internal Revenue Service.

h _____

_____

¹⁰After the President's speech, Special Prosecutor Leon Jaworski issued a statement declaring that "there has been no agreement or understanding of any sort between the President and his representatives and the special prosecutor relating in any way to the President's resignation."

i _____

_____

¹¹Jaworski said that his office "was not asking for any such agreement or understanding and offered none."

¹²His office had been informed yesterday afternoon of the President's decision, Jaworski said, but he had to **disclaim** any participation by his office in the President's decision to resign.

¹³Mr. Nixon's brief speech was given in firm tones, and he appeared to be in complete control of his emotions. The absence of rancor contrasted sharply with the "farewell" he delivered in 1962 after being defeated for the governorship of California.

j _____

_____

■ Check your answers in the Answer Key and write the number correct in the scoring box.
■ Look for the right answers to any you had wrong.

NUMBER CORRECT _____ (Possible 10)
(1 point for each answer)

■ Consider the slant of the *Washington Post* story. Answer these questions about it.

1 Fill in short answers to as many of these 5W + H questions as you can from the lead paragraph alone. For those questions that are not answered in the first paragraph, write "no answer."

  a Where? _____

  b When? _____

  c Who? _____

  d What? _____

  e Why? _____

  f How? _____

       (½ point each)

2 The *Washington Post* story says the main reason for President Nixon's resignation was (Circle the letter of the correct answer.)

  a pressure from party leaders and public
  b to help America
  c a sense of bitterness

3 The main stress of this *Washington Post* front-page story is on

  a the sadness of the resignation
  b the fact that Nixon avoided talking about the charges against him
  c the change in leadership from one President to another

4 The *Washington Post* article seems to suggest

  a a belief in Nixon as a good President
  b the possibility that Nixon had done wrong during his term of office
  c strong support for Mr. Ford in place of President Nixon

5 The headline of this story

  a does not suggest the slant of this story
  b does suggest the slant of this story

The End of a Presidency

Article

■ Check with your teacher or with the manual for the correct answers, and write the number correct in the scoring box.
■ Look for the right answers to any you had wrong.

NUMBER CORRECT _____ (Possible 5)
(½ point for each answer)

The Chicago Tribune

■ The third story is from the *Chicago Tribune* of the same date and records the same event.
■ Read it carefully and consider the slant it presents. Make Paragraph Key notes as you read.

NIXON RESIGNS

'America Needs A Full-time President'

By Frank Starr and
Aldo Beckman
Chicago Tribune Press Service

[1]WASHINGTON, Aug. 8—President Nixon tonight announced his decision to resign as the 37th President of the United States to avoid impeachment for his role in the Watergate scandal.

a _____
_____

[2]The **unprecedented** but orderly transfer of power to Vice-President Ford will occur at noon tomorrow, with no interruption of government operation expected.

b _____
_____

[3]Nixon's resignation, the first ever by an American President, came 21 months after he had won a second term by one of the largest margins in history.

c _____
_____

[4]But it also climaxed a scandal that grew out of that election and was still developing on Monday, when the President admitted his own early knowledge of the Watergate break-in and cover-up and then dramatically lost his most loyal supporters in the Congress.

d _____
_____

e _____
_____

■ Check your answers in the Answer Key and write the number correct in the scoring box.
■ Add your scores for the three Paragraph Keys, and record this score on the Development Chart.
■ Look for the right answers to any you had wrong.

NUMBER CORRECT _____ (Possible 5)
(1 point for each answer)

■ Consider the slant of the *Chicago Tribune* story. Answer these questions about it.

1 Fill in short answers to as many of these 5W + H questions as you can from the lead paragraph only. For those questions that are not answered in the first paragraph, write "no answer."

a Where? _____

b When? _____

c Who? _____

d What? _____

e Why? _____

f How? _____

(½ point each)

2 The *Chicago Tribune* story suggests that the main reason for President Nixon's resignation was

a to avoid impeachment

b to help America

c a sense of bitterness

3 The main stress of the *Chicago Tribune* front-page story is on

a the sadness of the resignation

b the change in leadership from one President to another

c the Watergate scandal and Nixon's part in it

4 The *Chicago Tribune* seems to be

a in favor of Nixon

b against Nixon

c undecided

5 The headlines of this story

a do not suggest the slant of the story

b do suggest the slant of the story

■ Check with your teacher or with the manual for the correct answers, and write the number correct in the scoring box.

■ Add your scores for the three sets of questions, and record the total on the Development Chart.

■ Look for the right answers to any you had wrong.

NUMBER CORRECT _____ (Possible 5)
(½ point for each answer)

The End of a Presidency
★ Personal Opinion

★ Personal Opinion

Here again are the ten words used for special study with this article. Select the correct word to fill in the blank in each of the sentences, then complete each sentence **in your own words** so it expresses your ideas on the topic.

| abhorrent | combative | disclaimed | landslide | sworn in |
| arduous | conciliatory | impeachment | misdemeanor | unprecedented |

1 I believe that before a President is _____ to office,

. . . .

2 To my mind the most _____ thing about a scandal involving a President is

. . . .

3 It is not wise to _____ any knowledge of an incident if

. . . .

4 I think a _____ becomes a crime when

. . . .

5 In order to win a _____ victory, a candidate must

. . . .

6 I think that removing Nixon from office by _____ would have been

. . . .

7 I think one of the most _____ and exhausting jobs is that of

. . . .

8 It is necessary for one country to make a _____ move toward another when

. . . .

9 Nixon was the first President to resign. I think this _____ move made people

think. . . . .

10 A President has to be patient and tactful most of the time, but there are times that call for a

_____ attitude, such as when. . . . .

Check with your teacher or with the manual for the correct answers.

Record your score.

NUMBER CORRECT _____ (Possible 20)
(2 points for each word)

The End of a Presidency
★ Speed Exercise

★ Speed Exercise

■ (One minute allowed for reading only. Teacher timed or self-timed.)

What is news?   It is supposed to be information   that is likely to have an effect
on most people   in the community.   And there was a time   when newspapers were just that,
and people would really look forward   to the arrival of the newspaper
to catch up on local happenings.   But now newspapers are dead.   In the last ten years
many newspapers have gone out of business.   Why is this?   There are perhaps many reasons.
We are no longer a nation of readers.   We are a nation of viewers.
And so we would rather look at the news   than read about it.   And we would rather hear
about what is on sale at the local store   than read about it.
Watching the news on television is much easier   than reading it in a newspaper.
We need to use our imagination   when visualizing a story from the newspaper.
But when we watch the news on television,   we don't have to use our imagination.
Television animates the news   and visualizes the stories for us.
Another reason may be that there is no time to read newspapers anymore.
The pace of life is too fast.   There is not much leisure time   in life anymore.
Once you could read the newspaper   as you went home on the train.
Now the train is a super-express,   and you get home in no time at all.
And besides, trains are so crowded   there is no room to open a newspaper.
Then when you get home,   what do you do?   There are kids to take care of;
there is shopping to be done;   there are TV shows to watch.   There is no time to read.
Perhaps, too, we are sick of the stories   in the newspaper.
It is not very good news most of the time.   Perhaps people have stopped reading newspapers
because the news is just too often bad.   All we get is news of war and crimes,
high prices and shortages.   So who needs the newspaper?   (329 words)

1 Today newspapers are _____

2 Reasons for this:

    a _____

    b _____

    c _____

    d _____

NUMBER CORRECT _____ (Possible 20)
Score 10 points if you read the whole article,
and 2 points for each correct answer. Check
your answers by looking back at the article.
Deduct ½ point for each line you did not read.

Reading the Editorial

■ The news in a newspaper is presented as *hard news* or *editorial*. Hard news reports facts and gives the reader a precise account of an event that has occurred. An editorial interprets the news. It gives the reader a deeper or broader perspective of the news. It is given the name editorial because it is prepared by the chief editor of a newspaper or the chief editor's staff. The editorial gives opinions about and interpretations of a particular aspect of the news.

■ An editorial differs from a hard news story in these ways:

1 An editorial gives opinions as well as facts.
2 An editorial is presented in a different shape. Rather than taking the inverted pyramid shape, it is presented like this:

Introduction
B
O
D
Y
Conclusion

■ The introduction gives the main hypothesis of the editorial. Each paragraph in the body is equally important, and each paragraph presents one important point relevant to the hypothesis. The conclusion makes a strong, final point. It is as important to the story as any of the other paragraphs.

■ This next article contains two editorials. They may seem difficult to read; but if you take one paragraph at a time and read with questions in mind, you will be able to understand the editorials.

Interpretive Journalism
Word Study, Dictionary Definitions

Word Study—Etymology Review

■ Many words in English come from other languages with by far the greatest number coming from Latin and Greek. At one time it was common for people to learn Latin to aid their understanding of English.

■ Now that Latin is not commonly learned, you have to rely on the dictionary to provide the etymology of words for you. Understanding the origin of a word can often help you with its meaning.

★ ■ Here is the list of ten words chosen for special study with this article. All of them come originally from other languages. Using the Dictionary Definitions to help you, write the language from which each of these words originated and its original meaning.

WORD	LANGUAGE	MEANING
1 conspiracy		
2 crave		
3 cynical		
4 degradation		
5 mute		
6 nurture		
7 slight		
8 tantalize		
9 tenacity		
10 vent		

■ Check your answers in the Answer Key.
■ Record your score.

NUMBER CORRECT _____ (Possible 10)
(1 point for each correct row)

Dictionary Definitions

conspiracy (kən spir' ə sē), *n., pl.* **-cies. 1** act of conspiring; secret planning with others to do something unlawful or wrong, especially against a government, public personage, etc. **2** a plot or intrigue. (Latin *com* with + *spirare* to breathe)

crave (krāv), *v.* **craved; craving. 1** to long for greatly; yearn for; desire strongly. **2** to ask earnestly for; beg. (Old English *crafian* to demand)

cynical (sin' ə kəl), *adj.* **1** doubting the sincerity and goodness of others. **2** sneering; sarcastic. (Latin *cynicus*, from Greek *kyon* dog)

degradation (deg' rə da' shən), *n.* **1** a degraded condition; debasement; degeneracy. **2** a wearing away by erosion. (Latin *de* down + *gradus* grade)

mute (myüt), **muted; muting.** —*adj.* **1** not making any sound; silent. **2** unable to speak; dumb. **3** not pronounced; silent. —*n.* **1** person who cannot speak, usually because of deafness, loss of or damage to the tongue, etc. **2** clip, pad or other device used to soften or muffle the sound of a musical instrument. **3** a silent letter. —*v.* to deaden or soften the sound of (a tone, voice, musical instrument,

etc.) with or as if with a mute. (Latin *mutus* unable to speak)

nurture (nér' chər), *v.* **-tured; -turing. 1** to bring up; care for; foster; rear; train. **2** to nourish. —*n.* **1** the bringing up; rearing; training; education. **2** nourishment. (Latin *nutrire* to feed)

slight (slīt), *adj.* **1** not much; not important; small. **2** not big around; slender. **3** frail, flimsy. —*v.* to treat as of little value; pay too little attention to. —*n.* slighting treatment; act of neglect. (Perhaps Old English *sliht* level, as in *eorth-slihtes* level with the ground)

tantalize (tan' tl īz), v. **-lized; lizing**. to torment or tease by keeping something desired in sight but out of reach, or by holding out hopes that are repeatedly disappointed. (Greek *Tantalus* Tantalus in Greek myths was the son of Zeus and was punished in the lower world by having to stand up to his chin in water, under

branches laden with fruit. Each receded from his reach whenever he tried to eat or drink.)
tenacity (ti nas' ə tē), n. **1** firmness in holding fast. **2** stubbornness; persistence. **3** ability to remember. **4** firmness in holding together; toughness. **5** stickiness. (Latin *tenere* to hold)
vent (vent), n. **1** hole or opening,

especially one serving as an outlet. **2** a way out; outlet; escape. **3** free expression. **4** the excretory opening at the end of the digestive tract, especially in birds, reptiles, amphibians, etc. **5** a small window in an automobile. —v. **1** to let out, express freely. **2** to make a vent in. (Latin *ventus* wind)

Using the Words

■ Choose the right word from the Dictionary Definitions to complete the blank in each of the following sentences. The verbs may be used in the present or the past tense.

1 A person who reacts to a _____ as if it were a major insult is probably too sensitive.

2 Most of us need to _____ our anger from time to time when something really annoys us..

3 Children who have committed minor misdemeanors should not suffer the _____ of being imprisoned with hardened criminals.

4 Many of us have been _____ by a momentary vision of success that vanished before anything ever came of it.

5 It takes considerable _____ to hold on to your beliefs when everyone else in the world is against you.

6 A child who has been _____ in an atmosphere of genuine love usually grows up to be a loving parent.

7 It is hard to have to be a _____ witness to a situation you do not like but cannot change.

8 It is good to learn to question information that is given to you as factual, but you have to guard against becoming too _____ .

9 Most people _____ the opportunity to have a good job and still have plenty of leisure time.

10 The idea of any President being a part of a _____ to take away the rights of the people is unthinkable to most Americans.

■ Check your answers in the Answer Key.
■ Record your score.

NUMBER CORRECT _____ (Possible 10)
(1 point for each answer)

Interpretive Journalism

Article

Paragraph Key

■ Make a brief summary note on the important point of each paragraph. Be sure to note the hypothesis in the first paragraph of each editorial.

(The *Washington Post Editorial*)

¹Now that it is over, now that the long ordeal has ended for the man and the nation, now that the angry emotions have been **vented** into the vacuum created by his departure, what one can feel is compassion for Richard Nixon and renewed confidence in the country he left behind.

a _____
_____

²He wanted so much to be President. The office **tantalized** and terrified him for 13 years before it came into his possession. And like any passion too long **nurtured** before it is fulfilled, it turned into something monstrous, something he could not control.

b _____
_____

³Had Dwight Eisenhower's heart not been so strong when that first severe coronary attack came in 1953, had Richard Nixon, then 42, unembittered and awed by his fortune, become President accidentally, he might have made something quite different of it, for those were simpler times and his was a less complicated character. His advisors then were men like Bruce Harlow, Bill Rogers and Jim Mitchell; **cynical**, secretive men like John Mitchell and Bob Haldeman had not even entered Nixon's life.

c _____
_____

⁴But that was not to be, and in the 13 years before the Presidency was his, he suffered a series of humiliations that would have embittered and perhaps destroyed most men: the abortive "dump Nixon" drive of 1956, undertaken with Eisenhower's unspoken blessing; the heartbreakingly narrow and clouded loss to John Kennedy; the defeat in the California governorship race in 1962; the "last press conference" and its permanently embittering effects on his relations with the press.

d _____
_____

⁵All this and much more—the thousands of petty, personal **slights** that came to him as he wandered from Washington to California to New York and around the world—he carried with him when he finally came to the Oval Office.

e _____
_____

⁶What we now understand is that someone who **craved** presidential power as much as Richard Nixon did may not be trusted with its possession; but most of us did not know it then, in 1968, and he may not have known it either. Those of us in the press who had witnessed the long story admired the personal **tenacity** and technique which marked his climb back from political ruin to the Presidency.

f _____

_____

⁷There is no ignoring or supporting the abuse of power that took place in his Presidency, or, what is almost worse, his cynical misuse of people and **degradation** of institutions. But in the end, Richard Nixon himself came to understand that he had lost the confidence of the people who had elected him, and he gave up what he had paid such a price to obtain.

g _____

_____

⁸Like Lyndon Johnson before him, he came—through pain—to accept that the Presidency belongs to the people, not to any individual, and that when a President cannot lead, it is time to stand aside.

h _____

_____

⁹Because the American people, in their **mute** strength, were able to bring this message home twice in six years to even their most powerful elective representative, American democracy has not only survived this ordeal, but has been justified.

i _____

_____

¹⁰The constitutional process did not fail us, and new leadership will soon be lawfully installed.

j _____

_____

(The *Chicago Tribune* Editorial)

¹The rumors have ceased. The bitter controversy is suddenly stilled. The President of the United States has resigned—effective at noon today.

a _____

_____

²In a graceful and touching farewell address, he announced what was clearly the most painful decision of his career. He admitted no more than wrong judgments, however, and attributed his decision solely to loss of political support in Congress. He said he has made it in the national interest, not his own.

b _____

_____

³Mr. Nixon's decision is best not only for this country, but also his party and himself. If he hadn't chosen to resign, he would surely have been removed from office after a painful ordeal of impeachment. Yet we cannot escape from the fact that this is the first time in the nearly 200 years of the Republic's history that a President has left office other than through death or the end of his term.

c _____

_____

⁴And it comes just 10 months after Spiro Agnew became the first Vice-President to resign under fire.

d _____

_____

⁵It is an occasion not for joy, but rather for gratitude, relief, and a revival of hope. The monstrous apparition called Watergate no longer blocks the road ahead and obscures the sky. It can now be left to the courts and to history to be sorted out and dealt with as the facts may warrant.

e _____

_____

⁶We are no longer crippled by the Presidency of a man who had isolated himself from the world of reality and somehow persuaded himself that it was in his interest, or the country's—we don't know which—to pretend that a President can do no wrong.

f _____

_____

⁷He tried to save himself while his closest associates were marched off to jail for their participation in a **conspiracy** in which it now appears he was the guiding conspirator.

g _____

_____

⁸And yet our feelings toward Mr. Nixon must be of sorrow rather than anger, and of mercy rather than revenge. His weaknesses are more of blind ambition and poor judgment than deliberate contempt for the law. He has paid the heaviest price a man in public office can pay. His downfall will be recorded forever as evidence that no one is above the law and that Presidents must live up to the standards expected of their office.

h _____

_____

⁹Unless there are new and startling disclosures, which we do not foresee, there is nothing to be gained by pursuing Mr. Nixon with criminal charges. Despite his achievements, the damage he has done to the country in the last two years cannot be measured in terms of days in prison or dollars of a fine.

i _____

_____

¹⁰Let us rather look now to Mr. Ford and the future.

j _____

_____

- ▪ Write in your Finishing Time and subtract to find your Total Reading Time.
- ▪ Record your Total Reading Time on the Development Chart.
- ▪ Check your answers in the Answer Key.
- ▪ Record your score.

NUMBER CORRECT _____ (Possible 20)
(1 point for each answer)

Summary

■ The summary of an editorial article is best achieved by first outlining the main hypothesis and then listing the points the writer uses to support that hypothesis.

■ In each of these editorials, the hypothesis is briefly stated in the first paragraph. Since both of these articles are extracts from longer editorials, the outlines below do not include entries for the conclusions.

Washington Post editorial:

1 Hypothesis: _____ (Paragraph 1)

2 Reasons: _____ (Paragraphs 2–6)

3 Nixon learned _____ (Paragraph 7)

4 And he learned _____ (Paragraph 8)

5 The American people learned _____ (Paragraphs 9, 10)

Chicago Tribune editorial:

6 Hypothesis: _____ (Paragraph 1)

7 The decision was good for _____ (Paragraph 3)

8 And for _____ (Paragraph 3)

9 This is an occasion for _____ (Paragraph 5)

10 For Nixon we should feel _____ (Paragraph 8)

■ Check with your teacher or with the manual for the correct answers.

■ Record your score.

NUMBER CORRECT _____ (Possible 10)
(1 point for each answer)

Interpretive Journalism
Recalling the Details

Recalling the Details

■ Richard Nixon was the first American President ever to resign from office, and his action is an important part of history. The reasons for the resignation will probably be debated for generations. It is worth considering the ideas that were put forward at the actual time of the resignation. Review your Paragraph Key notes, or your summary, and then complete this exercise.

1 The *Washington Post* article suggests that one factor that led to Nixon's downfall was

  a poor advisors
  b his temper
  c Lyndon Johnson

2 The article also suggests that another contributing factor was

  a his lack of tenacity
  b his great desire to become President
  c his attitude toward Congress

3 Mr. Nixon's attempts to become President lasted for

  a 15 years
  b 8 years
  c 13 years

4 The *Washington Post* article

  a says that Nixon should be imprisoned
  b makes no comment on whether or not he should be punished
  c says he should be allowed to be completely free

5 The overall tone of this article is

  a very harsh
  b completely forgiving
  c generally kind

6 The *Chicago Tribune* article says Mr. Nixon gave as his reason for resigning

  a the fact that he did not have enough support from Congress
  b the fact that he admitted wrongdoing
  c the fact that Spiro Agnew had already resigned

7 This article says that if Mr. Nixon had not resigned

  a his troubles would have blown over
  b he would have been impeached
  c he would have gone on to another term as President

8 The *Chicago Tribune* writer says Mr. Nixon's main weakness was

  a deliberate contempt for the law
  b hunger for power
  c blind ambition combined with poor judgment

9 The article suggests that Nixon's resignation should remind us

  a that Presidential candidates cannot be trusted
  b not to vote for a person who has wanted to be President for a long time
  c that no one in America is above the law

10 This article suggests that

  a the Watergate problems are over
  b Watergate will continue to be a major issue when Ford becomes President
  c the Watergate problems are largely responsible for Nixon's downfall

■ Check with your teacher or with the manual for the correct answers.
■ Record your score.

NUMBER CORRECT _____ (Possible 10)
(1 point for each answer)

Interpretive Journalism
★ Personal Opinion

★ Personal Opinion

■ Here again are the ten words used for special study with this article. Select the correct word to fill in the blank in each of the following sentences, then complete each sentence **in your own words** so it expresses your ideas on the topic.

conspiracy   cynical   mute   slight   tenacity
crave   degradation   nurture   tantalize   vent

1 The most recent government coverup that seems to me like a _____ was.......................................

2 I believe that if we want to _____ the ideals of democracy in this country, we will have to.......................................

3 Journalists who _____ their personal feelings about national leaders in the press ....

4 An unpleasant incident to which I was forced to be a _____ witness involved ....

5 People who _____ power for a long time are likely to ....

6 The state of _____ into which many people fall when they lose their jobs could be helped by.......................................

7 If there is one thing I am doubtful, or even _____ , about when it comes to politics, it is.......................................

8 The _____ of the investigators who patiently strove to find out the truth about Watergate was.......................................

9 In order to hold the attention of their readers over a period of time, the press may _____ them by.......................................

10 I believe the worst _____ to the American people resulting from this whole scandal was.......................................

■ Check with your teacher or with the manual for the correct answers.
■ Record your score.

NUMBER CORRECT _____ (Possible 20)
(2 points for each word)

Interpretive Journalism
★ Speed Exercise

★ Speed Exercise

■ (One minute allowed for reading only. Teacher timed or self-timed.) For this speed article, you will be reading a brief summary of the Declaration of Independence.

We believe that the following is true: All people are created equal.
And God has given all people   certain rights that cannot be taken away.
Among these rights are the right to life,   the right to freedom,   and the right to find happiness.
We believe that the best way   to hold onto these rights   is to have a government
which has been chosen by the people.
We believe that whenever a government   tries to destroy or take away   these rights,
then it is the right of the people   to alter or to abolish the government.
And the people should be able to set up a new government   that will serve their best interests.
It is obviously wise   that a government which has been in power   for a long period of time
should not be changed without good reason.   It is also true
that people would rather put up with troubles they know,   if they can possibly stand them,
than make a change.   But when there have been a lot of abuses   and a number of plots
to take away the power of the people,   then the people have the right
to get rid of that government.   It is their duty to find new leaders   to take care of the future.
The people of the colonies   have suffered such wrongs.   After suffering these wrongs,
we have humbly asked for compensation   from the King of England.
Our attempt to rectify and adjust the situation   has brought on only more harm and injury.
And it is this suffering   which forces us to alter   our form of government.
We must free ourselves   from the King of England   and his oppressive government.
Long has been the patient sufferance   of these colonies,   but now there is this necessity
which forces us to alter   our system of government.
The history of the present King of Great Britain   is a history   of repeated wrongs and evils,
all aimed at having total domination   over these states.   (327 words)

1 The Declaration of Independence holds it true that _____ .

2 It also states that government should be _____ .

3 When a government is bad, the people should _____ .

4 Changes should not be made _____ .

5 American people had suffered much abuse from _____ .

NUMBER CORRECT _____ (Possible 20)
Score 10 points if you read the whole article,
and 2 points for each correct answer. Check
your answers by looking back at the article.
Deduct ½ point for each line you did not read.

SECTION I.
Reading Suggests the Future

Judging Suppositions

■ No one can predict the future entirely. It is possible, however, to look at future trends in certain matters so we can plan to avoid future problems. It is wise to do this.

■ You can read about future trends in many books, magazines, and research articles. It is your responsibility to read these things carefully. You should think about and discuss the possible changes they suggest, and decide what, if anything, we should all do about them.

■ As you read about the future, you should notice the difference between *facts* and *suppositions*. Facts give you support and evidence. Suppositions do not. Suppositions are like guesses. There might be good reasons for the guesses, but they are still not facts.

■ Written suppositions usually use such words as "might," "perhaps," and "seems," so look for these words as you read about the future. Suppositions are not necessarily wrong, but they should not be seen or talked about as fact.

■ As you read this article, look for the suppositions, think about them, and discuss them.

Where Has All the Air Gone?
Word Study, Dictionary Definitions

Word Study—Using Technical Words

■ In your reading, you may come across technical words that are new to you. You may not always need to learn and remember their technical meanings, but it is necessary to understand their use in the context of what you are reading. It is important, therefore, to find the best definition to help you understand what you are reading.

★ ■ Here are definitions of ten phrases that are used in this article. Use the Dictionary Definitions to find the name of the substance being named in each definition.

1 A major ingredient of natural gas _____

2 Informal expression for pure air _____

3 Metallic element used in nuclear fuels _____

4 Poisonous gas formed by incomplete burning of air _____

5 Highly poisonous brown gas _____

6 Colorless, gaseous compound used in dyes _____

7 Gas or liquid that is irritating _____

8 Radioactive element used in radiotherapy _____

9 Odorless gas used in beverages and fire extinguishers _____

10 Element once used in aerosol propellants _____

■ Check your answers in the Answer Key.
■ Record your score.

NUMBER CORRECT _____ (Possible 10)
(1 point for each answer)

Dictionary Definitions

carbon dioxide *n.* a heavy, colorless, odorless gas, present in the atmosphere or formed when any fuel containing carbon is burned, widely used to form carbonated water, as dry ice, in fire extinguishers, etc.

carbon monoxide, *n.* a colorless, odorless, very poisonous gas, formed when carbon burns with an insufficient supply of air. It is part of the exhaust gases of automobile engines.

chlorofluorocarbon (klor' o floor' o kar' bən), *n.* any of various carbons consisting of carbon, hydrogen, chlorine, and fluoride, once used as aerosol propellants and refrigerants.

formaldehyde (for mal' də hīd), *n.* a colorless gas with a sharp, irritating odor, used in a water solution as a disinfectant and preservative, and often used in manufacture of dyes.

methane (meth' ān), *n.* a colorless, odorless, flammable gas, CH_4, the simplest of the hydrocarbons; marsh gas. Methane is formed naturally by the decomposition of plant or other organic matter, as in marshes, petroleum wells, vol-

canoes, and coal mines. It is obtained commercially from natural gas.

nitrogen dioxide (nit' trə jən di ox' īd), *n.* a highly toxic brownish gas, used as an industrial chemical and also released as an air pollutant during the burning of fossil fuels. It reacts with water and oxygen to form nitric acid.

ozone (o' zōn), *n.* a form of oxygen with a sharp, pungent odor, produced by electricity and present in the air, especially after a thunderstorm. It is a strong oxidizing agent produced for commercial use and is also a toxic pollutant present in smog. INFORMAL. pure, fresh air.

radon (rā' don), *n.* a heavy, radioactive, gaseous element formed by the decay of radium. It is used in radiotherapy for the treatment of cancer.

uranium (yoo ra' nē əm), *n.* a very heavy white, radioactive metallic element occurring in pitchblende and certain other minerals, used in research, nuclear fuels, and nuclear weapons.

sulfur dioxide, *n.* a heavy, colorless gas that has a sharp odor and causes severe irritation. Used as a bleach, disinfectant, preservative, etc.

Using the Words

■ Select the correct phrase from the Dictionary Definitions to fill in the blanks in the following sentences.

1 CH₄ is the symbol for _____ , which is an important source of hydrogen.

2 Some early aerosol products were very dangerous because of their high _____ content.

3 The price of _____ rose dramatically after the creation of the atomic bomb.

4 Sitting in a closed car with the engine running can be dangerous because of the _____ that is given off by the exhaust.

5 There is growing fear that the pure _____ layer above the earth is being destroyed by pollution.

6 Animal specimens in laboratories are usually preserved in _____ .

7 Factories that use sulfuric acid must protect their workers against the _____ , which can cause skin and eye irritations.

8 Without _____ , it would not be possible to have sparkling drinks such as soda water.

9 Unlike most gases, which are colorless, _____ has a distinctly brown shade.

10 Too much radiotherapy can be dangerous because of the presence of _____ , which is a radioactive element.

■ Check your answers in the Answer Key.
■ Record your score.

NUMBER CORRECT _____ (Possible 10)
(1 point for each answer)

Where Has All the Air Gone?
Article

Time Key

Finishing Time   _____

Starting Time   _____

Total Reading Time _____ minutes

Paragraph Key

■ Make notes on the contents of each paragraph as you read.

¹Throughout history, humans have lived with perils over which they have no control—stronger creatures, hostile elements, mysterious diseases. One by one such threats have been tamed and replaced by one of our own making—air pollution.

a _____
_____

²Air pollution is modern man's wolf at the door, says Dr. Irving J. Selikoff, called by some the father of pollution health effects. "If you look at the studies and the experiments with guinea pigs and mice," he says, "it looks like we should all get off the face of the earth. But we don't really know what many of the things in the air do to people. It may take 50 years to know that. Can we wait that long?"

b _____
_____

³What is not known about air pollution may be the biggest problem we face. We are in a time of technical change, resulting in some 65,000 chemical compounds being put into our environment each year. Some are proven cancer-causing substances, and many more are suspected of being so.

c _____
_____

⁴Left on its own, our planet can deal with natural pollutants. For millions of years such pollutants have been present in our ecosystem, constantly changing form. They pass through plant and animal tissues, sink into the sea, return to the earth, and rise into the air naturally to begin the cycle again. Each atom of oxygen completes the cycle approximately once every 2,000 years.

d _____
_____

⁵Now the question is whether earth can cope with all the extra pollutants man is adding, such as the 70 million tons of sulfur that we release each year. Can the plants absorb the additional nitrogen oxides (NO_x) we create with the miniature lightning bolts inside our car cylinders? Can the atmosphere take on the extra load of **carbon dioxide** (CO_2), **methane**, man-made **ozone**, and **chlorofluorocarbon** coolers? Scientists say these could raise the world's temperatures by what they call a "greenhouse effect."

e _____
_____

⁶During the past two centuries, CO_2 in the atmosphere has increased dramatically. The probable causes are the burning of fossil fuels and the clearing and burning of forests by farmers.

f _____
_____

Adapted from "Are We Poisoning Our Air?" by Noel Grove, *National Geographic Magazine*, vol. 171, no. 4 (April, 1987).

Where Has All the Air Gone?
Article

7Scientists worry that the growing burden of CO_2 and other gases might change earth's climate. Like panes of glass in a greenhouse, CO_2 allows most solar radiation to penetrate the atmosphere, but prevents part of the heat given back by land and bodies of water from escaping into space. As CO_2 accumulates, enough heat may be trapped to gradually warm the atmosphere.

8Researchers estimate that earth's average temperature could rise 2.5°F to 7.5°F (1.5°C to 4.5°C) by the middle of the next century if greenhouse gases continue to increase at the current rate.

9The world's rainfall patterns could shift, too, bringing heavy rain to previously arid regions such as the Sahel in Africa and droughts to productive farmlands such as the U.S. Midwest.

10The impact would be even greater at the Poles, where average temperatures might rise as much as 18°F (10°C). If the West Antarctic ice sheet melted, as it did. once before, 120,000 years ago, ocean levels could rise as much as 15 or 20 feet, flooding many cities and farm regions.

11Lead is another major pollutant of our atmosphere. Between 75 and 95 percent of the lead we breathe or take in with food or drink accumulates in our bones and tissues, threatening to cause irreversible brain and kidney damage.

12Young children are most at risk because their nervous systems are still developing. Too much lead in a child's system can decrease intelligence, shorten the learning span, create learning disabilities, or cause hyperactivity. Perhaps 20% of all preschool children have excessive blood lead levels.

13Elevated blood lead levels in adult males have been linked to high blood pressure. An estimated 60,000 to 70,000 heart attacks per decade might be prevented if the average blood lead level of all Americans was reduced by one-third. Getting rid of leaded gasoline is already helping. But is this enough?

14Air pollution goes on all around us. Even in the home and the office we are not safe. Pollution levels indoors can be ten times higher than those outdoors, especially in buildings that have been made airtight for energy conservation.

15**Radon** is a colorless, odorless, radioactive gas, which is found naturally in some soils containing decaying **uranium**. This can seep its way undetected into basements. From this and other causes, a million families in the United States are thought to be exposed to radiation levels even higher than those faced by uranium miners.

16Poisonous fumes enter the home or workplace in many ways. Newly installed carpets, furniture, plywood, and some foam insulation give off **formaldehyde**, which causes headaches, impaired breathing, and irritated eyes, nose, and throat. Kerosene heaters, gas ranges, and wood stoves that

g _____

h _____

i _____

j _____

k _____

l _____

m _____

n _____

o _____

p _____

Where Has All the Air Gone?
Article

do not have proper vents can put out unhealthy amounts of **carbon monoxide** and **nitrogen dioxide**.

¹⁷In offices, copying machines give off poisonous ozone. Dry-cleaning fluids, disinfectants, paints, and pesticides can all leak chemical vapors. Cigarettes, wood stoves, dryers, and asbestos insulation can put hazardous particles into the air.

q _____

_____

¹⁸Biological pollutants add other worries. Bacteria may be drawn into air-conditioning systems from rooftop puddles or they may breed in kitchens, baths, bedside humidifiers, or spaces above office ceilings. Fungi grow in cellars. Even pets can cause allergies from the scurf and dandruff in their coats.

r _____

_____

¹⁹There are some possible remedies for all this: ventilate when cooking with gas; never use unvented kerosene heaters; open fireplace dampers fully when using a fire; filter pollen from the air; stop smoking. But the question remains: Are things getting worse? Are our problems growing every time we breathe or every time we drive an automobile?

s _____

_____

²⁰The Environmental Protection Agency (EPA) says that nationally the air quality has improved since 1975 if we judge by the commonly known air particles that are monitored, such as **sulfur dioxide**, carbon monoxide, nitrogen dioxide, ozone, and lead. And yet, the Agency points out that nearly 80 million people live in countries where ozone levels exceed air-quality standards, 61 million breathe too much carbon monoxide, and 32.6 million share air space with too many particles.

t _____

_____

²¹As Roger Revelle, University of California professor of science and public policy, once said, "Mankind is in the process of conducting a major, unintentional experiment. In a short space of geological time we are feeding back into the atmosphere the fossil fuels that have slowly accumulated over the past 500 million years . . . ."

²²Now that the chemical era has joined the age of combustion, that experiment has expanded. Almost breathlessly, we await the outcome. We are our own guinea pigs.

- ■ Write in your Finishing Time and subtract to find your Total Reading Time.
- ■ Record your Total Reading Time on the Development Chart.
- ■ Check your answers in the Answer Key.
- ■ Record your score.

NUMBER CORRECT _____ (Possible 20)
(1 point for each answer)

Summary

■ This article contains suppositions and facts. Your summary should list both. Reread your Paragraph Key notes and make a summary of the suppositions about air pollution problems, and the facts about pollutants in the house and office:

Suppositions:

1 Air pollution problem _____

2 World temperatures _____

3 Rainfall _____

4 Rise in polar temperatures _____

5 Percentage of children with high blood lead levels _____

6 Heart attacks that might be avoided _____

Known pollutants in home and office:

7 _____

8 _____

9 _____

10 _____

■ Check with your teacher or with the manual for the correct answers.
■ Record your score.

NUMBER CORRECT _____ (Possible 10)
(1 point for each answer)

Where Has All the Air Gone?

Recalling the Details

Recalling the Details

■ Air is vital to life, so it is important for all of us to be aware of the purity of the air we breathe. Your understanding of possible present and future dangers to our pure air will be increased if you can recall the details of this article.

■ Reread your Paragraph Key and your summary and then complete this page. Be sure to recognize the difference between facts and suppositions.

1 With the future of air pollution

    a we know almost everything about it
    b we know nothing about it
    c we do not know as much as we need to

2 The present revolution has put into our air

    a 650,000 commercial compounds
    b 65,000 tons of commercial compounds
    c 65,000 commercial compounds

3 Earth naturally

    a deals with natural pollutants
    b has no pollutants
    c absorbs pollutants into the sea

4 The "greenhouse effect" results in

    a lowering world temperatures
    b raising world temperatures
    c lowering the world's CO_2 level

5 The melting of the Antarctic ice sheet could

    a raise ocean levels by 15 to 20 feet
    b make new drought areas
    c increase the CO_2 level of the air

6 Increased blood lead level in children

    a always lowers intelligence
    b might result in learning difficulties
    c occurs in perhaps 50% of our children

7 Studies of adult men with high blood lead levels suggest

    a it causes high blood pressure
    b little or no effect in 60,000 cases
    c a possible link with high blood pressure

8 Newly installed furniture can give off

    a radon
    b formaldehyde
    c noxious ozone

9 The EPA suggests that since 1975 the quality of our air

    a has improved
    b has not been tested
    c has gotten worse

10 From this article we can conclude

    a we have no need to worry about our air quality
    b we lack evidence about the future of air quality
    c our air is getting worse all the time

■ Check with your teacher or with the manual for the correct answers.
■ Record your score.

NUMBER CORRECT _____ (Possible 10)
(1 point for each answer)

Where Has All the Air Gone?
★ Personal Opinion

★ Personal Opinion

■ Here again are the ten phrases used for special study with this article. Select the correct phrase to fill in the blank in each of the following sentences, then complete each sentence **in your own words** so it expresses your ideas on the topic.

carbon dioxide	chlorofluorocarbon	methane	ozone	uranium
carbon monoxide	formaldehyde	nitrogen dioxide	radon	sulfur dioxide

1 I believe that aerosol cans containing _____ are

. . . .

2 Natural gas, which contains _____ , is very dangerous

. . . .

3 In my opinion, the idea that earth's _____ layer is being destroyed is

. . . .

4 Drinks that contain _____ can be dangerous if

. . . .

5 You can protect yourself from the _____ from an automobile exhaust by

. . . .

6 _____ is needed to make atom bombs. In my opinion these bombs

. . . .

7 If you find high levels of natural _____ in your house you should

. . . .

8 One way to control smog and its accompanying _____ might be

. . . .

9 Workers who are exposed to the _____ in sulfuric acid should

. . . .

10 _____ , which is sometimes given off by newly installed carpets, can also be

used for. . . . .

■ Check with your teacher or with the manual for the correct answers.
■ Record your score.

NUMBER CORRECT _____ (Possible 20)
(2 points for each word)

Where Has All the Air Gone?

★ Speed Exercise

★ Speed Exercise

■ (One minute only allowed for reading. Teacher timed or self-timed.)

The world has seen considerable change   throughout the last century.
It is hard to imagine that   not so long ago, the farm was   the most important focus of society.
These days, very few know anything about farm life.   Indeed, there are many people living
in cities who have never seen a farm.   Today, science and technology are the major focus
of society.   Because of this emphasis on   science and technology,   many of us feel alienated
from our society.   Most of us   can learn to understand animals and plants   quite easily.
Many of us, on the other hand,   have a lot of trouble understanding technological things
without a great deal of study.   So today it is harder for us   to take charge of our own lives.
This may not be very healthy for us.   Some people think we should halt
the march of technology before it gets   out of hand.   But then we have to
consider if we would like to live   without all the things   that technology has given us.
Most people would like to have a robot   to do all of their dirty work for them.
But will we be able to control the robots?   Will they take over?   Is it possible
that people could disappear from Earth completely?
As long as robots cannot think for themselves,   we are safe.   But technology is already at work
improving robots by giving them a type of "brain."   Is it possible that when robots learn to think
they will decide they do not need people?
Some people believe that schools should teach   a lot more about technology.
They argue that if all children learn   to use computers, there will be no need   to fear them.
They say that   the world of tomorrow   could be a world of leisure.
Therefore, children should be taught   to use computers and taught to use
their leisure more effectively.   Some schools have already added
computer language to the subjects they teach,   but there are not too many
that teach anything about leisure.   (335 words)

1 The focus of life a century ago _____ .

2 Today the focus is _____ .

3 Some people think _____ .

4 Others think _____ .

5 They argue the world of tomorrow _____ .

NUMBER CORRECT _____ (Possible 20)
Score 10 points if you read the whole article,
and 2 points for each correct answer. Check
your answers by looking back at the article.
Deduct ½ point for each line you did not read.

The Scholarly Article

scholar 1 a student in schools. **2** a learned person; a person having much knowledge.

■ It is the second meaning of the word that is being used when we discuss the scholarly article.

■ Those who are learned or experienced in a profession frequently write about it. Usually, their writing will fall into one of the following categories:

1 The report of an "experiment" within the profession.
2 Observations and criticisms of the existing state of the profession.
3 Suggestions or recommendations for improving some aspect of the profession.

■ While the first and second types are particularly relevant to others in the profession, it is the third type that is most useful to the general public. Where the profession is one that touches all our lives—such as education—it is important to be aware of possible changes and consider their possible effects. As you read the next article, think about your own reactions to the changes suggested.

Our Changing Schools
Word Study, Dictionary Definitions

Word Study—Antonyms

■ An *antonym* is a word that has an opposite or nearly opposite meaning to another word: Hot is the *antonym* of cold.

■ One way of ensuring that you understand a word fully is to see if you can provide an accurate antonym for it. This also helps expand your vocabulary.

★ ■ The following table contains ten words chosen for special study with this article and ten antonyms for these words. In the parentheses beside the words, write in the number of the appropriate antonym. Use the Dictionary Definitions to help you if you are uncertain of the meanings of any list words.

WORD LIST	ANTONYM LIST
1 compliance ( )	1 democratic
2 conservative ( )	2 disobedience
3 diminish ( )	3 actually
4 impenetrable ( )	4 unintelligent
5 intellectual ( )	5 abstain
6 internalize ( )	6 unnecessary
7 perpetrate ( )	7 ignore
8 relevant ( )	8 immoderate
9 totalitarian ( )	9 increase
10 virtually ( )	10 enterable

■ Check your answers in the Answer Key.
■ Record your score.

NUMBER CORRECT _____ (Possible 10)
(1 point for each answer)

Dictionary Definitions

compliance (kəm plī′ əns), *n*. **1** agreeing with or doing as another wishes; yielding to a request or command. **2** tendency to yield to others. **3 in compliance with**, complying with, according to. (Italian *complire*, Spanish *cumplir*, Latin *complere* fulfill, complete)
conservative (kən ser′ və tiv), *adj*. **1** inclined to keep things as they are or return to what they were in the past; opposed to abrupt change in traditions. **2** not inclined to take risks; cautious; moderate. (Latin *consevare*, *com* with + *sevare* to preserve)

diminish (də min′ ish), *v*. **1** make smaller; lessen; reduce. **2** lessen the importance, power, or reputation of; degrade. **3** (in architecture) to cause to taper. (Latin *dis* apart + *minus* less)
impenetrable (im pen′ ə trə bəl), *adj*. **1** that cannot be penetrated, pierced, or passed. **2** impossible to explain or understand. **3** not open to ideas, influences, etc. (Latin *im* not + *penetratum* gone through, pierced)
intellectual (in′ tə lek′ chü əl), *adj*. **1** needing or using intelligence. **2** of the intellect. **3** having or show-

ing intelligence. (Latin *inter* between + *legere* to choose)
internalize (in ter′ nl īz), *v*. incorporate consciously or subconsciously the ideas, values, mannerisms, etc., of another person or group into one's own personality. (Latin *internus* within)
perpetrate (per′ pə trāt), *v*. do or commit (a crime, fraud, trick, or anything bad or foolish). (Latin *per* thoroughly + *patrare* perform)
relevant (rel′ əv ənt), *adj*. bearing upon or connected with the matter in hand; to the point. (Latin *relevantem* relieving, refreshing,

re back + *levis* light)
totalitarian (to tal' ə ter ē ən), *adj.* of or having to do with a government controlled by one political group that suppresses all opposition, often with force, and that controls many aspects of citizens' lives. (Medieval Latin *totalis*, Latin *totus* all)
virtually (ver' tu' ə lē), *adv.* being in effect although not in name; for all practical purposes; actual; real:

The battle was won with so great a loss of soldiers that it was virtually a defeat. (Italian *virtu* excellence, Latin *virtutem* virtue)

Using the Words

■ Choose the right word from the Word List to complete each of the following sentences.

1 _____ anyone who has ever been a student believes there is room for improvement in education.

2 Computer science is a subject that is _____ to the needs of the business world these days.

3 Students are usually expected to act in _____ with the rules of the school.

4 Many high schools teach both technical and _____ subjects.

5 It is much easier to learn something if you can _____ it and understand it.

6 It is often claimed that private schools take a more _____ attitude to education than high schools.

7 There is no such thing as freedom of speech under a _____ government.

8 Students who do not have some form of higher education may well _____ their chances of getting a good job.

9 A student who finds the complexities of a subject quite _____ might be better to drop the subject.

10 We do not expect our schools to _____ the same difficulties that many young people face in society.

■ Check your answers in the Answer Key.
■ Record your score.

NUMBER CORRECT _____ (Possible 10)
(1 point for each answer)

Our Changing Schools
Article

a ————————————

b ————————————

  ————————————

[1]There are five major areas that need to be considered in the process of improving schools in the U.S.A. These five major areas are 1. Intentions, 2. Structure, 3. Curriculum, 4. Teaching, and 5. Evaluation.

Intentions

c ————————————

[2]Given the findings of recent studies of schools, we need to reaffirm our commitment to making teaching **relevant** to students. This intention has implications for increasing rather than decreasing the teachers' role in determining curriculum.

  ————————————

d ————————————

[3]Teachers deal with real children, not abstract 7th graders; and it is teachers who must make the curricular adjustments, not only in pace and in mode of teaching, but in contents and example so that students are motivated by more than a direct **compliance** to other people's desires.

  ————————————

e ————————————

[4]Students need to have a stake in what they learn, and not only in the grades they might receive. In our desire to standardize curriculums and to apply common standards, we have almost lost sight of the importance of genuinely meaningful learning.

  ————————————

f ————————————

  ————————————

g ————————————

[5]Related to meaningful learning is the need to provide special programs giving students opportunities to pursue **intellectual** and artistic interests. By developing school programs that give students opportunities to develop their special abilities and talents, we can better save them and our culture.

  ————————————

h ————————————

[6]In **totalitarian** societies, the state shapes children into its own image. In democracies, we say we wish to cultivate the talent and aptitudes that all of us possess. Surely, such values should be reflected in our school programs.

  ————————————

Structure

i ————————————

[7]The existing secondary school structure separates teacher from teacher and divides subject matter into small units with **virtually impenetrable** boundaries. It also **perpetrates** a feeling of isolation among students.

  ————————————

Adapted from "The Ecology of School Improvement" by Elliot Eisner, *Educational Leadership*, vol. 45, no. 5 (February, 1988).

Our Changing Schools
Article

⁸Many students come from single-parent homes. Often that parent works, and other relatives may be hundreds or thousands of miles away. Even neighborhoods lack a sense of community.

j _____

_____

⁹In short, our students often have limited contacts with caring adults who know them well. Given these circumstances, what do we offer them in high schools? We give them the same conditions at school that they have at home. Fourteen-year-olds enter a high school of over a thousand persons with no adult formally responsible for their non-academic needs.

k _____

_____

¹⁰Teachers must focus on other matters; and where counselors are employed, the ratio of students to counselors is often about 1:400. It is unreasonable to expect counselors to provide care to students with whom they can have little contact and cannot really know. We must think of ways to structure the school days so that such care is provided.

l _____

_____

Curriculum

¹¹It is common for each school subject to be treated as a separate unit without any relationship to any other. Students study American history and American literature as if they came from two worlds that have nothing to do with each other. Learning is more meaningful if the inter-relationship of subject matter is apparent to the students.

m _____

_____

¹²For example, the impact of science and technology on American social life in late 19th century America can be revealed through novels, history, art, and science. Our major aim in science education is not only to train professional scientists but also to help the ordinary citizen understand science as a part of the ebb and flow of culture. Examining its relationship to culture, therefore, is crucial.

n _____

_____

¹³A curriculum that isolates science from cultural and historical context **diminishes** its relevance and its appeal for most students.

o _____

_____

¹⁴Building bridges between subjects has another potential benefit for one of the serious problems we encounter in schools, namely, the tendency for students to separate life-relevant from school-relevant learning. The aim of curriculum and teaching is not simply to help students meet the demands of schooling, but to help them use what they learn to meet the demands of life.

p _____

_____

¹⁵What this means in practice is that both the curriculum and teaching should help students **internalize** what they have learned and relate it to life outside of school.

q _____

Our Changing Schools
Article

Teaching

 [16]We have structured our schools in ways that make it difficult for teachers to improve their teaching abilities. School administrators, in this regard, are no better off than teachers. How can we de-isolate teachers and administrators? How can we provide the support and the critical feedback that will help them become reflective practitioners? Ballet dancers, who practice their art to perfection, have mirrors to see for themselves how they are doing. Where are our teachers' mirrors?

r _____

_____

Evaluation

 [17]Our standard method of evaluation is a narrow range of achievement tests which are inconsistent with much of what we need. They are too narrow, they neglect personal forms of achievement, they encourage educationally **conservative** practices, they foster a grade-oriented attitude, and they direct our students' attentions to very limited goals.

s _____

_____

 [18]One of our major tasks is to invent better ways to reveal to the public what they have a right to know, namely how we perform as professionals and how their children perform as students. As yet, we have made little headway in inventing such methods.

t _____

_____

- Write in your Finishing Time and subtract to find your Total Reading Time.
- Record your Total Reading Time on the Development Chart.
- Check your answers in the Answer Key.
- Record your score.

NUMBER CORRECT _____ (Possible 20)
(1 point for each answer)

Summary

■ Your summary of this article should list each of the five areas of educational improvement, together with the main change needed in each.

■ Reread your Paragraph Key and then complete the summary.

1 Area _____

2 Needed change _____

3 Area _____

4 Needed change _____

5 Area _____

6 Needed change _____

7 Area _____

8 Needed change _____

9 Area _____

10 Needed change _____

■ Check with your teacher or with the manual for the correct answers.

■ Record your score.

NUMBER CORRECT _____ (Possible 10)
(1 point for each answer)

Our Changing Schools
Recalling the Details

Recalling the Details

■ Your summary has outlined five main areas for educational improvement. From that summary and your Paragraph Key notes, you should be able to complete more of the details of each of these areas of improvement.

1 Eisner says the real intention of teaching should be

    a decreasing teacher load
    b putting more importance on grades
    c providing genuinely meaningful learning

2 There is a need to provide better opportunities for

    a special abilities and talents
    b commonly applied standards
    c a fairer grading system

3 Shaping children in its own image is the aim of

    a democratic societies
    b republics
    c totalitarian societies

4 The structure of the modern school should

    a back up home teaching
    b compensate for lack of home care
    c teach students how to make friends

5 A major problem of the modern curriculum is

    a separation of subjects into individual units
    b too little American history being taught
    c a lack of science teaching

6 A good curriculum should provide

    a school-relevant learning
    b university-relevant learning
    c life-relevant learning

7 A major problem for teachers is

    a the lack of opportunities to improve their performance
    b isolation from students
    c the lack of assistance from administrators

8 Present evaluation methods

    a provide inaccurate grades
    b are quite adequate
    c provide students with limited goals

9 The real goal of evaluation should be to

    a show how teachers and students perform
    b give employers a guide to student ability
    c provide continuous teacher feedback

10 This article suggests that Eisner believes American education is

    a completely off track
    b in need of major revision
    c in need of slight changes only

■ Check with your teacher or with the manual for the correct answers.
■ Record your score.

NUMBER CORRECT _____ (Possible 10)
(1 point for each answer)

★ Personal Opinion

■ Here again are the ten words used for special study with this article. Select the correct word to fill in the blank in each of the following sentences, then complete each sentence **in your own words** so it expresses your ideas on the topic.

compliance	diminish	intellectual	perpetrate	totalitarian
conservative	impenetrable	internalize	relevant	virtually

1 In the question of whether high schools should concentrate on technical or _____ subjects, I believe.......................................

2 The subject I am studying that is most _____ to my future job needs is ....

3 One current mistake in education that I hope schools will not _____ in the future is.......................................

4 If I had to choose between attending a liberal or a _____ school, I would choose ....because ....

5 One subject that always held _____ difficulties for me was ....

6 If there is one thing that is sure to _____ my interest in a subject it is ....

7 I find it much easier to understand and _____ something I am learning if ....

8 One subject I believe _____ every high school student should take is ....

9 The aspect of a _____ government I would find hardest to live with would be.......................................

10 I would like to see more schools in _____ with a philosophy of teaching that ....

■ Check with your teacher or with the manual for the correct answers.
■ Record your score.

NUMBER CORRECT _____ (Possible 20)
(2 points for each word)

Our Changing Schools
★ Speed Exercise

★ Speed Exercise

▪ (One minute only allowed for reading. Teacher timed or self-timed.)

The human mind has powers   that sometimes seem to be limitless.   The truth may well be
that most of us   are not using our minds at anywhere near   their full capacity.
It is only when   we hear of people with unusual mental abilities
that we question what the mind can do.   Many stories have been told
about people who can predict the future.   And many stories have been told
of people with other mental powers.   Some of these people   claim they can bend iron bars
with their bare hands.   Others claim they can talk   to the animals.
Still others claim they have   the power to communicate   with spirits of people who had died.
There are a number of psychics   who believe they can read another person's mind,
even when that person   is not present in the same room or place.

Of course not everyone believes   the truth of these claims.   Indeed, some people
who boast of supernatural powers   cannot be believed.   They have been proven   to be frauds.
On the other hand,   there are those who really do   seem to have the powers they claim.
It is always hard   to prove which of these claims   can be believed and which cannot.

All the claims, however,   do prove one thing.   They prove that currently we do not know
all there is to know about the human mind.   According to some researchers,
we know almost nothing   about the human mind.   They maintain that most of us
use about one tenth   of the mind power we possess.   Some researchers claim
that if we trained our minds,   we could do amazing things.   There are courses you can take
to train your mind,   and they promise to teach you   how to use your mind
to gain power over other minds.   But most of us get tired   just using our minds
the way we use them now.   Doing any more mental work   is something most of us
would not choose to do.   (339 words)

List five things that people claim they can do with mental power:

1 _____

2 _____

3 _____

4 _____

5 _____

NUMBER CORRECT _____ (Possible 20)
Score 10 points if you read the whole article,
and 2 points for each correct answer. Check
your answers by looking back at the article.
Deduct ½ point for each line you did not read.

Detecting Emotional Appeal

■ Facts are not always sufficient to attract the reader's attention. Sometimes it is necessary to employ *emotional appeal* as well. This means the writer starts the article by attracting your attention through your emotions. The writer makes you angry or sad or defensive about the subject before giving you the facts.

■ Emotional appeal is often successful in attracting attention. As the reader, however, you must be sure that the emotional appeal is appropriate. Be sure the writer is not evoking an emotion that attempts to disguise the effects of the facts. Usually, it would be inappropriate, for example, for a writer to evoke amusement before discussing the facts of a person's death.

■ Emotional appeal often is directed through a personal story since most of us become more easily involved with people than with facts.

■ This next article begins with an emotional appeal. As you read the article, be aware of this emotional appeal and consider its appropriateness to the subject matter.

The Perils of Plastic
Word Study, Dictionary Definitions

Word Study—Dictionary Review

■ Frequent use of a dictionary will give you greater ability with understanding and using words. The more words you know, the more you will enjoy reading.

■ Throughout this course, you have learned that a dictionary provides various types of information about words. This exercise will help you review this information.

★ ■ Here are the ten words chosen for special study with this article. From among them you are asked to find: 4 *restrictive labels*, 2 *inflected forms*, 1 word that has different meanings in different English-speaking countries, 1 word derived from Old French, 1 word taken directly from a Latin root, and 1 word using a Latin prefix and root. Use each word only once. Beside each word write the category into which it fits and the meaning of the word.

WORD LIST	CATEGORY	MEANING
1 arid	_____	_____
2 buoyant	_____	_____
3 debris	_____	_____
4 degradable	_____	_____
5 designate	_____	_____
6 exigencies	_____	_____
7 signatory	_____	_____
8 staccato	_____	_____
9 synthetic	_____	_____
10 trillion	_____	_____

■ Check your answers in the Answer Key.
■ Record your score.

NUMBER CORRECT _____ (Possible 10)
(1 point for each answer)

Dictionary Definitions

arid (ar′ id), *adj*. **1** having very little rainfall: dry. **2** unfruitful because of lack of moisture; barren. **3** uninteresting and empty; dull. (Latin *aridus, arere* be dry)

buoyant (boi′ ənt, bü′ yənt), *adj*. **1** able to float. **2** able to keep things afloat or aloft. **3** tending to rise. **4** cheerful, lighthearted. (Old French *boie* chain, fetter, Latin *boaie*)

debris (de brē′, dā′ brē), *n*. **1** the remains of anything broken down or destroyed; ruins, rubbish. **2** (in geology) a mass of large fragments worn away from rock. (French *debris*)

degradable (di grad ə bl), *adj*. **1** able to be reduced in rank, esp. as a punishment. **2** bringing into dishonor or contempt. **3** lowering in character or quality; debasing. **4** being worn down by erosion. **5** (in chemistry) decomposing or breaking down, esp. large molecules into simpler substances by oxidation, heat, bacteria, etc. (Late Latin *degredare*, Latin *de* down + *gradus* grade)

designate (dez′ ig nāt), *v*. **1** mark out, point out, indicate definitely; show. **2** name, entitle. (Latin *designare* to mark out, *de* + *signum* mark)

exigency (ek′ sə jen sē), *n., pl.* **-cies. 1** situation demanding prompt action or attention; urgent case; emergency. **2** often **exigencies** *pl.* an urgent need; demand for prompt action or attention. (Latin *ex* out + *agere* to drive)

signatory (sig' nə tor' ē), *n., pl.* **-ries 1** a signer of a document. **2** country, company, etc., on whose behalf a person signs a document. (Late Latin *signatura*, Latin *signum* sign)

staccato (stə ka' to), *adj.* **1** MUSIC. with breaks between the successive tones; disconnected; detached. **2** abrupt. (Italian, literally, detached)

synthetic (sin thet' ik), *adj.* **1** of, having to do with, or involving synthesis. **2** made artificially by combining parts or elements into a whole. **3** not real or genuine. **4** LINGUISTICS. characterized by the use of affixes and inflectional endings rather than by the use of separate words, such as auxiliary verbs and prepositions to express the same idea. Latin is a synthetic language while English is analytic. (Greek *syn* together + *tithenai* to put)

trillion (tril' yən), *n.* **1** (in the United States, Canada, and France) 1 followed by 12 zeros (1,000,000,000,000). **2** (in Great Britain and Germany) 1 followed by 18 zeroes (1,000,000,000,000,000,000). (Latin *tri* three + *mille* thousand)

Using the Words

■ Choose the correct word from the Word List to complete the blank in each of the following sentences.

1 It has been estimated that more than a _____ plastic products are produced in the world each day.

2 The United States was a major _____ to the treaty that ended World War II.

3 The highest incidence of starvation occurs in the most _____ parts of the world.

4 _____ fabrics are generally much easier to care for than natural fibers such as linen and cotton.

5 It is usual for people to _____ their successors in their wills.

6 A good swimmer can remain _____ for many hours.

7 A sharp, _____ voice can be irritating to listen to for a long period of time.

8 It is wise to know where hotel exits are in case of fire or other _____ .

9 There is already so much _____ in our air that it is becoming dangerous to breathe.

10 Only naturally _____ things should ever be tossed aside in the wilderness.

■ Check your answers in the Answer Key.
■ Record your score.

NUMBER CORRECT _____ (Possible 10)
(1 point for each answer)

The Perils of Plastic
Article

Paragraph Key

■ Make notes on the content of each paragraph.

¹It is dawn on the Gulf of Mexico, nature's rush hour. Sunbathers and pleasure boaters, sleeping off the **arid** heat of July, haven't yet descended on the shore. All along the water's edge, seabirds strut and dive for fish, while ghost crabs and ground squirrels scurry for food. But this morning there's a human intrusion. A large, bearded man slowly drives a tan pickup truck down the beach, his right hand gripping the steering wheel, his left continuously punching a portable computer to record what the tide has brought in.

a _____

_____

²As Tony Amos jabs computer keys programmed for the most common discoveries, he rattles off the items in the **staccato** tone of an inventory clerk:

b _____

_____

³"Plastic bottle, plastic bottle, plastic bag, Styrofoam, plastic glove, plastic lids, foam packaging, plastic rope, plastic produce sack, Karo syrup jug, six-pack ring, another glove, Styrofoam cup, cup, plastic bag, plastic fishing line, plastic bleach bottle, plastic egg carton, piece of plastic net, 50-pound plastic bag of sea salt, Bic Lighter."

c _____

_____

⁴Finally he brakes and gets out to inspect a specimen for which there is a special computer key **designated** "dead." A three-foot-long reddish fish, its scales shimmering in the sun, has been washed ashore. The fish is ringed tightly by a black plastic gasket, which has caused a deep gash and eroded the gills. Apparently, months earlier, the fish had darted into the gasket, which had lodged behind its gill cover. As the fish grew, the plastic ring became a noose, damaging the gills and thus cutting off the animal's supply of oxygen.

d _____

_____

⁵Amos has come to expect such casualties. An oceanographer at the University of Texas Marine Science Institute who has combed the same seven and a half miles of beach every other day for ten years, he is one of a growing number of scientists who are documenting plastic pollution of the ocean and its perils for the creatures that live there.

e _____

_____

⁶The problem extends far beyond the Gulf. Throughout the world, important water bodies—especially the oceans—have become virtual wastebins for tons of plastic products dumped daily by commercial

f _____

_____

Adapted from "Plastic Reaps a Grim Harvest in the Oceans of the World" by Michael Weisskopf, a reporter for the *Washington Post*. Written for *Smithsonian Magazine* (March, 1988).

fishermen, military vessels, merchant ships, passenger liners, pleasure boats, offshore oil and gas drilling operations, the plastic industry and sewage treatment plants.

[7]No one knows how much plastic pollutes the seas. In 1975, the National Academy of Science estimated that seven million tons of garbage are dumped into the world's oceans every year. There is no overall breakdown for plastics, but the Academy itemized trash from several specific sources. Measured in terms of weight, less than 1 percent of that litter was categorized as plastic. But some experts believe such findings greatly understate the problem because plastic is so much lighter than other debris.

g _____

_____

[8]The production of plastic has more than doubled since 1975. Plastic soft drink bottles, for instance, were not introduced until the late '70s. This dramatic increase is reflected in more recent studies of marine debris. A 1985 report estimated that merchant ships dump 450,000 plastic containers each day into international waters.

h _____

_____

[9]Another major aspect of the problem is the vast amount of plastic that is washed ashore. Mustang Island and other tourist beaches along the Gulf of Mexico look like cluttered landfills.

i _____

_____

[10]One three-hour-long cleanup of 157 miles of Texas shoreline in September 1987 reaped 31,773 plastic bags, 30,295 plastic bottles, 15,631 plastic six-pack rings, 28,540 plastic lids, 1,914 disposable diapers, 1,040 tampon applicators and 7,460 plastic milk jugs.

j _____

_____

[11]It is one of the sad ironies of modern times that the synthetic developed by man to outlast and outperform products made from natural material is now ravaging nature in the process.

k _____

_____

[12]Since the **exigencies** of World War II spurred large-scale production of plastic as a substitute for scarce resources, it has become the favorite American material—more durable than wood and rubber, lighter than metals, safer than glass and less expensive than leather. It is present in virtually every product line from Army helmets to artificial hearts to Styrofoam cups.

l _____

_____

[13]Today, the plastic industry occupies a major place in the U.S. economy, employing more than one million workers in almost every state and in 1985 producing $138 billion in finished goods. The 1.2 **trillion** cubic inches of plastic manufactured in that year was nearly double the combined output of steel, aluminum and copper.

m _____

_____

[14]Yet the very durability of the **synthetic** has created a massive disposal problem, especially in the marine environment where sea-goers traditionally unload their domestic wastes and gear.

[15]Perhaps it is not plastics themselves that are the problem, but rather the way people dispose of them. Regardless of where the blame lies, the problem has caught up with us. Whereas other materials degrade relatively

n _____

_____

The Perils of Plastic
Article

quickly or sink to the bottom, plastic persists. **Buoyant**, it floats on the surface and can be easily mistaken for food. Often transparent, it nets or entwines animals that cannot see it. It is the most common type of sea litter today.

¹⁶However, there is some sign of hope. A key turning point occurred in 1984 when a conference on marine **debris** was held in Honolulu by the National Marine Fisheries Service (a division of NOAA, the National Oceanic and Atmospheric Administration).

¹⁷The meeting brought into focus the scope of the problem and led to the founding of NOAA's Marine Entanglement Research Program. Thus, beginning on December 31, 1988, it became illegal for ships registered in **signatory** nations, and all other ships within the waters of these countries that prohibit dumping, to discard plastics into the ocean.

¹⁸The plastic industry also is addressing the problem of plastic disposal. One spotlight is turned on **degradable** plastics; the technology for some types is already in place, and research continues for wider and appropriate applications. Several companies now offer degradable resins for sale, and a few manufacturers in the United States, Italy and Canada are making degradable plastic bags. A photodegradable agricultural mulch has been available for several years, and to comply with laws in 11 states, manufacturers have developed six-pack rings that also break down in sunlight.

¹⁹There has been some progress, too, in the area of recycling. Plastic industry sources say that, in this country, 20 percent of all plastic soft drink bottles are being recycled. Technology is also available for "comingled" recycling—mixing different types of plastics in the recycling process—and that process is now being used to produce a new building material called plastic lumber.

²⁰Meanwhile, back on Mustang Island, Tony Amos drives his truck along the beach every other morning, documenting the plastic debris that the tide has brought in. People in his line of work don't tend to get overly optimistic. "I have pictures of girls in bikinis lying among piles of the stuff on the beach," says Amos. "People have almost got used to this. Maybe it'll become acceptable—part of the environment." It's something to think about.

o _____
_____

p _____
_____

q _____
_____

r _____
_____

s _____
_____

t _____
_____

- Write in your Finishing Time and subtract to find your Total Reading Time.
- Record your Total Reading Time on the Development Chart.
- Check your answers in the Answer Key.
- Record your score.
- Look for the right answers to any you had wrong.

NUMBER CORRECT _____ (Possible 20)
(1 point for each answer)

Summary

■ This article begins with an emotional appeal to the reader. This is an important part of the article because it attracts the reader's attention. It should not, however, be included in your summary.

■ Your summary should contain only the facts about plastic pollution and the efforts being made to combat it.

■ Reread your Paragraph Key notes if necessary before completing this summary.

1 Name of researcher _____

2 Researching _____

3 Large-scale plastic production began increasing in _____

4 Ships dump each day _____

5 Effect of this _____

6 Plastic's advantages _____

7 Industry employs _____

8 Turning point _____

9 Beginning December 1988 _____

10 Plastic industry now _____

■ Check with your teacher or with the manual for the correct answers.

■ Record your score.

NUMBER CORRECT _____ (Possible 10)
(1 point for each answer)

The Perils of Plastic
Recalling the Details

Recalling the Details

■ This article describes a situation that is a threat to the whole world. In order to understand the true meaning of this threat, you should be able to recall specific details of it.

■ Reread your Paragraph Key and your summary if necessary before completing this page.

1 Plastic trash has a fatal effect on

  a many forms of marine life
  b fish only
  c birds and fish only

2 In 1975, daily dumping into the ocean included 7 million tons of

  a plastic bottles
  b general plastics
  c general garbage

3 In 1985, ships dumped plastic containers at the daily rate of

  a 450
  b 4,500
  c 450,000

4 Which of the following is NOT listed as an advantage of plastic?

  a more durable than rubber
  b less expensive than glass
  c lighter than metals

5 In 1985, plastic production was almost double that of

  a steel, aluminum, and copper
  b steel, iron, and aluminum
  c aluminum, copper, and glass

6 The program founded in 1984 by NOAA was called

  a the Plastic Pollution Program
  b the Marine Plastic Research Program
  c the Marine Entanglement Research Program

7 By December 1988, it will be illegal for plastic to be dumped by

  a any ship using the oceans
  b signatories to the 1984 agreement
  c signatories to the Geneva agreement

8 In 1988, 11 states in the United States had laws about

  a six-pack rings
  b plastic bottles
  c degradable plastics

9 The number of soft drink bottles being recycled is

  a 50%
  b 20%
  c 5%

10 It seems likely that people will

  a give strong support to overcoming the plastics problem
  b become accustomed to plastic trash
  c demand more degradable plastics

■ Check with your teacher or with the manual for the correct answers.
■ Record your score.

NUMBER CORRECT _____ (Possible 10)
(1 point for each answer)

The Perils of Plastic

★ Personal Opinion

★ Personal Opinion

■ Here again are the ten words used for special study with this article. Select the correct word to fill in the blank in each of the following sentences, then complete each sentence **in your own words** so it expresses your ideas on the topic.

arid   debris   designate   signatory   synthetic
buoyant   degradable   exigencies   staccato   trillion

1 The fact that plastic is _____ and will not sink easily means

   that...

2 Because plastic is not naturally _____ , I think we should

   ....

3 To help overcome the immediate _____ of the plastic problem, I would suggest

   ....

4 One answer to the problem of how to dispose of plastic _____ might be

   ....

5 One area of the world that I would _____ as still being remarkably free from

   pollution is...

6 The number of _____ and therefore uninhabitable places in the world is

   increasing because...

7 If I were asked to become a _____ to a petition demanding degradable plastics,

   I would...

8 If I were to inherit a _____ dollars, I would spend it on

   ....

9 One increasingly common sound in the modern world is the _____ tapping

   of...

10 I believe that one of the most valuable uses of _____ materials is

   ....

■ Check with your teacher or with the manual
  for the correct answers.
■ Record your score.

NUMBER CORRECT _____ (Possible 20)
(2 points for each word)

The Perils of Plastic
★ Speed Exercise

★ Speed Exercise

■ (One minute allowed for reading only. Teacher timed or self-timed.)

What will the future be like?   Most people want to know   the answer to that question.
They want to know   their own futures.   They also want to know   the future of the world.
What changes lie ahead   for those who will be alive   one hundred years from now?
Will computers take   the place of schools?   Will there still be post offices?
Perhaps, instead, all communication   will be sent by computer   or by satellite.
Will there still be automobiles?   It is hard to know   the answers to those questions.
One answer is sure.   Things will be different   in a hundred years.   Consider the changes
that have been made   in the past century.   And these days,   change is occurring more often,
and it is happening more dramatically.   So the next century   should see radical change.
The biggest changes   may occur in such things as
transport, communication, and labor-saving devices in the home.   There may also be
marked changes in education.   You may do a lot more   of your study at home.
The noted future-writer Alvin Toffler   maintains that in the future,
much office work will also be done   in the home.   People will have
computer terminals at home.   These will be connected with   main terminals in the main office.
You will be able to sit at home   and do your part of the work,   and yet be part of the office team.
That sounds great.   No more traffic.   No more special office wardrobe.
No more brown bag lunches.   The only drawback is   that working at home may be lonely.
There will be no one   with whom to have lunch,
and no one with whom to share the latest gossip.   For some employees, it is people
who make the job.   Mr. Toffler believes   you can overcome that problem.
He suggests you can have lunch   with people who live near you.
Since they will be working at home also,   you can all meet each week
for lunch and exchange gossip.   And the added bonus is more leisure time.
If you do not have to travel to work,   you can spend more time on pursuits you enjoy.
(350 words)

List five major changes that may occur in the next 100 years:

1 _____

2 _____

3 _____

4 _____

5 _____

NUMBER CORRECT _____ (Possible 20)
Score 10 points if you read the whole article,
and 2 points for each correct answer. Check
your answers by looking back at the article.
Deduct ½ point for each line you did not read.

SECTION J.
Reading Provides Relaxation

Reading a Story

■ The reading you have completed so far in this course has been informational, with the intent of educating you on subjects that may be new or only partially known to you. This last section presents another type of reading—reading for relaxation—and it deals with reading stories.

■ Stories can be true or fictional, yet all have a theme and all express a point of view. It is largely through the point of view taken that the author reveals the important aspect of life shown in the theme.

■ The first story in this section is an extract from a true story written as an autobiography. As you read it consider:

1 The author's point of view.
2 The theme it illustrates.
3 The tone of the writing. (Is it serious, tragic, funny, charming, educational, or does it fall into a different category altogether?)

Alan's Funny Leg
Word Study, Dictionary Definitions

Word Study—Dictionary Review

■ Throughout this course, you have had practice with words and with the dictionary. You have also had practice using the following information from the dictionary:

pronunciation   inflected forms
parts of speech   etymology
restrictive labels   prefixes

■ By now you know the information you can expect to find in a dictionary entry. Most dictionaries contain the same type of information, although they do not all present it in the same order.

★ ■ Here is some information about the ten words chosen for special study with this article. Use the Dictionary Definitions to identify which word goes with which description. Use each word only once.

DESCRIPTION	WORD
1 A noun using the prefix *ad*-up to	_____
2 A noun of uncertain origin	_____
3 A noun using the Latin prefix for "back"	_____
4 A noun that has a restrictive label	_____
5 A verb that has a restrictive label	_____
6 A word that is the same in both the noun and adjective form	_____
7 An irregular verb that has an inflected form	_____
8 An adjective derived from Old French	_____
9 A noun derived from a phrase	_____
10 A noun with an inflected form	_____

■ Check your answers in the Answer Key.
■ Record your score.

NUMBER CORRECT _____ (Possible 10)
(1 point for each answer)

Dictionary Definitions

aggressiveness (ə gres' iv nəs), *n.*
1 the taking of the first step in a quarrel or war. **2** offensiveness. **3** extreme activity, energy. —*adj.* aggressive. (Latin *ad* up to + *gradi* to step)
anomaly (ə nom' ə lē), *n., pl.* **-lies.**
1 something that deviates from the norm or the rule. **2** irregularity. (Greek *an* not + *homalos* even)
circus (sér' kəs), *n.* **1** a traveling show of acrobats, clowns, riders, and wild animals. **2** the performers who give the show. **3** the circular area, often covered by a large circular tent, in which such a performance is given. **4** INFORMAL. an amusing person or thing; a lively time. (Latin *ring*)
familiar (fə mil' yər), *adj.* **1** known from constant association; well-known. **2** of everyday use; common; ordinary. **3** well-acquainted; versed. **4** extremely close, intimate. **5** informal; unceremonious. —*n.* **1** an intimate friend or close acquaintance. **2** spirit or demon supposed to serve a particular person. (Latin *familiaris* family)
handicap (han' dē kap'), *n.* **1** something that puts a person at a disadvantage; hindrance. **2** race, contest, game in which the poorer contestants are given certain advantages and the better ones are given certain disadvantages, so all have an equal chance to win. (from *hand in cap*; with reference to an old wagering game)
harness (här' nis), *v.* **1** put harness on. **2** cause to produce power. **3** ARCHAIC. put armor on.

(Old French *harneis* tackle, gear)
imply (im plī'), *v.* **-plied; -plying**
1 mean without saying so;
express indirectly; suggest.
2 involve as a necessary part or
condition. **3** signify; mean. (Latin
in in + *plicare* to fold)

overt (ō' vėrt', ō vėrt'), *adj.* open or
public; evident, not hidden. (Old
French *ovrir* to open)
puzzlement (puz' əl mənt), *n.* **1** a
puzzled condition. **2** something
that is confusing, perplexing.
(origin uncertain)

revulsion (ri vul' shən), *n.* **1** a sudden, violent change or reaction. **2**
a drawing or a being drawn back
or away, especially suddenly or
violently. (Latin *re* back + *vellere*
tear away)

Using the Words

■ Select the right word from the Dictionary Definitions to complete the blank in each of the following sentences.

1 People are inclined to turn away in _____ from something that is ugly or hurtful to observe.

2 Many people find life a _____ with little or no apparent meaning.

3 Silence is often used to _____ consent.

4 It may be necessary to _____ all possible resources if the world energy shortage is to be overcome.

5 A child with a _____ should be treated as much as possible in the way other children are treated.

6 It is much easier to do well in a sport that is _____ to you than in one you do not know.

7 Some people believe it is cruel to make animals perform in a _____ .

8 Throughout the United States there is a clear and _____ distrust of communism.

9 Frequently, people will develop an attitude of _____ if they find themselves constantly being criticized.

10 It is a strange _____ of freedom that it can sometimes lead to anarchy.

■ Check your answers in the Answer Key.
■ Record your score.

NUMBER CORRECT _____ (Possible 10)
(1 point for each answer)

Alan's Funny Leg
Article

Paragraph Key

■ Make a brief note on the content of each paragraph.

¹The word "crippled" to me suggested something that could be applied to other people, but not to me. But since I heard so many people refer to me as crippled, I was forced to concede that I must fit this description. At the same time, I realized that while being crippled was obviously a distressing state for some people, with me it didn't matter.

a _____

_____

²The crippled child is not conscious of the **handicap implied** by his useless legs. They are often inconvenient or annoying, but he is confident that they will never prevent him from doing what he wants to do or being whatever he wishes to be. If he considers them a handicap, it is because he has been told they are.

b _____

_____

³Children make no distinction between the one who is lame and the one who has the full use of his limbs. They will ask a boy on crutches to run here and there for them and complain when he is slow.

c _____

_____

⁴In childhood, a useless leg does not bring with it a sense of shame. It is only when one learns to interpret the glance of people unable to hide their feelings that one experiences a desire to avoid them.

d _____

_____

⁵Strangely enough, this **overt** glance of distaste only comes from those who have weak bodies. That is, from people who carry with them a consciousness of some physical inferiority. It never comes from people who are strong and healthy. It is those under the threat of helplessness who quail when confronted with it in another.

e _____

_____

⁶A useless leg or a twisted limb is freely discussed by children. "Come and see Alan's funny leg. He can put it over his head." "How did you get that sore leg?"

f _____

_____

⁷The pained mother hearing her son announce bluntly, "Here's Alan, Mom. His leg is all crooked," hastens to stop him talking. She forgets that she is looking at two happy little boys—her son, who is proud of his exhibit, and Alan, who is happy to be able to provide it.

g _____

_____

⁸A crippled limb often adds importance to its owner, and he is sometimes privileged because of it. In **circus** games I accepted the role of donkey because of my "four legs." After a great display of kicking and bucking, I would see the benefits of my handicap and would enjoy being able to do this.

h _____

_____

From *I Can Jump Puddles*, by Alan Marshall, F. W. Cheshire, Australia 1955.

Alan's Funny Leg

Article

⁹Children's sense of humor is not restricted by adult ideas of good taste and tact. The children often laughed at the spectacle of me on crutches. And they shouted with merriment when I fell over. I joined in their laughter, gripped by some sense of absurdity that made a stumble on crutches a hilarious thing.

i _____

¹⁰When high fences had to be negotiated, I was often pushed over, and the collapse of those taking my weight was regarded as extremely funny. And it was seen as funny not only for those helping me, but for me as well.

j _____

¹¹I was happy. I had no pain and I could walk. But the grown-up people who visited our home did not expect me to be happy. They called my happiness "courage."

k _____

¹²Most grown-up people talk freely about children in front of them as if children are incapable of understanding references to themselves. "He's a happy kid despite his affliction, Mrs. Marshall," they would say as if surprised that this were so.

l _____

¹³"Why shouldn't I be happy?" I thought. The suggestion that I should not be happy troubled me. It implied the presence in my life of some disaster that I did not recognize, but which would catch up with me some day. I wondered what it was, and at last concluded they imagined my leg pained me.

m _____

¹⁴"My leg doesn't hurt," I'd say brightly to those who expressed surprised approval of my smiling face. "Look!" I would say, lifting my bad leg with my hands and placing it over my head.

n _____

¹⁵This made some people shudder, and my **puzzlement** increased. My legs were so **familiar** to me that I viewed them as one would view normal limbs and not as objects that should cause **revulsion**.

o _____

¹⁶Some parents told their children to be gentle with me, or they corrected any unfeeling attitude in their children. This only confused the children. Some children, as a result of the counseling of their parents, would try to "make things easier" for me and protect me from the treatment I was getting from their mates. "Don't bump him; you'll hurt his leg," they would say.

p _____

¹⁷But I wanted to be bumped. Although I was not naturally aggressive, I developed an **aggressiveness** to counter what I regarded as unnecessary and humiliating concessions.

q _____

¹⁸I had a normal mind, so my attitude to life was that of a normal child, and my crippled limbs could not alter this attitude. When I was treated as someone different from other children, I had to learn to deal with those influences that would **harness** my mind to my crippled body.

r _____

Alan's Funny Leg
Article

¹⁹There is not a state of mind peculiar to crippled children. Those who stumble on crutches or fall or automatically use their hands to move a paralyzed limb are not thinking in terms of frustration and **anomaly**. They are not occupied with the difficulty of getting from one place to another. They are occupied with the goal of getting there, as are all children who run across a field or walk up a street.

²⁰Suffering because of being crippled is not for you in your childhood. It is reserved for those men and women who look at you.

s _____

_____

t _____

_____

■ Write in your Finishing Time and subtract to find your Total Reading Time.
■ Record your Total Reading Time on the Development Chart.
■ Check your answers in the Answer Key.
■ Record your score.

NUMBER CORRECT _____ (Possible 20)
(1 point for each answer)

Summary

■ There are two points of view included in Alan Marshall's story: Alan's view and the adults' view of crippled children. These viewpoints are expressed throughout the article. Your summary should bring together these comments under the headings below.
■ See if you can complete the summary without looking back at your Paragraph Key notes.

The child's attitude:

1 Alan had confidence that _____

2 He had no sense of _____

3 He realized crippled children often get _____

4 His attitude of life was _____

5 He did not think about _____

Adults' attitudes:

6 Those who felt distaste _____

7 Their advice to other children _____

8 They praised crippled children for _____

9 Crippled limbs affected them _____ _____

10 They expected Alan's attitude to be _____

■ Check with your teacher or with the manual
for the correct answers.
■ Record your score.

NUMBER CORRECT _____ (Possible 10)
(1 point for each answer)

Alan's Funny Leg
Recalling the Details

Recalling the Details

■ This extract is taken from an autobiography of a man who, as a child, was crippled with poliomyelitis. The details of the story reveal how the author dealt with his difficulties and give a clear understanding of his personal attitude about his handicap.

■ See if you can complete this exercise on the details of the story without referring to your summary or your Paragraph Key notes.

1 Alan accepted that he was crippled when convinced by

   a his inability to be like other children
   b other people's constant reference to his condition
   c the cruelty of other people

2 His most frequent reaction to his handicap was

   a annoyance and inconvenience
   b pain and anger
   c revulsion

3 Those who viewed his affliction with distaste were

   a adults who were healthy
   b children who were healthy
   c those who felt threatened by physical weakness

4 Other children treated Alan

   a as if they were afraid of him
   b like any other child
   c with revulsion

5 He found that children frequently

   a showed interest in his handicap
   b pretended they did not notice his handicap
   c ridiculed him

6 His story shows that children

   a have a cruel sense of humor
   b have a sense of humor not restricted by adult ideas
   c share the same sense of humor as adults

7 It surprised him that adults commented on his

   a happiness
   b misery
   c anger

8 Alan's sense of aggression was a result of

   a his anger at life's unfair treatment of him
   b other children treating him roughly
   c trying to avoid being overprotected

9 Alan's story shows that crippled children

   a need sympathy and special care
   b would prefer to be accepted as ordinary children
   c become aggressive adults

10 From this article, the reader can infer that Alan's point of view is:

   a adults should treat crippled children the way other children treat them
   b adults are insensitive, foolish people
   c most people are cruel to crippled children

■ Check with your teacher or with the manual for the correct answers.

■ Record your score.

NUMBER CORRECT _____ (Possible 10)
(1 point for each answer)

★ Personal Opinion

■ Here again are the ten words used for special study with this article. Select the correct word to fill in the blank in each of the following sentences, then complete each sentence **in your own words** so it expresses your ideas on the topic.

aggressiveness	circus	handicap	implied	puzzlement
anomaly	familiar	harness	overt	revulsion

1 If a child displays unusual hostility and _____ , it may be because of

....

2 I think it is a strange _____ in a free country that

....

3 One thing about life that is almost constantly a _____ to me is

....

4 I think for me the most difficult _____ or disability to cope with would be

....

5 One thing that causes me feelings of disgust and _____ is

....

6 On the subject of using trained animals in a _____ , I think

....

7 The typical _____ reaction to a person with severe handicaps is

....

8 One ability of mine that I would like to _____ and make better use of is

....

9 If a person is physically handicapped, it should not be _____ that

....

10 The type of handicap with which I am personally most _____ is

....

■ Check with your teacher or with the manual for the correct answers.
■ Record your score.

NUMBER CORRECT _____ (Possible 20)
(2 points for each word)

Alan's Funny Leg

★ Speed Exercise

★ Speed Exercise

■ (One minute only allowed for reading. Teacher timed or self-timed.)

Many articles and books   have been written   about neglected and abused children.
One of the most beautiful books   on this subject   is called *No Language but a Cry*.
It was written   by Dr. Richard D'Ambrosio.   It is also   one of the most disturbing books
on this subject.   It is a true story.   It tells of a little girl   who was so abused by her parents
when she was a baby   that she withdrew from life completely.   She would not talk.
She could hardly walk.   At the age of 12   she was in a home   for children who were
hopelessly retarded.

But the nuns who ran the home   would not think of her   as hopeless.
They showed her love   all the time,   even though she did not seem
to understand it or accept it.   And then they found Dr. D'Ambrosio.   He agreed to see
what he could do to help.

It was a long, hard job.   For a very long time   he seemed to be getting   nowhere at all.
But he did not give up.   For years he got no response from Laura.   He would talk to her
and take her for walks.   He would show her toys of all sorts.
But she showed no interest in anything.

Then he found out   that she liked candy.   So he brought her candy bars every day.
It was the only thing   she had ever taken from him.   The final break came when the doctor
made a dollhouse for Laura.   With this dollhouse   he finally brought Laura
back to the world.   The scene in which Laura talks to him   for the first time
is surely one of the most moving things   you could ever read.   This is a book
that everyone should read.

A book dealing with another side of child abuse   is *Throwaway Children*,
by Lisa A. Richette.   This tells about the treatment of children   who come before the courts
for various crimes.   The book shows that our justice system,   as it relates to children,
is very poor.   Our treatment of children,   both before they come to trial
and after they have been convicted,   is something we should be ashamed of.   (360 words)

1 The first book mentioned is _____ .

2 It is about _____ .

3 The second book mentioned is _____ .

4 It tells about _____ .

5 Both books are dealing with _____ .

NUMBER CORRECT _____ (Possible 20)
Score 10 points if you read the whole article,
and 2 points for each correct answer. Check
your answers by looking back at the article.
Deduct ½ point for each line you did not read.

Discovering Irony

■ Almost everybody enjoys a good story. Reading a story is relaxing in a way that is different from a movie. Reading allows you to use your imagination to envisage and interpret the story, so that it becomes a very personal experience.

■ A good story also reflects on life, enriching your understanding of what can happen in people's lives. Stories can cover a full range of experiences— exciting, horrifying, funny, tragic, even ironic.

■ *Irony* is a situation or outcome that is the opposite of what would naturally be expected. *Example*: There is *irony* in the fact that the turtle won the race, even though the hare is usually the faster runner.

■ This story is based on *irony*. As you read it, look for:

1 The character of "the hero."
2 The nature of the people with whom he is in conflict.
3 The expected outcome of this conflict.
4 The events and circumstances that cause his life to take a new direction.
5 The ironic conclusion.

The Verger
Word Study, Dictionary Definitions

Word Study—Meaning from Context

■ Many words have more than one meaning. Often you can find the meaning from the context of the word in the sentence.

■ The following sentences contain the ten words chosen for special study with this article. Try to find the correct meaning of each underlined word from the context. Then check your answers with the Dictionary Definitions. In the parentheses, write the number of the correct definition for each word.

1 A democracy does not believe in an aristocratic class. ( )

2 The cashier reported the theft of a large sum of money. ( )

3 The employee said he would rather resign than demean himself by taking a lesser position. ( )

4 A smile can sometimes disarm an angry person. ( )

5 A good student may be rewarded for exemplary behavior. ( )

6 The punk kid took out a fag and tried to look cool. ( )

7 A child who is given too much latitude may become hard to handle. ( )

8 Many people in America have no notion of what life is like in the developing countries. ( )

9 Sometimes it seems that only providence can save you from a terrible problem. ( )

10 Priests put on their robes in the vestry before beginning the church service. ( )

■ Check your answers in the Answer Key.
■ Record your score.

NUMBER CORRECT _____ (Possible 10)
(1 point for each answer)

Dictionary Definitions

aristocratic (ə ris′ tə krat′ ik), *adj.* **1** of or connected with aristocrats: *the aristocratic class*. **2** in keeping with the character of an aristocrat; stylish or grand: *an aristocratic air*. **3** snobbish; exclusive. **4** favoring aristocrats or government by aristocrats. (< Late Latin *aristocratia* < Greek *aristokratia* < *aristos* best + *kratos* rule)

cashier (ka shir′), *n.* **1** person who has charge of money in a bank, or in any business. (< French *caissier* treasurer < *caisse*). **2** *v.t.* dismiss from service for some dishonorable act; discharge in disgrace. (< Dutch *casseren* < Old French *casser* or *quasser* < Latin *quassere* to break)

demean (di mēn′), *v.t.* **1** lower in dignity or standing; humble; degrade: *demean oneself by*

insulting a friend. **2** behave or conduct (oneself). (< Old French *demener* < *de* + *mener* to lead)

disarm (dis ärm′), *v.t.* **1** take weapons away from. **2** remove anger or suspicion from; make friendly: *The speaker's honesty disarmed the angry crowd*. **3** make harmless: *disarm a bomb by removing the fuse*. (< *dis* + Middle English *armes* (pl.) weapons < Latin *arma*)—**disarming**, *adj.* allaying criticism or hostility.

exemplary (eg zem′ plə rē), *adj.* **1** worth imitating, serving as a model or pattern: *exemplary conduct*. **2** serving as a warning to others: *exemplary punishment*. **3** serving as an example; typical.

fag (fag), *n.* **1** drudgery. **2** drudge. **3** BRITISH. boy who waits on an older boy in certain schools.

4 SLANG. cigarette.

latitude (lat′ ə tüd, lat′ ə tyüd), *n.* **1** distance north or south of the equator, measured in degrees. A degree of latitude is about 69 miles. **2** place or region having a certain latitude: *Polar bears live in the cold latitudes*. **3** room to act or think; freedom from narrow rules; scope. (< Latin *latitudo* < *latus* wide)

notion (nō′ shən), *n.* **1** idea; understanding: *He has no notion of what I mean*. **2** opinion; view, belief: *modern notions about raising children*. **3** intention. **4** inclination or desire; whim; fancy: *A sudden notion to take a trip*. **5** a foolish idea or opinion. **6 notions**, *pl.* U.S. small, useful articles; pins, needles, thread, tape, etc. (< Latin *notionem* < *noscere* know)

providence (prov' ə dəns), *n.*
1 God's care and help. **2 Provi-dence**, God. **3** instance of God's care and help. **4** a being provi-dent; prudence. (< Latin *providere* < *pro* forward + *videre* to see)

vestry (ves' trē), *n., pl.* **-tries.**
1 room in a church where vest-ments, and often the sacred ves-sels, etc., are kept. **2** room in a church or an attached building, used for Sunday School, prayer

meetings, etc. **3** (in the Church of England and the Protestant Epis-copal Church of America) an elected committee that helps manage church business. (< Latin *vestire* to clothe < *vestis* garment)

Using the Words

■ Select the correct word from the Dictionary Definitions to complete the blank in each of the following sentences.

1 A child's smile may _____ an angry parent.

2 Choir boys who sound so angelic in church are often very naughty while they are waiting in the _____ .

3 The word _____ is slang for cigarette.

4 Someone who has shown _____ , heroic behavior may be rewarded with a medal.

5 An _____ society believes in class distinction.

6 Few people are prepared to _____ themselves in public.

7 The work of a _____ has become easier with the introduction of computers.

8 Many a great discovery begins with a simple _____ .

9 A trusted employee can be given wide _____ in managing his or her job.

10 Some people think you have a better chance of being helped by _____ if you first help yourself.

■ Check your answers in the Answer Key.
■ Record your score.

NUMBER CORRECT _____ (Possible 10)
(1 point for each answer)

The Verger
Article

The Verger

By W. Somerset Maugham

Introduction: Albert Edward Foreman had been the verger of St. Peter's, Neville Square, for 16 years, and he had done his job faithfully and well. (A verger is a person who takes care of a church building.) With the appointment of a new vicar, however, Foreman suddenly found himself dismissed because it had been discovered that he could neither read nor write. Although it had obviously never affected his work for the church, the vicar and the churchwardens felt they could not have such an ignorant man working for them.

¹"We don't want to be harsh with you, Foreman," said the vicar, "but the churchwardens and I have quite made up our minds. We'll give you three months, and if at the end of that time you cannot read and write, I'm afraid you'll have to go."

²Albert Edward had never liked the new vicar. He'd said from the beginning that they'd made a mistake when they gave him St. Peter's. He wasn't the type of man they wanted with a classy congregation like that. And now he straightened himself a little. He knew his value and he wasn't going to allow himself to be put upon.

³"I'm very sorry, sir; I'm afraid it's no good. I'm too old a dog to learn new tricks. I've lived a good many years without knowing 'ow to read and write, and without wishin' to praise myself—self praise is no recommendation—I don't mind sayin' I've done my duty in that state of life in which it 'as pleased a merciful **providence** to place me, and if I *could* learn now I don't know as I'd want to."

⁴"In that case, Foreman, I'm afraid you must go."

⁵"Yes, sir, I quite understand. I shall be 'appy to 'and in my resignation as soon as you've found somebody to take my place."

Characters:

a _____

b _____

c _____

Foreman's nature:

d _____

e _____

f _____

Plot:

g _____

Extracted from "The Verger" by W. Somerset Maugham.

6But when Albert Edward, with his usual politeness, had closed the church door behind the vicar and the two churchwardens, he could not sustain the air of unruffled dignity with which he had borne the blow inflicted upon him, and his lips quivered. He walked slowly back to the **vestry** and hung up on its proper peg his verger's gown. He sighed as he thought of all the grand funerals and smart weddings it had seen. He tidied everything up, put on his coat, picked up his hat and walked down the aisle. He locked the church door behind him. He strolled across the square; but deep in his sad thoughts, he did not take the street that led him home, where a nice strong cup of tea awaited him—he took the wrong turning.

h _____

7He walked slowly along. His heart was heavy. He did not know what he should do with himself. He did not like the **notion** of going back to domestic service; after being his own master for so many years—for the vicar and churchwardens could say what they liked; he knew it was he that had run St. Peter's, Neville Square—he could scarcely **demean** himself by accepting a situation. He had saved a tidy sum, but not enough to live on without doing something; and life seemed to cost more every year. He had never thought he would be troubled with such questions. The vergers of St. Peter's, like the popes of Rome, were there for life. He had often thought of the pleasant reference the vicar would make, in his sermon at evensong the first Sunday after his death, to the long and faithful service and the **exemplary** character of their late verger, Albert Edward Foreman.

8He sighed deeply. Albert Edward was a nonsmoker and a nondrinker, but with a certain **latitude**; that is to say, he liked a glass of beer with his dinner and when he was tired he enjoyed a cigarette. It occurred to him now that one would comfort him and, since he did not carry them, he looked about him for a shop where he could buy a packet of Gold Flakes. He did not at once see one and walked on a little. It was a long street, with all sorts of shops in it; but there was not a single one where you could buy cigarettes.

i _____

9"That's strange," said Albert Edward. To make sure, he walked right up the street again. No, there was no doubt about it. He stopped and looked reflectively up and down.

10"I can't be the only man who walks along this street and wants a **fag**," he said. "I shouldn't wonder but what a fellow might do very well with a little shop here. Tobacco and sweets, you know."

11He gave a sudden start. "That's an idea," he said. "Strange 'ow things come to you when you least expect it."

j _____

12He turned, walked home, and had his tea.

13"You're very silent this afternoon, Albert," his wife remarked.

14"I'm thinkin'," he said. He considered the matter from every point of view, and next day he went along the street and by good luck found a little shop to let that looked as though it would exactly suit him. Twenty-

k _____

four hours later he had taken it, and when a month after that he left St. Peter's, Neville Square, for ever, Albert Edward Foreman set up in business as a tobacconist and newsagent. His wife said it was a dreadful comedown after being verger of St. Peter's; but he answered that you had to move with the time, the church wasn't what it was, and 'enceforward he was going to render unto Caesar what was Caesar's. Albert Edward did very well. He did so well that in a year or so it struck him that he might take a second shop and put a manager in it. He looked for another long street that hadn't got a tobacconist and when he found it, and a shop to let, took it and stocked it. This was a success, too. Then it occurred to him that if he could run two, he could run half a dozen; so he began walking about London, and whenever he found a long street that had no tobacconist, and a shop to let, he took it. In the course of ten years he had acquired no less than ten shops and he was making money hand over fist. He went round to all of them himself every Monday, collected the week's takings, and took them to the bank.

l _____

m _____

n _____

15One morning when he was there, paying in a bundle of notes and a heavy bag of silver, the **cashier** told him that the manager would like to see him. He was shown into an office and the manager shook hands with him.

16"Mr. Foreman, I wanted to have a talk to you about the money you've got on deposit with us. D' you know exactly how much it is?"

17"Not within a pound or two, sir, but I've got a pretty rough idea."

18"Apart from what you paid in this morning, it's a little over thirty thousand pounds. That's a very large sum to have on deposit and I should have thought you'd do better to invest it."

o _____

19"I wouldn't want to take no risk, sir. I know it's safe in the bank."

20"You needn't have the least anxiety. We'll make you out a list of absolutely gilt-edged securities. They'll bring you in a better rate of interest than we can possibly afford to give you."

p _____

21A troubled look settled on Mr. Foreman's distinguished face.

22"I've never 'ad anything to do with stocks and shares, and I'd 'ave to leave it all in your 'ands," he said.

23The manager smiled. "We'll do everything. All you'll have to do next time you come in is just to sign the transfers."

24"I could do that all right," said Albert uncertainly. "But 'ow should I know what I was signin'?"

q _____

25"I suppose you can read," said the manager a trifle sharply.

r _____

26Mr. Foreman gave him a **disarming** smile. "Well, that's just it, I can't. I know, it sounds funny like, but there it is! I can't read or write—only me name, an' I only learned to do that when I went into business."

27The manager was so surprised that he jumped up from his chair. "That's the most extraordinary thing I ever heard."

s _____

28"You see, it's like this, sir—I never 'ad the opportunity until it was too late, and then some 'ow I wouldn't. I got obstinate like."

29The manager stared at him as though he were a prehistoric monster. "And do you mean to say you've built up this important business and made a fortune of thirty thousand pounds without being able to read or write? Good Lord, man, what would you be now, if you had been able to?"

Irony:

30"I can tell you that, sir," said Mr. Foreman, a little smile on his still **aristocratic** features. "I'd be verger of St. Peter's, Neville Square."

t _____

- Write in your Finishing Time and subtract to find your Total Reading Time.
- Record your Total Reading Time on the Development Chart.
- Check your answers in the Answer Key.
- Record your score.
- Look for the right answers to any you had wrong.

NUMBER CORRECT _____ (Possible 20)
(1 point for each answer)

The Verger

Summary

■ In order to understand the irony of a story, you must understand the characters, the conflict, the climax, and the ironic conclusion. Your summary should cover all these points. Reread your Paragraph Key notes and complete this summary.

Characters:

1 Main _____

2 Secondary _____

3 Conflict between _____

4 Reason for conflict _____

5 Climax _____

6 Immediate result of climax _____

7 New idea _____

8 Action taken _____

9 Result _____

10 Irony _____

■ Check with your teacher or with the manual for the correct answers.
■ Record your score.

NUMBER CORRECT _____ (Possible 10)
(1 point for each answer)

Recalling the Details

■ Now that you have made a summary of the story, you should be able to fill out more of the details, which will give you a greater appreciation of the story.

■ Reread your Paragraph Key notes and your summary if necessary before completing this page.

1 The new vicar criticized Foreman for

   a not doing his duty
   b not being able to read and write
   c being too old for the job

2 Foreman refused to change his ways because

   a he did not want to please the new vicar
   b he was ready to retire in any case
   c he believed he was too old to change

3 His biggest worry after leaving his job was

   a what he would do with himself
   b explaining his job loss to his wife
   c how to take revenge on the new vicar

4 As he went home, he felt the need for

   a a drink
   b a cigarette
   c a holiday

5 When he tried to buy what he wanted, he found

   a there were none of the right shops in the area
   b he did not have enough money
   c he was afraid to ask for what he wanted

6 Ten years after leaving the church, he had acquired

   a 5 shops
   b 10 shops
   c 15 shops

7 Foreman's bank manager advised him to invest in

   a gilt-edged securities
   b more property
   c government bonds

8 Foreman thought he could not take this advice because

   a he had enough money already
   b he could not read
   c he had other plans of his own

9 The irony of this story comes in the fact that

   a Foreman finished up a wealthy man
   b he had revenge on the vicar in the end, even though he did not plan it
   c if he had been willing to change, he would not have been so successful

10 This story was written by

   a W. Somerset Maugham
   b Charles Dickens
   c Alan Paton

■ Check with your teacher or with the manual for the correct answers.
■ Record your score.

NUMBER CORRECT _____ (Possible 10)
(1 point for each answer)

The Verger
★ Personal Opinion

★ Personal Opinion

■ Here again are the ten words used for special study with this article. Select the correct word to fill in the blank in each of the following sentences, then complete each sentence **in your own words** so it expresses your ideas on the topic.

| aristocratic | demean | exemplary | latitude | providence |
| cashier | disarm | fag | notion | vestry |

1 One job I believe would give me the _____ I would like is

   ....

2 I believe the use of the word _____ for a cigarette is

   ....

3 The signing of the marriage registry in the _____ of the church marks the beginning of...

4 The job of _____ in a large company is often

   ....

5 One modern invention that began as a simple _____ is

   ....

6 I would not like to _____ myself by

   ....

7 I think people who believe _____ can change their lives

   ....

8 One method I use to _____ an angry person is

   ....

9 If I had to choose between living in a democratic and an _____ society, I would choose...

10 One person whose _____ behavior I would like to copy, is

   ....

■ Check with your teacher or with the manual for the correct answers.
■ Record your score.

NUMBER CORRECT _____ (Possible 20)
(2 points for each word)

★ Speed Exercise

■ (One minute only allowed for reading. Teacher timed or self-timed.)

This article contains 370 words.   And it does not have the words in groups.   Instead, there is only a space at the end of each sentence.   Otherwise it's printed like a regular book.

Can you read the whole of this article in one minute?   Don't worry too much if you can't.   It may be that you still need more practice.   If you have been reading other things this way, you may be reading the 370 words in a minute easily.   For many years, you may have been reading the wrong way. You may have been going back over words.   You may have been letting your eyes move too slowly. You may have been letting your mind wander.   So it might take you some time to break these old habits.   But they can be broken.   If you really want to read faster, you can.   All you have to do is keep practicing.   Soon you will not even have to think about it.   You will do it naturally.   You will enjoy reading more.

What is the hardest part of reading for you?   Is it understanding words?   If so, you should do some word practice every day.   Get a book on how to improve your vocabulary and work on it for 15 minutes a day.   Even two new words a day will make you 730 words richer by the end of the year. Do you have trouble with concentration?   Then you should practice reading with questions in your mind.   Answer them at the end of each paragraph.   Do you have trouble with reading quickly? Then you must practice the things we have done in these exercises.   Move your eyes forward all the time.   Move from left to right.   Do not look back.   Do not read every word.   Read for meaning.

Learn to skim by picking out the main nouns and the main verbs.   This is especially helpful when you are reading about a subject that you already know something about.   Remember that nouns will tell you the subject(s) of the article; verbs will tell you what those subjects are doing or thinking.

If you have trouble reading even simple words, you need help from a specialist who can diagnose your problems and prescribe treatment.   (370 words)

List 5 things that are important to good reading:

1 _____

2 _____

3 _____

4 _____

5 _____

NUMBER CORRECT _____ (Possible 20)
Score 10 points if you read the whole article, and 2 points for each correct answer. Check your answers by looking back at the article. Deduct ½ point for each line you did not read.

Reading Satire

◼ *Satire* is the use of sarcasm, irony, or wit to attack or ridicule a habit, idea, or custom. Writers may use satirical stories, poems, essays, or articles to express criticism or ridicule of common social habits.

◼ On the surface, the writer handles the subject with an apparently serious approach. As you read on, however, you will become aware of the implied criticisms and recognize the satirical style.

◼ When reading satire, you should look for the current social habit being discussed. Sometimes, this habit will be something we all accept without question. When the writer allows us to see it in a new light, we may begin to think about it in a new way.

◼ This next reading is a satire. As you read it, look for the *setting*, which will help you understand what the author is criticizing. Find out who the *characters* are and compare them with usual visitors to the chosen setting. Then consider the *name* the author gives to his subject. When you have finished reading, discuss the validity of the satire.

Bistromathics

Word Study, Dictionary Definitions

Word Study—Word Study Review

- This is the final Word Study in this book. Throughout the course, you have learned a great deal about word usage and about using a dictionary. If you continue an interest in words and find out as much as possible about new words you meet, you will continue to improve your reading and your understanding of things going on around you.

- The ten words chosen for special study with this article will be used to review some of the word study skills you have learned throughout this course. You should use the Dictionary Definitions to assist you in finding each of the words described below:

    1 Noun with inflected plural form meaning <u>difference</u> _____

    2 Noun originally from Czechoslovakian meaning <u>machine operating mechanically by remote control</u> _____

    3 Adjective with restrictive label ARCHAIC now meaning <u>keen, sharp</u> _____

    4 French noun used in English meaning <u>head waiter</u> _____

    5 Noun used in plural form meaning <u>limit, border</u> _____

    6 Noun using the Latin prefix *sub* meaning <u>existence in the mind only</u> _____

    7 Adjective using the Latin root *stellar* meaning <u>between the stars</u> _____

    8 Greek noun with optional plural forms meaning <u>exceptional fact or occurrence</u>

    _____

    9 Noun meaning <u>clever management</u> or <u>unfair or dishonest treatment</u> _____

    10 Noun made from a Greek prefix meaning *near* with a Latin root, meaning similar to <u>knowledge based on observed fact</u> _____

- Check your answers in the Answer Key.
- Record your score.

NUMBER CORRECT _____ (Possible 10)
(1 point for each answer)

Dictionary Definitions

confines (kən fin′ z), *n.*, *pl.* boundary, border, limit. (Latin *confinium* < *com* together + *finis* end)
discrepancy (dis krep′ ən sē), *n.*, *pl.* **-cies. 1** lack of consistency; difference. **2** an example of inconsistency. (Latin *discrepantum* sounding differently *dis* away + *crepare* to sound)
interstellar (in′ tər stel′ ər), *adj.* situated or taking place between the stars; in the region of the stars. (Latin *inter* in + *stellar* star)
maitre d′ (mā′ trə də, ma′ tər dē′), *n.* INFORMAL. maitre d′hotel.
maitre d′hotel (me′ trə dō tel′), *pl.*

maitres d′hotel. 1 head waiter. **2** butler or steward. **3** a hotel manager. (French, literally master of the house)
manipulation (mə nip′ yə lā shun′), *n.* **1** the handling or treating of something especially skillfully. **2** clever management. **3** the changing of something for one's own purpose or advantage. **4** unfair or dishonest treatment. (Latin *manipulus* handful < *manus* hand + *plere* to fill)
parascience, *n.*
  para prefix **1** beside, near. **2** related or similar to. **3** disor-

dered condition (Greek *para* beside, near)
science (sī′ əns), *n.* **1** knowledge based on observed facts and tested truths arranged in an orderly system. **2** branch of such knowledge dealing with the phenomena of the universe and their laws; a physical or natural science. **3** skill based on training and practice; technique. **4** a particular branch of knowledge or study, especially as distinguished from art. **5 Science,** Christian Science. (Old French < Latin *scientia* knowledge <

scire to know)
phenomenon (fə nom' ə non), *n.*, *pl.* **-na** (or **-nons**). **1** fact, event, or circumstance that can be observed. **2** any sign, symptom, or manifestation. **3** any exceptional fact or occurrence. **4** an extraordinary or remarkable person or thing. A genius is sometimes called a phenomenon. (Greek *phainomenon* < *phainesthai* appear)

robot (ro' bot, ro' bət, rob' ət), *n.* **1** machine made in imitation of a human being; a mechanical device that does routine work in response to commands. **2** person who acts or works in a dull, mechanical way. **3** any machine or mechanical device that operates automatically or by remote controls. (Czech *robota* work, *robotnik* serf)

shrewd (shrüd), *adj.* **1** having a sharp mind; showing a keen wit; clever. **2** keen, sharp. **3** ARCHAIC. mean, mischievous. (OE *shrewed* bad-tempered, wicked)
subjectivity (sub' jek tiv' ə tē), *n.* existence in the mind only; tendency to view things through the medium of one's own individuality. (Latin *sub* under + *jacere* to throw)

Using the Words

■ Choose the correct word from the Dictionary Definitions to complete each of the following sentences. Do not use any word more than once.

1 The press is sometimes accused of _____ of the facts to make a good story.

2 Complaints in a good restaurant should be addressed to the _____ rather than to the waiter or waitress.

3 Some scientists believe that _____ space is occupied by life forms we cannot yet see.

4 Some people learn well in the strict _____ of a classroom, while others need to be in a more relaxed atmosphere.

5 It takes a _____ and experienced reader to understand all the details of a clever satire.

6 In some factories, the most unpleasant, tedious job has already been handed over to a _____ .

7 It is hard to avoid _____ when assessing the success of your own work.

8 Some experts see science fiction as a type of _____ rather than as a type of fiction.

9 There are many _____ between the medieval understanding of the universe and the knowledge we have today.

10 The speed with which computers were accepted by the business world has been something of a _____ .

■ Check your answers in the Answer Key.
■ Record your score.

NUMBER CORRECT _____ (Possible 10)
(1 point for each answer)

Bistromathics
Article

<table>
<tr><td>

Time Key

Finishing Time _____

Starting Time _____

Total Reading Time _____ minutes

</td><td>

Paragraph Key

■ Fill in the main points where indicated.

</td></tr>
</table>

Setting:

a _____

_____

Characters:

b _____

_____

¹It was all completely artificial. The **robot** customers were attended by a robot waiter, a robot wine waiter and a robot **maitre d'**. The furniture was artificial, the tablecloth artificial, and each particular piece of food was clearly capable of exhibiting all the mechanical characteristics of, say, a *pollo sorpreso*, without actually being one.

²And all participated in a little dance together—a complex routine involving the **manipulation** of menus, check pads, wallets, check books, credit cards, watches, pencils and paper napkins, which seemed to be hovering constantly on the edge of violence, but never actually getting anywhere.

³Slartibartfast hurried in, and then appeared to pass the time of day quite idly with the maitre d', while one of the customer robots, an autorory, slid slowly under the table, mentioning what he intended to do to some guy over some girl.

c Main character is

_____

_____

⁴Slartibartfast took over the seat that had been thus vacated and passed a **shrewd** eye over the menu. The tempo of the routine around the table seemed somehow imperceptibly to quicken. Arguments broke out, people attempted to prove things on napkins. They waved fiercely at each other, and attempted to examine each other's pieces of chicken. The waiter's hand began to move on the check pad more quickly than a human hand could manage, and then more quickly than a human eye could follow. The pace accelerated. Soon, an extraordinary and insistent politeness overwhelmed the group, and seconds later it seemed that a moment of consensus was suddenly achieved. A new vibration thrilled through the ship.

Action:

d _____

_____

e _____

_____

f _____

_____

g _____

_____

⁵Slartibartfast emerged from the glass room. "Bistromathics," he said. "The most powerful computational force known to **parascience**. Come to the room of Informational Illusions."

Satire:

h _____

_____

From Douglas Adams, *Life, the Universe and Everything*, Pocket Books, 1982. Reprinted by permission.

Bistromathics
Article

⁶He swept past and carried them, bewildered, in his wake.

⁷The Bistromathic Drive is a wonderful new method of crossing vast **interstellar** distances without all that dangerous mucking about with Improbability Factors.

⁸Bistromathics itself is simply a revolutionary new way of understanding the behavior of numbers. Just as Einstein observed that space was not an absolute but depended on the observer's movement in space, and that time was not an absolute, but depended on the observer's movement in time, so it is now realized that numbers are not absolute, but depend on the observer's movement in restaurants.

⁹The first nonabsolute number is the number of people for whom the table is reserved. This will vary during the course of the first three telephone calls to the restaurant, and then bear no apparent relation to the number of people who actually turn up, or to the number of people who subsequently join them after the show/match/party/gig, or to the number of people who leave when they see who else has turned up.

¹⁰The second nonabsolute number is the given time of arrival, which is known to be one of those most bizarre of mathematical concepts, a recipriversexcluson, a number whose existence can only be defined as being anything other than itself. In other words, the given time of arrival is the one moment of time at which it is impossible that any member of the party will arrive. Recipriversexclusons now play a vital part in many branches of math, including statistics and accountancy and also form the basic equations used to engineer the Somebody Else's Problem field.

¹¹The third and most mysterious piece of nonabsoluteness of all lies in the relationship between the number of items on the check, the cost of each item, the number of people at the table and what they are each prepared to pay for. (The number of people who have actually brought any money is only a sub**phenomenon** in this field.)

¹²The baffling **discrepancies** that used to occur at this point remained uninvestigated for centuries simply because no one took them seriously. They were at times put down to such things as politeness, rudeness, meanness, flashiness, tiredness, emotionality or the lateness of the hour, and completely forgotten about on the following morning. They were never tested under laboratory conditions, of course, because they never occurred in laboratories—not in reputable laboratories at least.

¹³And so it was only with the advent of pocket computers that the startling truth became finally apparent, and it was this:

¹⁴Numbers written on restaurant checks within the **confines** of restaurants do not follow the same mathematical laws as numbers written on any other pieces of paper in any other parts of the Universe.

i _____

j _____

k _____

l _____

m _____

n _____

o _____

p _____

q _____

r _____

[15]This single statement took the scientific world by storm. It completely revolutionized it. So many mathematical conferences got held in such good restaurants that many of the finest minds of a generation died of obesity and heart failure and the science of math was put back by years.

s _____

_____

[16]Slowly, however, the implications of the idea began to be understood. To begin with it had been too stark, too crazy, too much like what the man in the street would have said, "Oh yes, I could have told you that," about. Then some phrases like "Interactive **Subjectivity** Frameworks" were invented, and everybody was able to relax and get on with it.

t _____

_____

[17]The small group of monks who had taken up hanging around the major research institutes singing strange chants to the effect that the Universe was only a figment of its own imagination were eventually given a street theater grant and went away.

- Write in your Finishing Time and subtract to find your Total Reading Time.
- Record your Total Reading Time on the Development Chart.
- Check your answers in the Answer Key.
- Record your score.
- Look for the right answers to any you had wrong.

NUMBER CORRECT _____ (Possible 20)
(1 point for each answer)

Summary

■ When you summarize a *satire*, you should try to make a note of what is being satirized as well as including the main details of the story.

■ Reread your Paragraph Key notes if necessary, and then complete this page.

Story:

1 Main character _____

2 Other characters _____

3 Setting _____

4 Action _____

Satire:

5 Bistromathics is _____

6 Numbers depend on _____

7 First nonabsolute number _____

8 Second nonabsolute number _____

9 Third nonabsolute number _____

10 Final "startling truth" _____

■ Check with your teacher or with the manual for the correct answers.

■ Record your score.

NUMBER CORRECT _____ (Possible 10)
(1 point for each answer)

Bistromathics

Recalling the Details

■ In order to appreciate the comments the author is making on current social behavior, it is necessary to be aware of some of the details of his satire. Reread your Paragraph Key and your summary if necessary and then complete this page.

1 State the two words from which "Bistromathics" seems to be taken:

_____ and _____

2 The author's main comment is on

  a restaurant food and the eating of it
  b restaurant checks and the paying of them
  c restaurant management

3 Bistromathics is claimed as a new way of understanding the behavior of

  a numbers
  b restaurant clients
  c robots

4 Bistromathics is compared with Einstein's theory about

  a time
  b space
  c space and time

5 The first nonabsolute concerns the number of people

  a for whom the table is reserved
  b who fail to show up
  c prepared to pay for the meal

6 The second nonabsolute deals with recipriversexcluson, which is a number that

  a does not exist
  b is smaller than it seems
  c is anything other than itself

7 The third nonabsolute concerns

  a who will pay the check
  b everything concerned with the check
  c the total amount of the check

8 The final truth is that numbers on restaurant checks

  a do not follow usual mathematical laws
  b exactly obey usual mathematical laws
  c defy all interpretation

9 The satire comes in part from

  a the use of big words
  b the report-like nature of the writing
  c the criticism of restaurant food

10 The author's overall attitude seems to be one of

  a harsh criticism
  b surprised concern
  c utter confusion

■ Check with your teacher or with the manual for the correct answers.
■ Record your score.

NUMBER CORRECT _____ (Possible 10)
(1 point for each answer)

★ Personal Opinion

■ Here again are the ten words used for special study with this article. Select the correct word to fill in the blank in each of the following sentences, then complete each sentence **in your own words** so it expresses your ideas on the topic.

confines	interstellar	manipulation	phenomenon	shrewd
discrepancies	maitre d'	parascience	robot	subjectivity

1 I think the most remarkable _____ of recent years is

....

2 If I could have a _____ to work for me, I would like it to

....

3 One occasion when I found it hard to maintain my _____ and see the other

point of view was...

4 There are many _____ between the experts and me when it comes to

understanding...

5 I like to remain in the _____ of my own home when

....

6 The one thing at which I would like to be experienced and _____ is

....

7 If I were invited to go on an _____ space journey, I would

....

8 I think the most difficult part of having a restaurant job as a _____ would

be...

9 I believe I was the victim of someone else's _____ when

....

10 On the question of whether science fiction is _____ or fiction, I think

....

■ Check with your teacher or with the manual
for the correct answers.
■ Record your score.

NUMBER CORRECT _____ (Possible 20)
(2 points for each word)

Bistromathics
★ Speed Exercise

★ Speed Exercise

■ (One minute only allowed for reading. Teacher timed or self-timed.)

And now you are coming to the end of this course.   If you have worked hard, you will have found out a number of things.   You will know how to read faster.   You will know how to understand what you read.   And you will know how to remember as you read.   Now if you will continue to read like this, you will find reading much easier and much more useful.

But you will have learned other things as well.   The idea of this book was not just to teach you to read better.   One important thing you should now know is that reading is a means to an end, or a means to several ends.   There are a number of reasons why reading is important.   One of them is that it helps you with your schoolwork.   But in the long run that is not the most important reason.   School work is only a small part of your life.   And school work is also meant to lead to other things.   It leads to a better job perhaps.   But it might also help you to understand yourself better.   And that is something reading can do.   In this book you have read about a lot of different subjects.   You should have had some opinions about all of them.   If you have shared some of these opinions with other people, then it means you are reading well.   People who think about what they read and share what they read are more likely to be more interesting people.

So you have learned more about reading and you have found out something about a variety of different subjects.   Another thing you might have found out is that you now have more confidence in yourself.   Now you know that you can understand the printed word.   You can read well.

It might be interesting for you at this time to think about the subjects in this book.   Which of them did you find most interesting?   From which group of articles did you learn the most?   Was there any subject that you wanted to find out more about?   Did you do any further reading in any books or magazines about any one of these subjects?   Did you ever find yourself discussing any of these subjects with other people?   (380 words)

List 5 things that this reading says you could learn from studying this book:

1 _____

2 _____

3 _____

4 _____

5 _____

NUMBER CORRECT _____ (Possible 20)
Score 10 points if you read the whole article, and 2 points for each correct answer. Check your answers by looking back at the article. Deduct ½ point for each line you did not read.

Second Half Review

■ In the second half of this book you have practiced the following things:

1 Using new vocabulary
2 Using the dictionary to find:
   inflected forms
   restrictive labels
   etymology
   prefixes
3 Standard Business English
4 Finding the topic sentence

5 Reading:
   a report
   a newspaper story
   interpretive journalism
   a business memorandum
   a business letter
   graphs
   technical material

■ To be sure that you understand everything that has been done so far, the next few pages are made up of review exercises. Try to answer the review questions without looking back at the articles. You will find the number of the article where the answer can be found printed beside each question. If you cannot remember an answer, go back to the article and read that section again.

A. General Questions about Reading

■ Circle the letter of the right answer for each of the following. The article number where this information can be found is listed after the last answer choice. For this section of questions, most of the answers can be found in the first half of the book.

1 Speed reading is good

  a for everyone all the time
  b even if you don't understand what you read
  c only when it isn't necessary to understand every word   (7)

2 A good general reading speed is

  a 100 words per minute
  b 300 words per minute
  c 1,300 words per minute   (1)

3 The 5W + H Question Frame can help in

  a reading a story and an article
  b reading a bibliography and a newspaper story
  c reading an editorial and a report   (4 and 18)

4 A Paragraph Key

  a keeps you busy while you read
  b helps you remember the number of paragraphs in an article
  c helps you make sure you are understanding as you read   (1)

5 Reading is

  a important for school work only
  b important if you think about and use what you read
  c not very important in the modern world   (1)

6 When you read, your eyes move

  a from right to left
  b from left to right
  c either direction   (3)

7 When you come across a new word in reading, you should

  a stop reading and look it up right away
  b ignore it
  c mark it and look it up later if you cannot work out the meaning from the context   (1)

8 One important thing to remember when you read is

  a think about what you're reading and form opinions of your own
  b it is someone else's idea and therefore not important to you
  c everything you read is true   (1)

9 Good reading means you should

  a read everything the same way
  b use different types of reading for different types of materials
  c speed read everything   (1)

10 You should remember that good reading is

  a a talent that only a few people have
  b a skill that needs constant practice
  c a skill that will stay with you if you practice it once or twice   (1)

B. Questions about Particular Types of Reading

■ If you do not remember the information about the following types of reading, review the article that is numbered for you after each question.

1 A report contains four parts. They are

  a introduction, body, details, and recommendations

  b introduction, body, conclusion, and recommendations

  c introduction, body, conclusions, and bibliography (16)

2 The introduction of a report is made up of three parts. They are

  a problem, details, and conclusion

  b purpose, scope, and conclusion

  c problem, purpose, and scope (16)

3 The scope of a report tells us

  a how many people were involved in preparing the report

  b how much research was done for it

  c what parts of the subject the report will cover (16)

4 The body of the report is made up of

  a facts and tests

  b opinions and ideas

  c the names of the authors and the report (16)

5 A newspaper story comes in the shape of

  a a column

  b an inverted pyramid

  c a spiral (22)

6 The "lead" of a news story is

  a information that leads the reporter to the story

  b the headlines

  c the first paragraph, which answers the 5W + H questions (22)

7 A dateline is

  a the date on which the newspaper is published

  b the place where the story came from

  c the date on which the story happened (22)

8 Yellow journalism is

  a scandal sheet writing

  b good personal reporting

  c newspapers printed on yellow paper (22)

9 An editorial article differs from a news story because

  a it gives facts rather than opinions

  b it gives opinions rather than facts

  c it is fiction (24)

10 In the body of an editorial

  a all paragraphs are of equal importance

  b the paragraphs get less important as the article finishes

  c the final three paragraphs are the most important (24)

11 A by-line is

  a an advertisement

  b the name of the writer of a news story or article

  c an extra line added to the bottom of a page (22)

12 Hard news means

  a facts of daily news

  b news that is difficult to understand

  c news that is printed in heavy type (24)

13 A memorandum is

   a an informal business note
   b a formal business letter
   c either of the above (19)

14 A memorandum is usually

   a sent from one department to another in the same business
   b sent to a person in another business
   c written by hand (19)

15 The plural of the word "memorandum" is

   a memoranda
   b memorandums
   c either of the above (19)

16 When you have read a memo, you should always

   a return it to the sender
   b make notes about anything it asks you to do
   c file it immediately (19)

17 A good business letter uses

   a formal, old-style language
   b clear, concise language
   c a lot of abbreviations (20)

18 When you read a business letter you should

   a make notes on what it is about
   b give it to someone else to read
   c file it immediately (20)

19 In a letter of application, "marital status" means

   a record of war service
   b previous employment
   c whether you are married, single, divorced, etc. (20)

20 When you read a letter of application you should

   a form an opinion about the applicant
   b make a note of any information not supplied
   c trust your memory to recall the details of the letter (20)

21 Satirical writing

   a is strictly factual
   b ridicules common habits
   c is used in business (30)

22 Irony means

   a the opposite of what is expected
   b having a sad ending
   c ridiculing common habits (29)

23 Suppositions in writing usually begin with words such as

   a definitely, factual, exactly
   b might, perhaps, seems
   c should, ought, must (25)

24 Emotional appeal in an article

   a indicates poor writing style
   b is never used with facts
   c can engage the reader's attention (27)

25 All stories contain a

   a theme
   b indication of source
   c list of characters (28)

C. General Information about the Dictionary

■ If you need to review any of these terms, you will find their definitions in the Glossary.

1 Etymology means

  a the pronunciation of a word
  b the history of a word
  c the spelling of a word

2 A restrictive label indicates

  a alternative spelling
  b that the word is foreign
  c special uses of the word

3 The restrictive label "SLANG" means the word or meaning is

  a foreign
  b old-fashioned
  c used in very informal speaking

4 An antonym is

  a an opposite meaning
  b a similar meaning
  c a plural form

5 An autobiography is a story about a person, written by

  a someone else
  b the person himself/herself
  c a newspaper writer

6 [in' də jes' chən] This type of print indicates

  a a foreign language
  b a restrictive label
  c a pronunciation key

7 A prefix is

  a a beginning on a word
  b a word meaning the same as another
  c a special word ending

8 A synonym is

  a a word of opposite meaning
  b a word of similar meaning
  c a type of restrictive label

9 A dictionary gives the spelling of a word, and it is helpful to know that a dictionary

  a gives one spelling form only for each word
  b gives alternative forms of spelling, where they exist
  c gives alternative spellings for only the most common words

10 One important thing to remember about dictionaries is

  a they are not all the same
  b they are all the same
  c intelligent people never have to use a dictionary

D. Practice with Synonyms and Antonyms

■ Here is a list of words that you have studied in the second half of this course. Select the correct synonym and antonym for each of these words. Write the number of the synonym in the first set of parentheses, and the number of the antonym in the second set of parentheses. The number of the article in which the word appears is given in the far right column, if you need to review a word.

WORD	SYNONYM	ANTONYM	ARTICLE #
1 ( ) ( ) abhorrent	**1** known	**1** freedom	23
2 ( ) ( ) unprecedented	**2** unconquerable	**2** disagree	23

WORD	SYNONYM	ANTONYM	ARTICLE#
3 ( ) ( ) familiar	3 open	3 obscure	28
4 ( ) ( ) incarceration	4 shrewd	4 common	29
5 ( ) ( ) comply	5 imprisonment	5 hidden	19
6 ( ) ( ) invincible	6 hateful	6 starve	18
7 ( ) ( ) eminent	7 nourish	7 conquerable	18
8 ( ) ( ) overt	8 agree	8 naive	28
9 ( ) ( ) astute	9 unknown	9 unknown	21
10 ( ) ( ) nurture	10 distinguished	10 likeable	24

E. Practice with Irregular Inflected Forms

■ In the second half of this course, you have learned that inflected forms are used in both nouns and verbs. The following nouns have inflected forms in the plural. See if you can provide the correct form. The numbers of the articles in which these words appear is indicated in the right-hand column.

WORD	PLURAL	ARTICLE #
1 emergency	_____	17
2 coronary	_____	17
3 facility	_____	17
4 basis	_____	17
5 tendency	_____	17
6 heredity	_____	17
7 diagnosis	_____	17
8 conspiracy	_____	24
9 exigency	_____	27
10 anomaly	_____	28

■ Here are five irregular verbs that have inflected forms in the past tense. The regular past tense is formed by adding "ed" to the end of the verb. These verbs are different. Write the correct past tense for each of them. The number of the article in which the verb was introduced is in the right-hand column.

VERB	PAST TENSE	ARTICLE #
1 identify	_____	17
2 tantalize	_____	24
3 gauge	_____	19
4 imply	_____	28
5 comply	_____	19

F. Practice with Prefixes and Roots

■ Choosing from the prefixes and roots listed here, provide a one-word alternative for each of the definitions below.

PREFIXES AND ROOTS

de	from	*pendere*	to hang
ab	away	*struere*	to build
in	in	*ferre*	to bring
inter	between	*cedere*	to go
re	back	*trahere*	to draw

DEFINITIONS	WORD
1 mutual reliance	_____
2 withdrawal	_____
3 acting or serving as a means	_____
4 conclusion from evidence	_____
5 summary	_____

G. Using Words in Context

■ Here are ten words from the second half of this book used in sentences. Choose and circle the letter of the correct definition of each word.

1 When you insult a friend, you <u>demean</u> yourself. (**a** upgrade **b** amuse **c** degrade) (29)

2 It is something of an <u>anomaly</u> to think that jobs that save people work can also put them out of work (**a** irregularity **b** absurdity **c** crime) (28)

3 In primitive societies, news could be widely <u>broadcast</u> by means of runners who would carry the news from tribe to tribe by word of mouth. (**a** spread **b** radioed **c** televised) (16)

4 Many people have <u>ambivalent</u> feelings about mercy killing. (**a** conflicting **b** antagonist **c** supportive) (18)

5 In some societies today, men are still expected to prove their manhood by taking all sorts of risks that put their lives in <u>jeopardy</u>, just to show that they are strong. (**a** the spotlight **b** danger **c** the news) (22)

6 It takes a good deal of <u>tenacity</u> to hold on to your beliefs when everyone is criticizing you. (**a** foolishness **b** faith **c** firmness) (24)

7 Pope John was famous for the <u>conciliatory</u> moves he made toward various nations of the world. (**a** peacemaking **b** missionary **c** warlike) (23)

8 Most parents hope their children will not <u>perpetrate</u> the foolishness of the previous generation. (**a** forget about **b** understand **c** commit) (26)

9 A skull and crossbones is often used to <u>designate</u> danger. (**a** scare away **b** indicate **c** lessen the effects of)

10 It is a shame that governments often get bogged down with so much <u>trivia</u> that they hardly have time to govern adequately. (**a** argument **b** trifles **c** red tape) (19)

■ Check your answers to all of the Second Half Review exercises in the Answer Key.

ANSWER KEY

ARTICLE 1: READING MADE EASY

★ WORD STUDY

1 freeze	6 panic
2 impact	7 picnic
3 improve	8 read
4 judge	9 reader
5 judging	10 reading

USING THE WORDS

1 5
2 2
3 1 (only one meaning given)
4 4
5 1

PARAGRAPH KEY

(Your answers do not have to be exactly the same as these, but they should reflect the same ideas.)

a   reading is a skill that needs practice
b   playing football
c   coach
d   work
e   concentrate
f   words; meanings
g   look up later
h   too slowly
i   after reading
j   remember
k   summary
l   lists main points
m discussing it
n   recall details
o   questions in mind
p   different ways to read different things
q   150 words per minute
r   read without saying
s   daily practice
t   be a better reader

ARTICLE 2: WHAT'S IN A TEXTBOOK?

★ WORD STUDY

1 glos sar y	4 ar ti cle
2 con tents	5 in dex
3 bib li o graphy	6 ti tle
7 top ic	9 pref ace
8 syl la ble	10 ta ble

USING THE WORDS

1 contents	6 index
2 preface	7 title
3 topic	8 article
4 syllable	9 bibliography
5 glossary	10 table

PARAGRAPH KEY

(Your answers do not have to be exactly the same as these, but they should reflect the same ideas.)

a   will to learn
b   tool
c   using it
d   main parts
e   title
f   subtitle
g   table of contents
h   index
i   glossary
j   glossary is alphabetized
k   bibliography
l   make own glossary
m preface
n   chapters
o   this book has ten groups of articles
p   heading tells topic
q   summary at beginning or end of chapter
r   examine textbook
s   write own summary
t   textbook is tool

ARTICLE 3: WHY READ?

★ WORD STUDY

1 get by one's own efforts or actions
2 act of acquiring or getting
3 belief taught or held as true, especially by authority of a church
4 done with dogmatism; emphatically
5 known from constant association; well known
6 make well acquainted with something
7 a plural of medium
8 something that is in the middle in nature or degree; neither one extreme nor the other

9 what one thinks; belief not so strong as knowledge; judgment
10 obstinate or conceited with regard to one's own opinions

USING THE WORDS

1 opinion
2 familiarize
3 media
4 opinionated
5 dogmatically
6 acquire
7 medium
8 familiar
9 acquisition
10 dogma

PARAGRAPH KEY

(Your answers do not have to be exactly the same as these, but they should reflect the same ideas.)

a   why read?
b   acquire facts
c   newspaper
d   books
e   opinions
f   learn about people
g   opinionated
h   reread (when you choose)
i   new ideas
j   combining ideas
k   lead to further ideas
l   presents ideas about daily life
m   discuss ideas (from reading)
n   relaxing
o   crime stories
p   science fiction stories
q   love stories
r   at own speed (as often as you choose)
s   easily transported
t   use what you read

ARTICLE 4: DREAMS THAT CAME TRUE

★ WORD STUDY

1 (n) or (adj) non-professional
2 (n) respect
3 (n) collision
4 (adj) forthcoming
5 (n) biologist
6 (n) forewarning
7 (adj) sneering
8 (adj) unconscious
9 (adj) worthless
10 (v) press down

USING THE WORDS

1 impending
2 impact
3 premonition
4 scornful
5 deference
6 subconscious
7 naturalist
8 amateur
9 vain
10 weigh

PARAGRAPH KEY

(Your answers do not have to be exactly the same as these, but they should reflect the same ideas.)

a   Mary Daughtery
b   on a hill
c   at night
d   hand
e   arm
f   body
g   men
h   wicker basket
i   nonsense; canceled his ticket
j   crashed into a hill
k   Mary's dream (or omen of Mary's dream)
l   John Bradley
m   a week before field trip
n   country lane (beside a churchyard)
o   a large elm tree
p   laughed
q   uneasy
r   bridge
s   footpath
t   of Bradley's dream

ARTICLE 5: FACTS ABOUT DREAMS

★ WORD STUDY

1 n
2 v
3 adv
4 adj
5 adj
6 n
7 adv
8 n
9 n
10 adj

USING THE WORDS

1 theory
2 psychologist
3 visual
4 ascent
5 illogical
6 erratically
7 logical
8 paranoia
9 eliminate
10 placidly

PARAGRAPH KEY

(Your answers do not have to be exactly the same as these, but they should reflect the same ideas.)

a research done on dreams
b humans are information processors
c used when we are awake
d used for night (dreams)
e several times a night
f we are harder to wake
g night terrors, sleepwalking, etc.
h body limp; eyeballs move fast
i 10 minutes
j pulse of life
k right side of brain
l paranoia results
m just as bad as not dreaming
n help with problems (creativity)
o present
p past (two)
q future
r present (grand finale)
s daily life (what we're like in day)
t the truth

ARTICLE 6: THE MEANING OF DREAMS

★ WORD STUDY

1 a	6 a
2 b	7 c
3 b	8 a
4 a	9 b
5 b	10 c

USING THE WORDS

1 interval	6 unconscious
2 faculty	7 visualize
3 novice	8 consciousness
4 enhance	9 decipher
5 device	10 nocturnal

PARAGRAPH KEY

(Your answers do not have to be exactly the same as these, but they should reflect the same ideas.)

a what do dreams mean?
b dream is picture of feeling
c in dreams, we see things we felt
d give us chance to get head and heart together
e force us to think about problems
f not everybody remembers dreams (or all can remember dreams)
g relax; be ready to record dreams
h no one else can decipher dreams for you
i some common dream symbols
j flying = being able to do anything
k nudity = fear of being exposed or found out
l discovering money = hidden talents
m paralysis = enjoyment of something wrong
n she really wanted to attract men
o wild animals = show of power and strength
p symbols can be very individual
q write down and study dreams
r dreams can be key to self-understanding

ARTICLE 7: GETTING RICH YOUR OWN WAY

★ WORD STUDY

1 b	6 a
2 b	7 b
3 a	8 b
4 a	9 a
5 b	10 b

USING THE WORDS

1 uninhibited	6 bask
2 apparel	7 hit
3 surpass	8 spontaneity
4 stock	9 crucial
5 conglomerate	10 dictatorial

PARAGRAPH KEY

(Your answers do not have to be exactly the same as these, but they should reflect the same ideas.)

a don't need own business to be millionaire
b sample cases
c Harvey; shy music lover
d job with record company
e able to recognize potential hits
f did not like dictatorial position
g bosses made his decisions their own
h new company; he had one-third of stock

i Ralph; rigid behavior; fear of making fool of himself
j jars of acid broke and scarred worker
k designed new storage jars
l enjoyed design work
m too expensive; management would not proceed
n put up half the money himself and owned half the stock
o soon company grew bigger and more profitable
p parent company bought Ralph's share
q Ellen—seemed scatterbrained, but wasn't
r interest in designing apparel
s very tightfisted
t took over firm when boss died

ARTICLE 8: THE MAN WHO TURNED *EBONY* INTO GOLD

★ WORD STUDY

1 A; attack	distinction
2 A; collect	7 A; advise against
3 F; think up	8 A; include
4 A; discourage	9 A; begin
5 A; summarize	10 A/F; separate
6 A/F; make	

USING THE WORDS

1 compile	6 dissuade
2 encompass	7 segregate
3 digest	8 daunt
4 discriminate	9 bombard
5 conceive	10 initiate

PARAGRAPH KEY

(Your answers do not have to be exactly the same as these, but they should reflect the same ideas.)

a is a success
b John Harold Johnson, 1918
c segregated schools; up to eighth grade
d died
e a domestic
f high school in Chicago; did very well
g spoke at Urban League
h got a job
i own magazine/*Negro Digest*
j got money from mother/furniture
k invite subscribers

l ask for papers/bombard newsstands
m *Ebony*
n advertising
o a book
p other corporations advertised
q now has big publishing business
r vacation
s start small
t guidelines for all who want to start business

ARTICLE 9: FLEXTIME

★ WORD STUDY

1 com'bat'	struggle, fight
2 com'plex'	complicated
3 crit'ical	crucial
4 econ'omy	resource management
5 flaw'	defect (fault)
6 inter'pret	elucidate
7 legit'imate	lawful
8 mon'itor	check
9 predic'tor	prophet
10 tradi'tion	custom

USING THE WORDS

1 combat	6 predictor
2 flaw	7 monitor
3 tradition	8 legitimate
4 critical	9 economy
5 interpret	10 complex

PARAGRAPH KEY

(Your answers do not have to be exactly the same as these, but they should reflect the same ideas.)

a high absenteeism bad for business and economy
b illness excuse most often given
c fellow employees blame personality
d frequent absentee seen as "odd"
e absenteeism increases when overtime available; when workers low paid
f simple reward programs usually work
g well pay plans hard to judge
h deferring well pay not effective
i flextime one way to reduce absenteeism
j dislike of work best predictor of absenteeism
k dislike judged by number of absences

l   began in Germany 1967 to reduce rush-hour congestion
m   also helps job satisfaction and job turnover
n   also helps married women and mothers
o   may also help dual-career marriages
p   comparisons made of flextime schedules
q   group 1 = no choice; 2 = 4 times a year change; 3 = 2 week change; 4 = daily change
r   group 1 had highest absenteeism; others did not decrease with flexibility
s   group 2 had strongest attendance
t   flexibility plus long period of commitment best

ARTICLE 10: THE QUESTION OF ETHICS

★ WORD STUDY

1   conscientious; conscience, conscientiousness; X; conscientiously
2   concurrent; concurrence; concur; concurrently
3   consensual; consensus; consent; consensually
4   daunting; X; daunt; dauntingly
5   deplorable; deplorableness; deplore; deplorably
6   elective; elective, election; elect; electively
7   ethical; ethics; X; ethically
8   forbearing; forbearance; forbear; forbearingly
9   grappling; grapple; grapple; grapplingly
10 X; integrity; X; X

USING THE WORDS

1 daunting	6 forbearance
2 ethical	7 deplore
3 consensus	8 integrity
4 grapple	9 conscientously
5 elective	10 concurrence

PARAGRAPH KEY

(Your answers do not have to be exactly the same as these, but they should reflect the same ideas.)

a   tendency to ignore national ethics when economy good
b   moral weakness everywhere in America
c   question is: Who sets standard?
d   what is relationship between morals and public policy?
e   government policy must be based on what people believe
f   Donna Shalala: must have consensus on social behavior
g   Father Murray: how can we control power in society?
h   Stothe Kezios, Georgia Tech: uses case studies (*Challenger*)
i   he says: "Raise hell, stand firm"
j   Michael Josephson, Loyola Marymount: hard to be ethical in real world
k   Kirk Hanson, Stanford Business School: students afraid of pressure in fast track
l   John Silber, Boston: sees present belief in personal pleasure
m   Coles, Harvard: 1,000 students doing volunteer work
n   tolerance, kindness, forbearance, affection his key words
o   some claim these things cannot be taught
p   Michael Ratelle, Georgia attorney; favors ethics teaching in elementary schools
q   adopted curriculum with freedom code: citizenship; obligations; tolerance; kindness
r   33,000 classrooms, 45 states using freedom code
s   Albert Shanker, American Federation of Teachers: can't teach reading with comic books
t   should America seek new ethics? If so, who will set them?

ARTICLE 11: USING THE MIND TO HELP THE BODY

★ WORD STUDY

ADJECTIVE	NOUN	VERB	ADVERB
1 voluntary	volunteer	volunteer	voluntarily
2 X	exertion	exert	X
3 intervening	intervention	intervene	interveningly

ADJECTIVE	NOUN	VERB	ADVERB
4 reflex	reflex	X	X
5 afflicted	affliction	afflict	X
6 b			
7 a			
8 a			
9 a			
10 b			

USING THE WORDS

1 categorically	6 reflex		
2 voluntary	7 exertion		
3 vital	8 literally		
4 intervene	9 affliction		
5 physiological	10 syndrome		

PARAGRAPH KEY

(Your answers do not have to be exactly the same as these, but they should reflect the same ideas.)

a the process of learning voluntary control over automatic body functions
b science did not believe in mind over matter
c average person knows mind can do wondrous things

d winking is example of biofeedback
e we get feedback from mirror or parent
f same voluntary control used with interior body functions
g learn to normalize disturbed body functions
h finger temperature experiment
i note finger temperature
j relax, repeat phrases, and note temperature from time to time
k biofeedback can relax muscle tension and relieve many symptoms
l study and practice of it have just begun
m 8
n 9
o 10
p 11

ARTICLE 12: IS THERE A DOCTOR IN THE BODY?

★ WORD STUDY

ADJECTIVE	NOUN	VERB	ADVERB
1 adverse	adversity	X	adversely
2 X	alleviation	alleviate	X
3 arbitrary	arbitration	arbitrate	arbitrarily
4 beneficial	benefit	benefit	beneficially
5 contentious	contention	contend	contentiously
6 implicit	implication	imply	implicitly
7 material	material	materialize	materially
8 X	placebo	X	X
9 prescriptive	prescription	prescribe	prescriptively
10 skeptical	skeptic	X	skeptically

USING THE WORDS

1	arbitrarily	6	implicitly
2	placebo	7	prescription
3	adverse	8	alleviate
4	skeptic	9	beneficial
5	contend	10	materialize

PARAGRAPH KEY

(Your answers do not have to be exactly the same as these, but they should reflect the same ideas.)

a placebos
b harmless pill, etc., with no curative effect
c not yet understood
d mind is fooled
e makes wish for health a reality
f not always
g when used by doctor the patient trusts
h by doctor about new drug
i by nurse
j group told by doctor got higher results
k many things—seasickness to pain from operations
l group 1 given nothing; group 2 given placebo; group 3 given new drug that did not affect old age
m groups 2 and 3 showed some type of improvement; group 1 showed no improvement
n can be harmful
o do not want to try them
p for centuries
q tribal doctors in Africa
r not yet
s some nonbelievers in mind over matter cured by them
t (any answer that represents your opinion can be counted as correct)

ARTICLE 13: CLONING

★ WORD STUDY

1	b	6	a
2	c	7	b
3	a	8	b
4	c	9	c
5	a	10	a

USING THE WORDS

1	premise	6	replica
2	controversy	7	detriment
3	trait	8	countermand
4	genetic	9	reprisal
5	potential	10	progenitor

PARAGRAPH KEY

(Your answers do not have to be exactly the same as these, but they should reflect the same ideas.)

a two sexes necessary for reproduction
b this premise being challenged
c cloning = single parent reproduction
d reproduction occurs when cell nucleus replaced with nucleus of another cell
e cloned child is exact replica of parent
f frogs have already been cloned
g frog had none of mother's characteristics
h scientists say it is possible to clone humans same as frogs
i cell taken from anywhere in donor's body
j parent is one who donates new cell nucleus
k cloning means anyone could be parent
l fear of social reprisals hold back scientific work
m cloning could change social structure
n cloning could be abused
o criminals could increase in number
p monsters could be formed through cloning
q should also consider moral question
r best people could be preserved
s cloning is already a fact
t should we try to prevent human cloning?

ARTICLE 14: NEW QUESTIONS ABOUT HUMAN BIRTH

★ WORD STUDY

1 nervous and mental disease, with brain damage, associated with senility
2 missing all or most of the brain
3 disease marked by frequent urination and insulin deficiency
4 experimenting with human pre-fetal organisms
5 unborn young from three months to birth
6 alteration of genes to change hereditary problems
7 starting life in an artificial environment

8 egg, eggs
9 nervous disorder of old people, with weakness and paralysis
10 substitute mother to carry baby to term

USING THE WORDS

1 Alzheimer's disease
2 surrogate motherhood
3 diabetes
4 anencephalic
5 fetus
6 embryo experimentation
7 genetic engineering
8 ovum
9 in vitro fertilization
10 Parkinson's disease

PARAGRAPH KEY

(Your answers do not have to be exactly the same as these, but they should reflect the same ideas.)

a new ways to create life bring questions
b 1 genetic engineering
  2 in vitro fertilization
  3 surrogate motherhood
  4 embryo experimentation
c genetic engineering = altering genes to change body
d might help diabetics to make insulin
e helps find fetal abnormalities
f 1 what if fetus deformed?
  2 can mother abort?
  3 has fetus rights?
  4 is fetus human?
g rights of unborn crucial to IVF and surrogacy
h IVF = sperm and ovum join in lab dish; embryo implanted in mother
i surrogacy is same, but uses substitute mother
j allows childless people to have babies
k both methods have questions
  1 mother changes mind?
  2 parents change minds?
  3 baby deformed?
  4 baby selling?
  5 moral questions?
l 1 better than adopting
  2 seen as baby selling
  3 gives child three parents
m churches and Pope against IVF and surrogacy
n should there be public policy on these things?
o when does life begin?
p 1 at joining of ovum and sperm
  2 when brain begins

3 when child is born
q using embryo tissue for curative purposes
r many anencephalic babies born each year
s they can be kept alive artificially and organs used
  1 is it right to do this?
t 1 women may abort for money
  2 is it all right to use fetuses from natural abortion?

ARTICLE 15: WHOSE BABY?

★ WORD STUDY

1 b	6 b
2 a	7 a
3 c	8 c
4 b	9 c
5 b	10 b

USING THE WORDS

1 dysmature
2 poll
3 universal
4 gynecologist
5 caesarean section
6 premature
7 obstetrician
8 unique
9 pediatrician
10 survey

PARAGRAPH KEY

(Your answers do not have to be exactly the same as these, but they should reflect the same ideas.)

a first surrogate grandmother, Pat Anthony, 48, triplets
b smallest underweight and underdeveloped
c caesarean section; conscious with anesthetic
d operation one hour; birth normal
e Mrs. Anthony's daughter, Karen Ferreira-Jorge, present
f smallest baby in incubator until stronger
g Mrs. Anthony ready to give babies to daughter—their biological mother
h most talked about pregnancy in S.A.'s history
i April 1987, droves of reporters trying to scoop the story
j Mrs. Anthony was to bear children for her daughter who could have no more

k implanted with ova from daughter, fertilized in vitro by son-in-law
l later learned she would have triplets
m *Star* survey on readers' reactions to surrogacy
n 72% women rejected it
o 12% would let another woman bear their children
p 15% would let mothers have their children for them
q 7% 35 and over would bear another woman's child
r survey showed sympathy for women who cannot conceive
s few women ready to do same thing as Mrs. Anthony; 48% favored adoption instead
t what is current situation?

FIRST HALF REVIEW

A. GENERAL QUESTIONS ABOUT READING

1 b		6 b	
2 c		7 a	
3 b		8 b	
4 a, c, d		9 a	
5 b		10 c	

B. REVIEW OF READING A TEXTBOOK

1 a, c, d
2 b
3 a
4 a
5 b

C. PRACTICE WITH SYNONYMS AND ANTONYMS

1 5		6 3	
2 8		7 7	
3 2		8 4	
4 10		9 9	
5 1		10 6	

D. PRACTICE WITH PARTS OF SPEECH

	ADJECTIVE	NOUN	VERB	ADVERB
1	ethical	ethics	X	ethically
2	concurrent	concurrence	concur	concurrently
3	voluntary	volunteer	volunteer	voluntarily
4	reflex	reflex	X	X
5	beneficial	benefit	benefit	beneficially
6	prescriptive	prescription	prescribe	prescriptively
7	afflicted	affliction	afflict	X
8	material	material	materialize	materially
9	arbitrary	arbitration or arbiter	arbitrate	arbitrarily
10	grappling	grapple	grapple	X

E. PRACTICE WITH PRONUNCIATION

1 consciousness; awareness
2 crucial; critical
3 physiological; dealing with bodily functions
4 placebo; harmless pill, shot, or capsule
5 gynecologist; women's doctor
6 progenitor; ancestor
7 psychologist; one who works with human behavior
8 skeptic; doubter
9 legitimate; legal
10 syndrome; group of symptoms

F. PRACTICE WITH DEFINITIONS

1	b	11	c
2	a	12	a
3	c	13	c
4	b	14	c
5	c	15	c
6	b	16	a
7	a	17	c
8	a	18	a
9	b	19	b
10	c	20	a

G. REVIEW OF INFORMATION FOR READING FASTER

1 b
2 c
3 a
4 b
5 b

ARTICLE 16: HIGH BLOOD PRESSURE

★ WORD STUDY

1	5	6	2
2	9	7	4
3	7	8	6
4	3	9	8
5	10	10	1

USING THE WORDS

1 stroke (4)		6 current (4)	
2 broadcast (1)		7 screen (2)	
3 lay (1)		8 conclusive (1)	
4 elevation (4)		9 field (6)	
5 tension (3)		10 resistance (1)	

PARAGRAPH KEY

(Your answers do not have to be exactly the same as these, but they should reflect the same ideas.)

Introduction:
a Problem: high blood pressure
b Purpose: to summarize current work
c Scope: for lay people
Body:
d silent, mysterious killer

e 1 in 6 have it; many don't know they do
f black females most prone to it
g simple test to detect it; treatment helps
h two methods of detection
Conclusions:
i too many people are ignorant about it
j more blacks than whites suffer from it
k room for more screening programs
Recommendations:
l everyone over 20 get a test
m set up more testing centers
n more information to the public

ARTICLE 17: YOUR RISK OF A HEART ATTACK

★ WORD STUDY

1 bases		6 heredities	
2 coronaries		7 tendencies	
3 diagnoses		8 to identify	
4 emergencies		9 to quit	
5 facilities		10 to squeeze	

USING THE WORDS

1 squeeze		6 bases	
2 quit		7 coronaries	
3 heredities		8 emergencies	
4 tendencies		9 identify	
5 diagnoses		10 facilities	

PARAGRAPH KEY

(Your answers do not have to be exactly the same as these, but they should reflect the same ideas.)

a clinical and statistical studies basis of current heart knowledge
b more risk factors, greater chance of heart attack

Major risk factors that cannot be changed:
c heredity
d race—black Americans more apt to get it
e male sex

Major risk factors that can be changed:
f cigarette smoking
g high blood pressure
h increased blood cholesterol levels

Other contributing risk factors:
i diabetes
j obesity
k physical inactivity
l stress possibly

Warning signals of heart attack:
m pressure, fullness, squeezing, or pain in center of chest
n pain spreading to shoulders, neck, or arms
o pain, dizziness, fainting, sweating, nausea
p not all signs of heart attack, but get help

What to do in an emergency:
q know cardiac care hospitals in area
r tell family and friends where nearest facility is
s keep list of emergency numbers handy
t get expert diagnosis

g through determination: diet, exercise, and semi-retirement
Story 2:
h Larry King
i 3:30 A.M.
j right side of body
k tPA
l balloon therapy
m stopped smoking
n heart-healthy diet
o walking exercise
p 3 medications
q aspirin to prevent clotting
r government requires more information
s some hospitals using drug on experimental basis
t drugs work if given in early stages

ARTICLE 18: THEY LIVED TO TELL THE TALE

★ WORD STUDY

1 showing conflicting feelings
2 walking; able to walk
3 outstanding
4 about to occur
5 show; manifest
6 unconquerable
7 disabled person
8 worthless
9 clearly
10 persistently

USING THE WORDS

1 ambivalent
2 invalids
3 imminent
4 patiently
5 eminent
6 ambulant
7 evince
8 patently
9 invalid
10 invincible

PARAGRAPH KEY

(Your answers do not have to be exactly the same as these, but they should reflect the same ideas.)

Introduction:
a stories of people who survived heart attacks
Story 1:
b Pearl Bailey
c 1972 and 1974
d Denver
e heart attacks
f forgot to take necessary care

ARTICLE 19: INTEROFFICE MEMORANDUM

★ WORD STUDY

	NOUN	VERB	ETYMOLOGY
1		V	Latin
2	N	V	Latin
3	N		Latin
4	N	V	Old French
5	N	V	Latin
6	N		Latin
7	N		Latin
8			Old French
9		V	Latin
10	N		Latin

USING THE WORDS

1 longevity
2 incentive
3 comply
4 solicit
5 gauge (or document)
6 implement
7 document (or gauge)
8 trivia
9 feasibility
10 paramount

PARAGRAPH KEY

(Your answers do not have to be exactly the same as these, but they should reflect the same ideas.)

a Jim Rader; Barbara Clarke; general health of employees

b study on health of employees
c discuss ideas with employees
d 12,000 sick hours per year
e loses 5 executives a year to heart and lung troubles
f suggestions for improved employee health
g changes in cafeteria food
h antismoking campaign
i exercise plans
j calisthenics program
k playing fields
l YMCA or YWCA membership
m lectures on heart care
n incentive plan to avoid heart trouble
o double benefits in health improvement
p solicit response from employees
q circulate brochure from Swan Company
r notify when memo complied with

ARTICLE 20: STANDARD BUSINESS ENGLISH

★ WORD STUDY

1 in re; as per
2 we are deeply grateful; beg your indulgence
3 please find enclosed; duplicate copy
4 kind favor; of recent date
5 your line; at your earliest convenience

USING THE WORDS

(Your answers do not have to be exactly the same as these, but they should be similar.)

1 copy
2 Thank you (for reading)
3 (state the actual date)
4 that you ordered
5 We are sorry
6 the products (or name the particular goods)
7 (state the actual date)
8 Thank you (for viewing)
9 We are enclosing
10 Regarding

PARAGRAPH KEY (Letter of Request)

(Your answers do not have to be exactly the same as these, but they should reflect the same ideas.)

a send copy of order
b look at brochure
c route brochure to department heads
d notice outstanding account
e give account to accounts department

PARAGRAPH KEY (Letter of Application)

(Your answers do not have to be exactly the same as these, but they should reflect the same ideas.)

a Terry Morgan
b manager
c high school and Indiana University (Business Administration)
d landscaping; construction work
e $550 a week
f John Crawley
g daytime except Thursday
h practical experience in work he'd be managing
i name and address of company
j date
k the applicant's age
l marital status

ARTICLE 21: JOBS OF THE FUTURE

★ WORD STUDY

	WORD	PREFIX(ES)	MEANING
1	abstract	abs	summary; theoretical
2	astuteness		shrewd
3	custom		habitual; usual
4	graphic		drawing; vivid
5	inference	in	conclusion
6	instrumental	in	played for music
7	interdependence	inter, de	mutual reliance
8	prolific	pro	fertile; abundance
9	recession	re	withdrawal; reduction
10	technical		industrial; mechanical

USING THE WORDS

1 (adj) prolific
2 (adj) graphic
3 (adj) abstract
4 (adj) instrumental
5 (adj) technical
6 (n) recession
7 (n) interdependence
8 (adj) customary
9 (adj) astute
10 (n) inference

PARAGRAPH KEY

(Your answers do not have to be exactly the same as these, but they should reflect the same ideas.)

a two categories of job: producing goods; providing services
b service group growing faster
c growth of certain industries
d 1984–1995
e administrators and clerical workers will need more training
f higher educational standard important for getting job
g proportion of workers with college background
h 1970s and early 1980s
i technology and service require engineers and scientists
j increase in need for computer workers and systems analysts
k service jobs include many different jobs
l biggest need for health workers
m growth of health services
n 1984–1995
o less need for clerical workers because of computers
p writers, entertainers always face stiff competition
q teachers needed: science, mathematics, computer sciences
r variety of jobs in sales work
s now need for higher training for sales people
t fast rise in sales employment

ARTICLE 22: READING A NEWSPAPER

★ WORD STUDY

1	4	4	7
2	6	5	10
3	8	6	9

7	2	9	5
8	3	10	1

USING THE WORDS

1	subsequent	6	5; column
2	1; jeopardy	7	2; originate
3	1; authenticity	8	2; chief *adj.*
4	2; story	9	4; yellow *adj.*
5	gist	10	2; invert

PARAGRAPH KEY

(Your answers do not have to be exactly the same as these, but they should reflect the same ideas.)

a good and bad newspapers provide information
b story shaped like inverted pyramid
c opening paragraph called lead
d subsequent paragraphs less important
e headline should attract attention and be accurate
f dateline at beginning of story
g tells where story originated
h by-line is reporter's name
i shows responsibility for authenticity
j news services
k 5 main ones
l question reliability if information not given
m reporter should get facts
n editor is in charge of layout and policy
o many papers interpret news
p on editorial page
q newspapers often biased
r yellow journalism is worst kind of reporting
s scandal sheets have little to do with real news
t learn to read intelligently

★ WORD STUDY

SYNONYM	ANTONYM
1 hateful (or repugnant, contrary, detestable)	1 likeable
2 difficult	2 easy
3 aggressive (or pugnacious)	3 peaceful
4 peacemaking	4 hostile
5 deny	5 acknowledge
6 accusation	6 acquittal
7 majority	7 minority
8 misdeed	8 lawful deed
9 admitted	9 removed
10 unknown	10 common

USING THE WORDS

1 disclaim	6 combative
2 sworn in	7 abhorrent
3 arduous	8 misdemeanor
4 landslide	9 impeachment
5 conciliatory	10 unprecedented

PARAGRAPH KEY

(Your answers do not have to be exactly the same as these, but they should reflect the same ideas.)

The *New York Times*
a   August 8, Nixon states he will resign, Ford to be sworn in
b   hoped it would start "process of healing"
c   regret for injuries done; acknowledged some judgments were wrong
d   appeared calm; first President to resign from office
e   leaving office is against his instincts, but he puts America first

The *Washington Post*
a   Nixon will resign
b   after two years of debate over Watergate
c   hopes to hasten process of healing
d   Ford praised Nixon's sacrifice
e   Nixon did not have strong political base in Congress
f   Nixon put America's interests first
g   he made no confessions to crimes
h   he did not refer to Judiciary Committee changes

i   Jaworski said there was not agreement between President and special prosecutor over resignation
j   Nixon was in control of his emotions

The *Chicago Tribune*
a   Nixon resigned in order to avoid impeachment
b   orderly transfer to Ford the next day
c   first resignation by a President
d   climax of scandal that grew out of his election
e   admitted knowledge of Watergate break-in and cover-up

ARTICLE 24: INTERPRETIVE JOURNALISM

★ WORD STUDY

LANGUAGE	MEANING
1 Latin	1 breathe
2 Old English	2 demand
3 Latin from Greek	3 dog
4 Latin	4 downgrade
5 Latin	5 unable to speak
6 Latin	6 to feed
7 Old English	7 level with ground
8 Greek	8 Tantulus from Greek mythology
9 Latin	9 to hold
10 Latin	10 wind

USING THE WORDS

1 slight	6 nurtured
2 vent	7 mute
3 degradation	8 cynical
4 tantalized	9 crave
5 tenacity	10 conspiracy

PARAGRAPH KEY

(Your answers do not have to be exactly the same as these, but they should reflect the same ideas.)

The *Washington Post*
a compassion for Nixon and confidence in the country
b wanted Presidency too long
c might have been different in 1953
d series of humiliations and defeats
e carried the insults with him into office
f untrustworthy but tenacious
g even Nixon saw he had lost confidence of people
h learned Presidency belongs to people
i democracy justified
j constitution victorious; new leadership soon

The *Chicago Tribune*
a resignation has ended the controversy
b blames loss of Congress support
c would have been impeached anyway
d 10 months after Agnew's resignation
e occasion for gratitude, relief, and hope
f no longer crippled by President isolated from reality
g was guiding conspirator
h we should feel sorrow, not anger
i punishing Nixon will not bring justice
j look to the future

ARTICLE 25: WHERE HAS ALL THE AIR GONE?

★ WORD STUDY

1 methane	6 formaldehdye
2 ozone	7 sulfur dioxide
3 uranium	8 radon
4 carbon monoxide	5 carbon dioxide
5 nitrogen oxide	10 chlorofluorocarbon

USING THE WORDS

1 methane	6 formaldehdye
2 chlorofluorocarbon	7 sulfur dioxide
3 uranium	8 carbon dioxide
4 carbon monoxide	9 nitrogen dioxide
5 ozone	10 radon

PARAGRAPH KEY

(Your answers do not have to be exactly the same as these, but they should reflect the same ideas.)

a earlier perils replaced by air pollution
b may take 50 years to find out what things in our air will do to us
c 65,000 commercial compounds in air—some cause cancer
d planet can deal with natural pollutants
e can earth cope with extra substances that can cause "greenhouse effect"?
f past two centuries—big increase in CO_2
g this might increase earth's temperature
h temperature could rise by 5°F or 3°C
i rainfall change; rain to Africa; drought to Midwest U.S.
j melting West Antarctic ice sheet could raise seas 15 to 20 ft
k lead danger; brain and kidney damage
l young children most risk; 20% may have too much lead
m high blood lead level causes high blood pressure in men
n pollution in home and office
o radon gets into basements; more uranium than miners
p formaldehyde from new carpets, furniture, CO, NO_2 from poor vents
q copiers—poisonous ozone; other hazards with other goods
r bacteria pollutants; allergies from pets; fungi in cellars
s there are remedies, but are things getting worse?
t EPA says air quality improved since 1975, but still problems throughout world

ARTICLE 26: OUR CHANGING SCHOOLS

★ WORD STUDY

1	2	6	7
2	8	7	5
3	9	8	6
4	10	9	1
5	4	10	3

USING THE WORDS

1 virtually
2 relevant
3 compliance
4 intellectual
5 internalize

6 conservative
7 totalitarian
8 diminish
9 impenetrable
10 perpetrate

PARAGRAPH KEY

(Your answers do not have to be exactly the same as these, but they should reflect the same ideas.)

a five areas for school improvement
b intentions, structure, curriculum, teaching, evaluation
c make teaching more relevant to students
d teachers should control curricular adjustments
e students should have stake in what they learn
f lost sight of meaningful learning
g need for opportunities for intellectual and artistic interests
h schools, like democracy, should encourage individual talent
i schools separate teachers and divide subjects into units
j many students often alone at home
k schools offer the same conditions
l teachers too busy to help; too few counselors
m subjects should be inter-related
n should teach relationship of science and culture
o otherwise science lacks relevance and appeal
p curriculum should teach life-relevant subjects
q students should relate subjects to life outside school
r need ways for teachers/administrators to improve
s evaluation gives limited goals for students
t need better ways to judge teachers and students

ARTICLE 27: THE PERILS OF PLASTIC

★ WORD STUDY

	WORD	CHARACTERISTIC	MEANING
1	arid	one Latin root	barren
2	buoyant	Old French	able to float
3	debris	restrictive label	ruins, rubbish
4	degradable	restrictive label	decomposing
5	designate	Lt *de* out + *signum* mark	show
6	exigencies	inflected form	emergency
7	signatory	inflected form	signer
8	staccato	restrictive label	disconnected
9	synthetic	restrictive label	made artificially
10	trillion	different meanings	1,000,000,000,000

USING THE WORDS

1 trillion
2 signatory
3 arid
4 synthetic
5 designate

6 buoyant
7 staccato
8 exigencies
9 debris
10 degradable

PARAGRAPH KEY

(Your answers do not have to be exactly the same as these, but they should reflect the same ideas.)

a beautiful beach; man in pickup with computer
b Tony Amos making inventory

c   list of plastic items found on beach
d   dead fish, killed by gasket
e   Amos is documenting plastic pollution of ocean
f   problem of plastic debris extends throughout world
g   plastic about 1% of garbage but may be more
h   1985, 450,000 plastic containers in sea each day
i   lots of waste on shore as well
j   enormous numbers of plastic articles collected in 3 hours
k   synthetics created to help are now ravaging nature
l   most favored American material; wide range of uses
m   major U.S. industry
n   problem is way people dispose of plastics
o   does not degrade easily, not easy to see
p   1984 conference on marine debris
q   1988 ban on dumping plastic in oceans
r   plastic industry beginning to make improvements
s   progress in recycling
t   people getting used to plastic pollution

ARTICLE 28: ALAN'S FUNNY LEG

★ WORD STUDY

1	aggressiveness	6	familiar
2	puzzlement	7	imply
3	revulsion	8	overt
4	circus	9	handicap
5	harness	10	anomaly

USING THE WORDS

1	revulsion	6	familiar
2	puzzlement	7	circus
3	imply	8	overt
4	harness	9	aggressiveness
5	handicap	10	anomaly

PARAGRAPH KEY

(Your answers do not have to be exactly the same as these, but they should reflect the same ideas.)

a   had to learn that "crippled" applied to him
b   crippled child unconscious of his handicap

c   children make no distinction between handicapped and normal children
d   has no sense of shame
e   distaste from the physically inferior
f   children discuss handicaps freely
g   parents stop children from talking about handicaps
h   a crippled limb often brings privileges
i   children's sense of humor not restricted to adults'
j   he and friends laughed at his difficulties
k   grown-ups called his happiness "courage"
l   grown-ups talk in front of children as if they're not there
m   thought he should be unhappy because of impending unknown disaster
n   told adults leg did not hurt
o   some adults reacted to him with revulsion
p   parents encouraged children to protect him
q   had to develop aggressiveness against this
r   had normal attitude to life
s   no special state of mind for crippled children
t   suffering is only for adults who see the crippled

ARTICLE 29: THE VERGER

★ WORD STUDY

1	1	6	4
2	1	7	3
3	1	8	1
4	2	9	1
5	1	10	1

USING THE WORDS

1	disarm	6	demean
2	vestry	7	cashier
3	fag	8	notion
4	exemplary	9	latitude
5	aristocratic	10	providence

PARAGRAPH KEY

(Your answers do not have to be exactly the same as these, but they should reflect the same ideas.)

a   vicar
b   Albert Edward Foreman
c   church wardens
d   knew his value; wasn't going to be put upon

e too old to learn new tricks
f had always done his duty
g dismissed
h took wrong turn on way home
i wanted a cigarette; no shop
j new ideas
k started a shop
l next year, started second shop
m ten years, ten shops
n took money to bank every Monday
o 30,000 pounds on deposit
p bank suggests gilt-edged securities
q wouldn't know what he was signing
r bank manager thought surely he could read
s most extraordinary thing bank manager heard
t would still have been verger if he could read and write

i new method of crossing interstellar distances
j new way of understanding behavior of numbers
k numbers depend on observer's movement in restaurant
l 1st nonabsolute number: number for whom table reserved
m 2nd nonabsolute number: given time of arrival
n relationship of check with other factors
o remained uninvestigated for centuries
p never tested under laboratory conditions
q pocket computers allowed truth to show
r numbers on restaurant checks not related to any other numbers
s scientific world taken by storm
t everybody able to relax

ARTICLE 30: BISTROMATHICS

★ WORD STUDY

1 discrepancy
2 robot
3 shrewd
4 maitre d' (maitre d' hotel)
5 confines
6 subjectivity
7 interstellar
8 phenomenon
9 manipulation
10 parascience

USING THE WORDS

1 manipulation
2 maitre d'
3 interstellar
4 confines
5 shrewd
6 robot
7 subjectivity
8 parascience
9 discrepancies
10 phenomenon

PARAGRAPH KEY

(Your answers do not have to be exactly the same as these, but they should reflect the same ideas.)

a restaurant with robots, artificial furniture
b robots
c Slartibartfast
d took seat and looked at menu
e arguments broke out
f waiter writing fast
g politeness overcame everyone
h bistromathics

SECOND HALF REVIEW

A. GENERAL QUESTIONS ABOUT READING

1 c	6 b
2 b	7 c
3 a	8 a
4 c	9 b
5 b	10 b

B. QUESTIONS ABOUT PARTICULAR TYPES OF READING

1 b	11 b	21 b
2 c	12 a	22 a
3 c	13 a	23 b
4 a	14 a	24 c
5 b	15 c	25 a
6 c	16 b	
7 b	17 b	
8 a	18 a	
9 b	19 c	
10 a	20 b	

C. GENERAL INFORMATION ABOUT THE DICTIONARY

1 b	6 c
2 c	7 a
3 c	8 b
4 a	9 b
5 b	10 a

D. PRACTICE WITH SYNONYMS AND ANTONYMS

1 6; 10
2 9; 4
3 1; 9
4 5; 1
5 8; 2

6 2; 7
7 10; 3
8 3; 5
9 4; 8
10 7; 6

E. PRACTICE WITH IRREGULAR INFLECTED FORMS

NOUNS
1 emergencies
2 coronaries
3 facilities
4 bases
5 tendencies
6 heredities
7 diagnoses
8 conspiracies
9 exigencies
10 anomalies

VERBS
1 identified
2 tantalized
3 gauged
4 implied
5 complied

F. PRACTICE WITH PREFIXES AND ROOTS

1 interdependence
2 recession
3 instrumental
4 inference
5 abstract

G. USING WORDS IN CONTEXT

1 c
2 a
3 a
4 a
5 b

6 c
7 a
8 c
9 b
10 b